Gems from the Quran and Hadith

To build a deeper relationship with the Book of God, this course explores
in detail selected sections of the Quran, Hadith, and Bible, covering
various aspects of our lives

Ghamidi Center of Islamic Learning
www.ghamidi.org   AN INITIATIVE OF AL-MAWRID US.

Publisher: Ghamidi Center of Islamic Learning - Al-Mawrid US
ISBN: 978-1-966600-30-5

Address: 3620 N Josey Ln, Suite 230 Carrollton, TX 75007
Website: www.ghamidicenter.com
Email: info@ghamidi.org

Chapter 1

Introduction to the Course

This chapter provides a brief introduction to the course.

Introduction

- The Quran is the final testament of God preserved in its original language. It is the ultimate source of guidance revealed for human beings through Prophet Muhammad and affirms everything revealed before in the form of religious scriptures (for example, the Gospel/Bible).

- As the Final Messenger of God, Prophet Muhammad practiced that guidance daily, as reported to us in Ahadith through a chain of narrators.

- Building on the foundation laid in Level 5, which covered various subjects related to the Quran sciences, this course will explore sections of the Quran, Hadith, and Bible relevant to faith and different aspects of our lives, and explain those passages in a style appropriate for teenagers.

- This course will provide our Muslim teenagers with an excellent opportunity to deepen their relationship with the Message of the Quran without delving into the complexities of Quranic Arabic.

Course Objectives

1
Apply the knowledge gained about the sciences of the Quran in Level 5 to the selected passages of the Quran and relevant Ahadith

2
Build the understanding of the Quran through reading various sections in detail and asking questions

3
Understand the relationship between the Quran and Hadith and how hadith should be understood in the light of the Quran

4
Appreciate the fact that there is nothing wrong with reading the Bible and benefit from the wisdom that it still offers

Structure of the course

- This is a two-part course, and Part 1 is on understanding the Quran.
- Part 2 applies the principles learned in Part 1 and covers Tafsir of selected sections of the Quran, titled "Gems from the Quran and Hadith."
- The brief descriptions of the two courses are given below

Understanding the Quran
Part 1

Covers various aspects of the Quran, including its style, topics, arrangement, coherence, collection, and transmission, which our youths must be aware of when approaching the Quran for a deeper understanding. Building on that foundation, we will explore various sections of the Quran relevant to faith and different aspects of our lives and explain those passages in a style appropriate for teenagers.

Gems from the Quran and Hadith
Part 2

Building on the foundation laid in Part 1, this course will explore additional selected sections of the Quran relevant to faith and various aspects of our lives, and explain those passages in a style suitable for teenagers. We will also explore various sayings of the Prophet and Bible passages relevant to the selected Quranic passages.

Why should we learn the Quran

- The Quran is a unique Book and the final guidance for mankind, following several Books that were given before and have since been lost to history.

- As we studied in Level 5, Understanding the Quran, its genre and style are distinct from those of books we generally read.

- Now that we have understood its genre, style, arrangement, and how it communicates with its various addressees, it is time for us to appreciate the message of the Quran.

- In this course, we will learn how the verses and Surahs are well-connected to a theme and a central message.

- A common misconception among Muslims and non-Muslims is that the Quran is a collection of disjointed verses that were compiled. For example, there are multiple opinions on who the actual addressee of a verse is.

- Similarly, the repetition of verses is understood to reinforce the message.

- We must keep in mind that some verses and commands are relevant to all times and places, while others are specific to their direct addressees.

- We will see that the Quran is a book that exhibits complete coherence, consistency, and flow, conveying its meanings with absolute clarity and without any ambiguity when the verses are understood in context.

Themes covered in this course

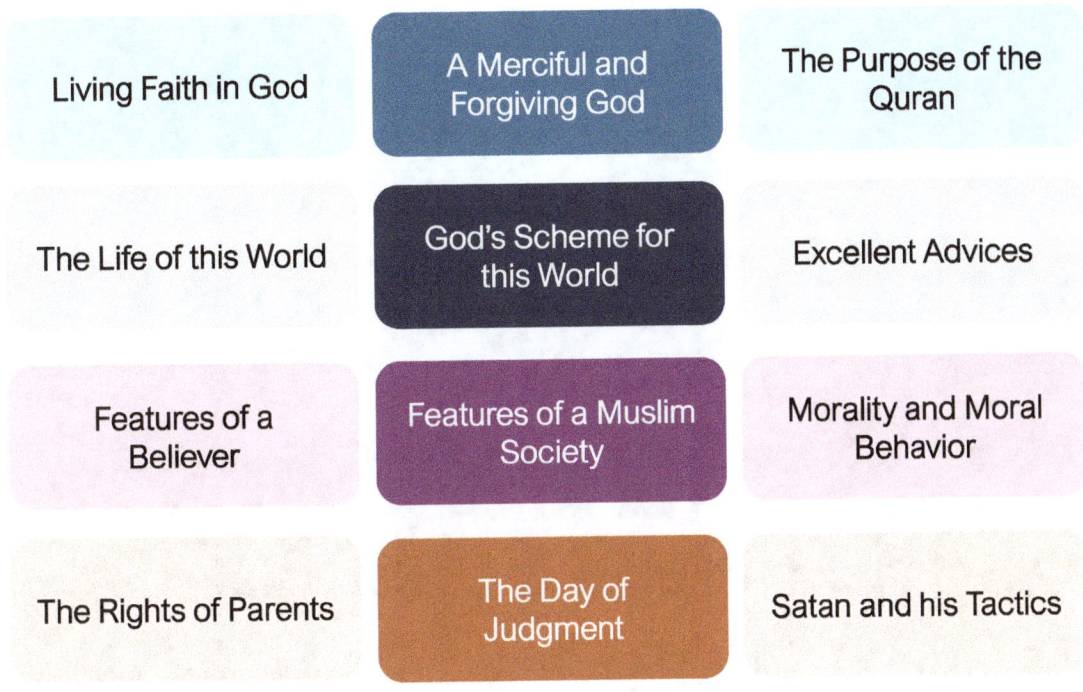

Living Faith in God	A Merciful and Forgiving God	The Purpose of the Quran
The Life of this World	God's Scheme for this World	Excellent Advices
Features of a Believer	Features of a Muslim Society	Morality and Moral Behavior
The Rights of Parents	The Day of Judgment	Satan and his Tactics

Why are we studying Ahadith and the Bible with the Quran

- Ahadith and other scriptures, like the Bible, serve as explanatory or illustrative texts when studying a topic in the Quran.

- Hadith reflects on how the Prophet practiced and explained the Quran's teachings on various topics. It often gives historical context, practical examples, beautiful advice, and additional details on Quranic directives.

- For example, when studying parental rights, Prophet Muhammad has given us valuable advice that substantiates the Quran's emphasis on this matter.

- Similarly, the Quran affirms that the Torah and the Gospel were originally divine books, so part of their wisdom remains intact. We should explore how God has been consistent in His message to all nations, as He does not change His mind regarding the matter of Truth.

- Studying them in the context of the Quran helps us understand the historical continuity of God's message.

- The study of the Hadith and the Bible is used to illuminate the Quran's message through examples from lived experiences and earlier revelations.

The Farahi School of
Thought
The 3 Giants

Imam Hamid Uddin Farahi
(1863 – 1930)

He is an 'extraordinary' genius from India, among the very few Islamic scholars who dedicated their lives to pondering over the Quran. For almost 50 years, Farahi reflected on the Quran, which remained his chief interest and focal point of all his writings. He is known for his work on Nazm, or Coherence in the Quran. He was instrumental in producing scholarly work on the theory that the verses and Surahs of the Quran are coherently interconnected. With this inherent coherence, he demonstrated that each verse in the Quran has only one interpretation.

Maulana Amin Ahsan Islahi
(1904 – 1997)

A Pakistani Muslim Scholar, best known for his Quran Tafsir, Tadabbur-e-Quran (Pondering on the Quran). Like his teacher, Farahi, he dedicated his life to pondering over the Quran. He took 22 years to finish his tafsir of the Quran. In addition to the 9-volume tafsir, he authored 21 books on various Islamic topics. What's unique about his tafsir is that he never went outside the Quran to explain it. He believed that the Quran explains itself.

Javed Ahmed Ghamidi

Born in 1952, Javed Ahmed Ghamidi is a Pakistani scholar, philosopher, and educationist of Islam, a student of Amin Ahsan Islahi. He founded the Al-Mawrid Institute of Islamic Sciences in Lahore, which is well-known for its Islamic research and education.

Besides his excellent Quran tafsir, Al-Bayan, his unique contribution is his extraordinary work, Al-Mizan. Al-Mizan is a unique book that describes Islam in its pure form, cleansed from Fiqh, Sufism, Philosophy, and other scholarly opinions from the past. He believes that God's Shariah is very limited and that one should avoid mixing human endeavors of understanding with God's Shariah.

External Resources

Annotated linguistic resource on Quran with Arabic grammar, syntax, and morphology for each word

https://corpus.quran.com/

Quran Tafseer by Javed Ahmed Ghamidi (Select English language)

https://www.javedahmedghamidi.org/#!/quran-home

Translation and Commentary by Abu Aala Maududi

https://islamicstudies.info/tafheem.php

Easy Quran Translation
https://www.clearquran.org/

Hadith Resources

https://ahadith.co.uk/

https://sunnah.com/

- What benefits do you want to get by attending this course?
- Have you read the Quran with a translation, and do you find it difficult to understand?

Important Notes

- You are required to attend all classes unless you have a valid reason to skip.
- Please send a note (or ask your parents) to your teacher on Google Classroom if you will skip a session.
- Attendance will be taken at the beginning of every class. Arriving in class 5 minutes after the start will be considered tardy.
- Three (3) tardies will be counted as one absence.
- Attendance will be counted toward your final assessment.
- Every student will be assessed via:
    - Participation in the class
    - Multiple Quizzes
    - Assignments
    - Semester Exam
    - End-of-Year Exam

Chapter 2

Introduction to the Quran

This chapter provides a brief introduction to the last book of God Almighty, the Quran. The next few chapters will provide a quick summary of what we studied in L5 before embarking on the journey to understand various passages of the Quran.

The main source of Islam

- For us now, Prophet Muhammad is the <u>ONLY</u> source of Islam. For something to be part of the religion of Islam, it must be given or sanctioned by Prophet Muhammad.
- Prophet Muhammad gave us this religion in two forms, which serve as our sources and form the corpus of religious knowledge: the Quran and the Sunnah.
- The Quran is the verbatim speech of God and His message to us in text form. The Sunnah is the practical aspects of the religion.
- Both the Quran and the Sunnah have been preserved in their original form amongst the Muslims and passed on from one generation to the next.
- Generally, Muslims attribute the Sunnah to Prophet Muhammad, but we must realize that we did not receive the Quran directly. Prophet Muhammad received it and gave it to us, making him its source for us as well.
- When it comes to authenticity, once it reached us, there is no difference between the Quran and the Sunnah. However, the Quran is the verbatim speech of God.

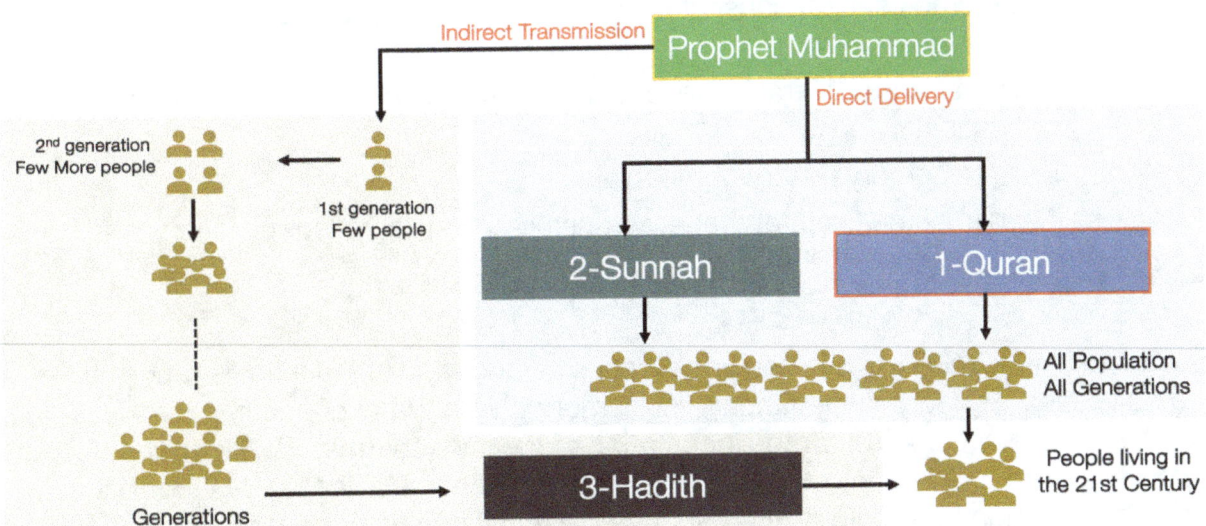

Hadith

Hadith is the historical record of Prophet Muhammad's actions, sayings, and approvals. It is another body of knowledge attributed to Prophet Muhammad. However, the method used for its transmission and preservation differs significantly from that of the Quran and the Sunnah, as shown in the picture. That's why Muslim scholars always consider Hadith as a secondary source of information about the main corpus of Islam.

The environment of revelation

- Knowing that the Quran was revealed in Arabic, which was spoken and written in the 7th century, is very important. The Quran was revealed in Classical Arabic, spoken in Makkah (Arabian Peninsula), in the 7th century (610-632 AD), by the tribe of Quraysh.

- The Prophet and the people around him spoke this language, but the Quran's articulacy and eloquence are inimitable. That period is called the 'Age of Jahiliyyah'. A clear understanding of the language of this period is essential to appreciate the message of the Quran.

- Some of the sources of the Classical Arabic language are:
  - The Quran itself (because it uses words in different contexts at different places).
  - Classical Arabic literature (especially poetry) reflects Arab culture and civilization.
  - Pre-7th-century history of the Arabs.
  - Ahadith of the Prophet that are transmitted verbatim (supplications and dialogues).

Walid Ibn Al Mughirah, one of the finest critics of language in Makkah, is reported to have said: "By God! None among you is more aware than I of poetry, neither battle songs nor eulogies nor the incantation of the jinn (charms). By God! The words spoken by this person (Muhammad) resemble none of these. By God! His words are delightful and lively. Its branches are full of fruit. Its roots are well-watered. It will definitely dominate [every other thing], and nothing will be able to dominate it, and it will crush everything below it." (Al Sirah al Nabawiyyah, vol. 1 Ibn Katheer)

Omar (RA) is reported to have said: "If you preserve your poetry, you will not go astray. People asked: "What are our poetic collections?" He said: "The poetry of the Jahiliyyah period, because it contains the tafsir of your Book and also the meaning of the words in your language." (Anwar al-tanzil wa asrar al-tawil, 2nd ed., vol. 3)

Religious groups – tradition of the Abrahamic religion

- At the time of the revelation of the Quran, the following groups were residing in the region:

Children of Ismail

Idol Worshippers: Due to greed and political rivalry, some people introduced idols into the Kaaba, and people started associating them as partners with God

Haneef: There were people among them who remained on the path of Prophet Ibrahim and Ismail. They used to be called Haneef (focused on one God)

Jews

They migrated from the Roman era and settled in the area, anticipating the coming of a prophet. They considered themselves God's chosen people and considered their leadership role as their right instead of a responsibility

Christians

The powerful Byzantine Empire was ruled by the Romans, who spread Christianity to neighboring countries and tribes. Countries that adopted Christianity as their religion were Abyssinia, Yemen, Syria, and many Arab tribes.

The Quran addresses these groups and uses historical references drawn from the history they were aware of.

The Final Divine Book on Religion

- This is not the first book of Islam. This is the **Last** book of Islam.
- It's the verbatim speech of God in which not a single dot was added or removed by Prophet Muhammad – the only original, authentic, unadulterated, and trustworthy Book of God on earth now.
- Historically, scholars of various religions agree that the Quran is the only divine text among the Abrahamic religions to have been preserved and remain available in its original language. No other religious text can claim that. What scholars of religion debate is whether it is from God or not.
- Because the Quran is preserved by God, it calls itself "Al Mizan" – the Scale and "Al Furqan" – The Distinguisher. Which means every other text should be read and understood in the light of the Quran.
- Scholars of the Quran who rely on external sources of knowledge (e.g., history, the Bible, and the Hadith) when explaining its verses can inadvertently contradict the Quran. Since the Quran is regarded as the final authority, external texts should be interpreted in accordance with the Quran.
- A hadith might explain what's already implied in the Quran but is overlooked, and the Prophet Muhammad would explain it to the Muslims, especially if they ask about it or if an occasion arises.
- Its relevance is eternal:
  - Brings us back to our real purpose in life.
  - Keeps us focused on death and what happens after (the Hereafter).
  - Explains matters required for the spiritual upbringing of humanity.
  - Provides moral guidance
  - Teachings are based on knowledge and reason; intuition also bears witness.
  - Addresses human psychology and emotions
  - Brings dead hearts to life.

Quran is protected and preserved

- The Arabic language is a living language, spoken and written throughout the world.
- Since the time of the Prophet Muhammad, thousands of Islamic scholars have studied, practiced, and mastered classical Arabic.
- The protection, preservation, originality, and authenticity of the Book require divine intervention; otherwise, it will be lost over time.

> إِنَّا نَحْنُ نَزَّلْنَا الذِّكْرَ وَإِنَّا لَهُ لَحَافِظُونَ
>
> It is We who revealed this Reminder, and We shall preserve it (15:9)

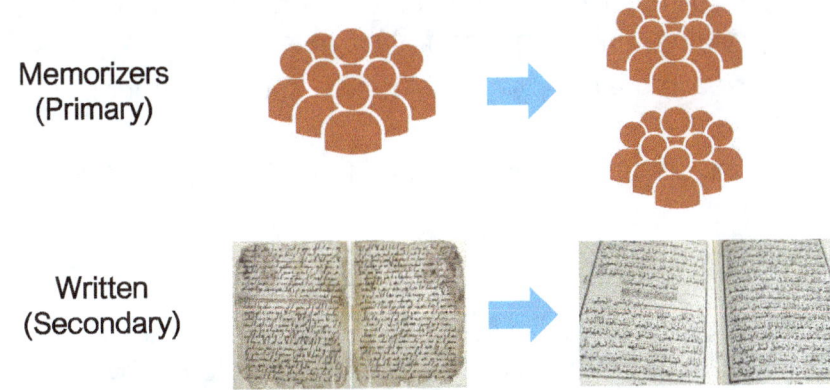

Memorizers (Primary)

Written (Secondary)

- This assurance was not given to any other religious text before.

Quran and other divine books

- It is a fact that other divine scriptures (Torah, Gospel, and Psalms) are not available in their original languages.
- That's why God called the Quran 'Muhaymin' over other divine books, meaning the Guardian or Protector. All religious texts and other Divine Books must be understood in the light of the Quran, provided the Quran addresses that topic.

وَأَنزَلْنَا إِلَيْكَ الْكِتَابَ بِالْحَقِّ مُصَدِّقًا لِّمَا بَيْنَ يَدَيْهِ مِنَ الْكِتَابِ وَمُهَيْمِنًا عَلَيْهِ ۖ فَاحْكُم بَيْنَهُم بِمَا أَنزَلَ اللَّهُ ۖ وَلَا تَتَّبِعْ أَهْوَاءَهُمْ عَمَّا جَاءَكَ مِنَ الْحَقِّ

And [O Prophet!] We have revealed the Book with the truth, confirming it before it and standing as its guardian. Therefore, give judgment among them according to the guidance revealed by God and do not yield to their whims by swerving from the truth revealed to you. (5:48)

Quran and Hadith

- The relationship between the Quran and Hadith is one of the core debates existed in the history of Muslim scholarship. To understand the message of the Quran and the relationship between the two, it is important to understand what Hadith is.

What is Hadith?

- Hadith is the historical record of Prophetic sayings, actions, and approvals.
- During the time of Prophet Muhammad, it was natural that the companions began writing down their interactions with Prophet Muhammad and recording them for their benefit. They used to narrate these interactions to people they met afterwards.
- This knowledge was naturally transmitted through generations, sometimes verbally and sometimes in written form (their notes).
- It practically turned into a body of knowledge a couple of hundred years after the prophet's death.
- Scholars then collected these texts in book form. For example, Sahih Bukhari.

The relationship

- As stated earlier, the Quran calls itself "Al Mizan" – the Scale and "Al Furqan" – The Distinguisher. Which means it is the scale and criterion by which all religious content must be judged. This includes Hadith as well.
- There is a common misconception that certain Ahadith supersede or contradict specific Quranic instructions, which runs counter to the Quran's own statements.
- Because if this is considered true, then there is no reason to believe that the Quran is the final authority, the scale, and the criterion of religion.
- The Quran is the standard by which everything else is judged as right or wrong.
- The Quran is a Furqan in the same sense, i.e., a book with the final and absolute verdict to distinguish truth from falsehood.
- A careful examination of those Ahadith that the scholars claim influence the Quran shows that they only explain or, most of the time, demonstrate what's already there or implied in the Quranic text.
- It is clear that when people were unable to comprehend certain stylistic features of the Quran, its background, and the implied meaning in specific verses, they also struggled to understand the Prophet's words on these topics.

Quran's Claim

اللَّهُ الَّذِي أَنزَلَ الْكِتَابَ بِالْحَقِّ وَالْمِيزَانَ

It is God who has revealed with truth the Book which is this scale [of justice]. (42:17)

تَبَارَكَ الَّذِي نَزَّلَ الْفُرْقَانَ عَلَىٰ عَبْدِهِ لِيَكُونَ لِلْعَالَمِينَ نَذِيرًا

Blessed be He who has revealed Al Furqan (the criterion) to His servant that it may warn the whole world. (25:1)

وَأَنزَلَ مَعَهُمُ الْكِتَابَ بِالْحَقِّ لِيَحْكُمَ بَيْنَ النَّاسِ فِيمَا اخْتَلَفُوا فِيهِ

And with these [prophets], He sent down His Book as the decisive truth so that it may settle these differences between people. (2:213)

وَأَنزَلْنَا مَعَهُمُ الْكِتَابَ وَالْمِيزَانَ لِيَقُومَ النَّاسُ بِالْقِسْطِ

And with these [messengers], We sent down Our Book, which is the Scale, so that [through it] people can adhere to justice [regarding what the truth is]. (57:25)

Quran and Science

- While studying the introduction to the Quran, it is important to understand that the Quran is **not** a book of science.

- Some recent scholars claim that many scientific facts discovered centuries later are mentioned in the Quran. This idea is promoted by those who believe the Quran contains scientifically accurate descriptions of natural phenomena that could not have been known at the time of its revelation, suggesting a divine origin for the text.

- The details will be discussed in a later chapter, but it is important to note that the Quran is a **literary** masterpiece revealed to the Prophet, providing guidance on religious matters and conveying news about the unseen. Science, on the other hand, is the intellectual and practical activity that encompasses the systematic study of the structure and behavior of the physical and natural world through observation and experimentation.

Our Questions	Science's Answers
(1) What is God's scheme for this universe?	✗
(2) What is the purpose of our lives in this world?	✗
(3) I have a unique personality; where does it come from, and where does it go when I die?	✗
(4) What is death, and what is life after death?	✗
(5) Which deeds are we accountable for, and when will we stand in front of God?	✗
(6) How should one prepare for that day to be successful?	✗

Our Questions	Quran's Answers
(1) Why is the sky blue?	✗
(2) What is the universe made of?	✗
(3) How do we get energy from the sun?	✗
(4) How do we treat bacterial infections?	✗
(5) How to improve the speed of a computer?	✗

Relationship between the Quran and Science

- As can be seen from the previous slides, the Quran and Science address two distinct domains of our lives and this universe.

- The aim of religion (or the Quran) is the moral purification of human beings so they can achieve success in the Hereafter.

- Science studies matter, the universe, and the laws within it – it provides answers to how, not why.

- The Quran alludes to various aspects of human nature, natural science, and history ONLY to substantiate its arguments.

- However, when the Quran mentions a scientific fact to substantiate an argument, it cannot conflict with the latest scientific facts (not theories), because the knowledge is said to come directly from God.

- Verses related to scientific phenomena must be interpreted literally, in accordance with the rules of the text.

It is not recommended to interpret science in the Quran or to interpret the Quran in light of scientific discoveries. Science is a progressive subject, and new research makes the older research obsolete.

Example of Quran and Science

- Scientific research has established that the brain is the center of human thought. Similarly, it has been established that the heart is unrelated to the thought process.

- The Quran uses literary metaphors and addresses the hearts.

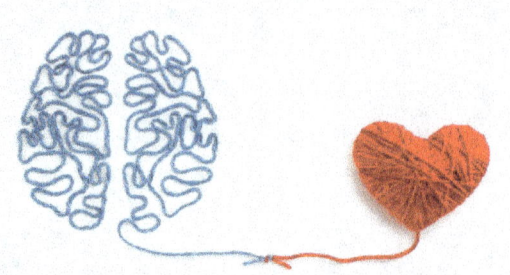

- It uses the word "heart" as a seat of thought and the center of all our emotions and thoughts. This metaphor is common in many languages. We usually say, "My heart is not in it." When we are emotionally down, we say, "It breaks my heart."

- Can we say that the Quran is scientifically wrong?

Reference: https://www.sciencenews.org/article/new-3-d-map-illuminates-little-brain-nerve-cells-within-heart

If Allah protected the Quran, why are there so many "versions" (called readings) of the Quran, which sometimes impact the command of Allah also?

Various Exegesis (*Tafsir*) of the Quran

For a student of the Quran, it is important to understand the various types of Tafsir (exegesis) produced by Muslim scholars. Understanding the methodology and thought behind a tafsir helps students understand why a *Mufassir* (Exegete) interpreted a verse of the Quran in a certain way.

History of Tafsir and *Tafsir Bil Mathoor*

- The Quran was revealed to Prophet Muhammad over a period of 23 years. During the revelation, a few incidents are reported in which people asked questions about a verse of the Quran, or Prophet Muhammad explained a verse to his companions for any reason.

- Naturally, the companions of the Prophet who heard this explanation of a verse or word of the Quran not only wrote it down for their benefit but also communicated it to others.

- Some of these companions later became scholars of the Quran, and when Islam spread among other nations whose languages were not Arabic, they began explaining Quranic verses as part of the study circle. Many study circles were founded at that time.

- This set the foundation for the science of Tafsir. The type of Tafsir based primarily on the interpretations and explanations of the Prophet's companions is called **Tafsir bil Mathoor**, or **Tafsir bil Riwayah**. For example, Tafsir-e-Tabari and Tafsir Ibn Kathir can be called the representative tafsirs of this type.

Tafsir bil-Ra'ey (Tafsir by Intellectual reasoning founded in the Quran)

- Tafsir bil-Ra'ey involves interpreting the Quran using rational analysis and intellectual reasoning, provided it does not contradict established Islamic principles. This method requires deep knowledge of Arabic, Islamic jurisprudence, and other related sciences. *Tafsir Qurtubi* is one example.

- This is a very broad category, and various Tafsir types fall under it.

Sufi Tafsir (Mystic Tafsir)

- Sufi *tafsir* is a method of interpreting the Quran that emphasizes its inner, spiritual meanings (hidden) over, or in addition to, its apparent, literal meanings (apparent). Sufis believe the Quran has multiple layers of meaning that can be accessed through spiritual practices and experiences rather than through linguistic or rational analysis alone.

Tafsir of Maulana Maududi

- The famous tafsir of Maulana Maududi, **Tafheem ul Quran**, is unique. Maulana Maududi viewed the Quran not merely as a religious text for recitation or abstract reflection, but as a "socio-religious institution" and a "revolutionary ideology" intended to transform society from the ground up. His interpretation emphasizes the practical application of Islamic principles in contemporary contexts. The *Tafhim al-Quran* is more than a traditional commentary; it incorporates discussions and debates on modern issues across various fields, including economics, sociology, history, and politics.

- A central theme of this tafsir is the concept of *Hakimiyya* (the sovereignty of God), arguing that all human governance must be subordinated to divine law (Shariah) and that achieving this MUST be the responsibility of every Muslim.

Tafsir of *Fikr-e-Farahi* (Farahi School of Thought)

- The tafsir methodology of the **Farahi school of thought** is distinct for its central emphasis on *Nazm*, the Quran's thematic and structural coherence.

- **Concept of *Nazm*:** The primary idea is that the Quran is a fully integrated, internally consistent book, where every verse and chapter is systematically connected to form a unified, cohesive message. Maulana Farahi argued that disregarding this internal order leads to sectarian differences, as verses taken out of context can have multiple meanings, while every word and verse of the Quran has only one meaning.

- The Farahi school emphasizes using the Quran itself (*tafsir al-Qur'an bi-al-Qur'an*) to explain difficult verses, with the inherent coherence and literary context serving as the primary guides.

Compare the Tafseer of Surah Al-Kauthar from the following:

1. Tafsir Ibn Kathir
2. Tafsir Qurtubi
3. Bayan al-Quran by Ashraf Ali Thanwi
4. Tafheem ul Quran
5. Tafsir of Maulana Amin Ahsan Islahi or Javed Ahmed Ghamidi

Chapter 3

Truth of the Quran
(Is the Quran from God?)

This chapter presents the case that the Quran is the Word of God.

Is the Quran the word of God?

Living in the 21st Century, the only sources of Islam are Prophet Muhammad and the Quran, which he gave us as the Book of Allah. Without ascertaining the truthfulness of the Quran and the Prophethood of Prophet Muhammad, we cannot be sure if we are on the right religion. Let's investigate a few universal truths that lead us to conclude that the Quran is not a human work and that Prophet Muhammad was a true Prophet of God because he presented this Quran to us.

Our sources of knowledge

- Three sources or mediums of knowledge shape how we understand the world, develop concepts, acquire skills, and make decisions. This is true in every field.
    - **Sensory perception** – it is the source of knowledge rooted in empiricism, the philosophical theory that all knowledge is derived from direct sensory experience. It involves using the five senses to gather information about the external world. Perception is considered the most direct and reliable source of knowledge because it provides immediate evidence of what is happening around us. However, sometimes, it can be deceptive.
    - **Inference** - the process of using existing evidence and reasoning to draw a conclusion or an educated guess about something that is not directly observed. It combines current knowledge with background knowledge to "read between the lines".
    - **History** - History is a source of knowledge because it provides an extensive evidential base for understanding how people and societies behave over time. The study of history is essential for understanding how the present came to be, as past events shape our current social, political, and cultural landscape.

Universal Truth

- A universal truth is a fact or a principle that is always true for all people, in all places, and at all times, until someone challenges it. They don't depend on someone's opinion, culture, or feelings – they remain true no matter what and are accepted by all.
- Some examples of universal truths are:

 The sun rises in the East
 All living things need water to survive
 Kindness makes life better for everyone
 Every action has a reaction

The process of deriving universal truths

- The picture below shows how we come to derive universal truths. To understand how we arrive at universal truths, start with the bottom-most layer: our sensory perception, and go upwards.

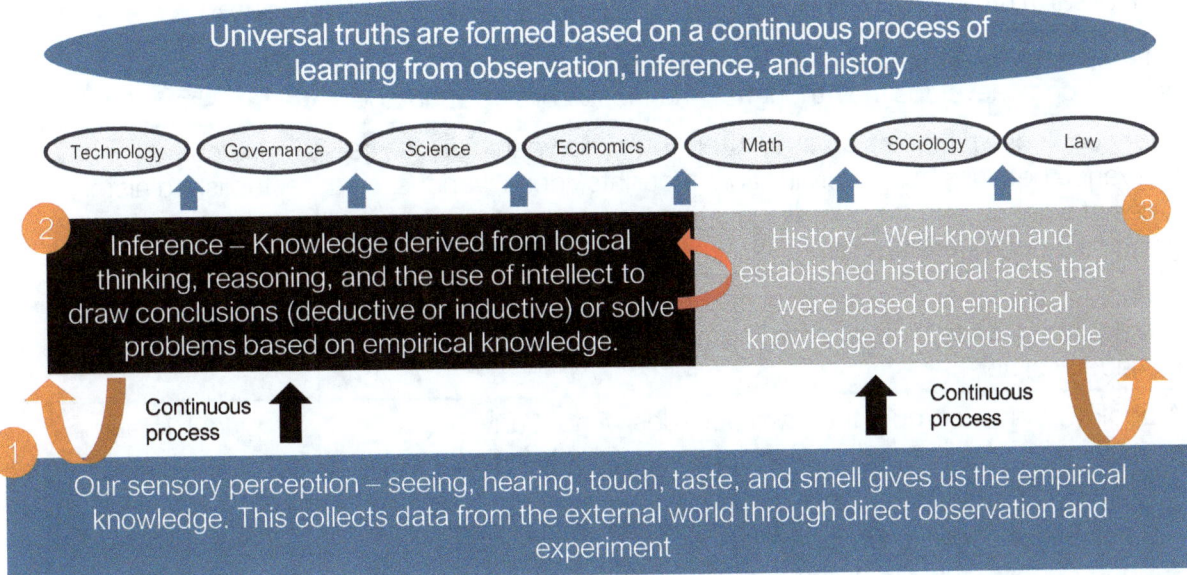

General Examples

Universal Truths	Source
Water maintains its level	Empirical
World War II occurred	Established history
Earth revolves around the sun	Empirical, Inference
A baby takes 6-9 months in a mother's womb to be born	Empirical
The universe is expanding	Empirical, Inference
The universe started at some point in time	Inference
All matter is formed of atoms and atoms are made of sub-atomic particles	Empirical, Inference
All crows are black	Empirical, Inference
Greece was the center of Western Philosophy	Established history
Socrates is the father of Western Philosophy	Established history

Some specific examples of universal truths

- Some specific examples of universal truths are shown here to make the case for Prophet Muhammad and the Quran. Let's review them.

Universal Truths	Source
An author who claims to write or present a high-quality scholarly work or book develops their thoughts and ideas from a young age.	Empirical, established history
Every book or writing has an age. After 100 or so years, it loses its relevance because human civilization, thoughts, ideas, various types of science, and discoveries progress, and it becomes only a great piece of historical work.	Empirical, established history
A book written over a couple of decades must go through a development, correction, and editing process before a final version is made available.	Empirical, established history
A book written over more than two decades without any development or editing will contain internal conflicts in its thoughts, ideas, and events.	Empirical, Inference
A person who challenges a powerful existing system with the support of only a few hundred people behind him never claims early on that in a few years, he and his supporters will be ruling the entire region over all the powerful nations around him.	Established history
A person who has never written an academic work cannot suddenly produce a high-quality scholarly work.	Empirical, inference, established history
A large book claims it will be protected forever, become easy to memorize, and be memorized by millions of people, cover to cover.	Empirical, established history

Now, let's look at some of the facts about the Quran and Prophet Muhammad in the light of the universal truths we just learned

Fact #1: No development in thoughts and ideas

- There is no sign in Prophet Muhammad's life that he **ever** went through the development of any of the thoughts and ideas presented in the Quran.

قُل لَّوْ شَاءَ اللَّهُ مَا تَلَوْتُهُ عَلَيْكُمْ وَلَا أَدْرَاكُم بِهِ ۖ فَقَدْ لَبِثْتُ فِيكُمْ عُمُرًا مِّن قَبْلِهِ ۚ أَفَلَا تَعْقِلُونَ

Tell them: "Had God pleased, I would never have recited this Quran to you, nor would He have made you aware of it. [It is His decision] because I have spent a lifetime among you (have you ever seen me writing or saying such a thing before). Do you not use your senses?" (10:16)

- The Quran is an ageless book. After 1455 years, it hasn't lost its relevance, even as human civilization, ideas, various sciences, and discoveries have made significant progress. Muslims still benefit from it to this day. It is still considered the center and focus of Islam.

Fact #2: No Contradictions in the Quran

- The Quran was revealed over a period of more than 23 years. Prophet Muhammad and his companions memorized it as it was revealed, without any editing. Even when it was written, it never underwent any editing. Still, it is free of internal contradictions in its thoughts, ideas, and events.

أَفَلَا يَتَدَبَّرُونَ الْقُرْآنَ ۚ وَلَوْ كَانَ مِنْ عِنْدِ غَيْرِ اللهِ لَوَجَدُوا فِيهِ اخْتِلَافًا كَثِيرًا

Do these people not ponder the Quran? Had it been from someone other than God, they would have found many (internal) contradictions in it. (Nisa: 82)

- The Quran was completed and written in 632 AD. Nothing in the Quran contradicts or conflicts with any facts associated with other sciences from that time until today.

وَ إِنَّهُ لَكِتَابٌ عَزِيزٌ ۙ لَا يَأْتِيهِ الْبَاطِلُ مِن بَيْنِ يَدَيْهِ وَلَا مِنْ خَلْفِهِ ۖ تَنزِيلٌ مِّنْ حَكِيمٍ حَمِيدٍ

In reality, this is a lofty Book. Wrong can neither enter it from its front (in the future) nor behind (in the history). It is revealed comprehensively from the Being, Who is an embodiment of wisdom and has praiseworthy attributes. (Fussilat: 42)

Fact #3: He was not a writer or author

- Prophet Muhammad did not know how to read or write academically before he presented the Quran. There were many poets and writers at that time, but he never uttered a single word before the Quran.

وَمَا كُنتَ تَتْلُو مِن قَبْلِهِ مِن كِتَابٍ وَلَا تَخُطُّهُ بِيَمِينِكَ ۖ إِذًا لَّارْتَابَ الْمُبْطِلُونَ

And, O Muhammad, you did not recite any book before this or write one with your right hand. Had this been the case, these disbelievers may get into doubts (Ankabut:48)

Fact #4: God protected the Quran

- The Quran states that God will protect this book until the Day of Judgment. The Quran, a 600+ page book, is the most memorized book in the world since the time of Prophet Muhammad. Kids as young as five (5) years old have memorized it cover-to-cover.

إِنَّا نَحْنُ نَزَّلْنَا الذِّكْرَ وَإِنَّا لَهُ لَحَافِظُونَ

It is Us who revealed this Reminder (Quran), and We shall preserve it (Raad:9)

Fact #5: Quran predicted his dominance early on

- Prophet Muhammad challenged the most powerful religious systems (Makkah was the hub of idol worship, and other neighboring powers were Christians and Fire Worshipers) with the support of only 10-20 people behind him.
- The Quran announced very early on that, in a few years, Islam would rule the entire region, subjugate all powerful nations around it, and dominate all other religions in that area.

هُوَ الَّذِي أَرْسَلَ رَسُولَهُ بِالْهُدَىٰ وَ دِينِ الْحَقِّ لِيُظْهِرَهُ عَلَى الدِّينِ كُلِّهِ ۚ وَ كَفَىٰ بِاللّٰهِ شَهِيدًا

He has sent His Messenger with guidance and the true religion so that it will prevail over all other religions. God is a Sufficient witness to this Truth. (Fath:28)

In less than 100 years, Muslims were ruling pretty much in the entire civilized world

Medinah

In this course, we will learn about the Quran. Before doing that, why is it first important to analyze whether the Quran is the book of God?

Chapter 4

Approaching the Quran
(Summary of L5 Topics)

This chapter summarizes what we studied in Level 5 before embarking on the journey of examining individual Quranic passages.

Quran's main message is very simple

1 There is one true God, and He has no partners. He is the Creator, and we are His creations.

2 This is a temporary life, and a new life will begin after this world comes to an end, and a new world will be created.

3 One Day, we will be held accountable for our beliefs and actions based on the concept of good/evil that is given to us by God.

Every human being can get this message from the Quran without any effort. A simple translation can deliver this message repeatedly. No scholarly discussions are required to get this message.

Scholars of the Quran agree that:

- The Quran is the easiest book for a common reader to grasp the main message of Islam because of its simplicity and its constant reminders throughout.

BUT,

- It is the most difficult book for scholars who want to dive deeper to understand the wisdom behind its choice of words, brevity, and relevance until the Day of Judgment.

Why is the Quran different from human writings?

- One of the most common objections raised against the Quran is that it is a collection of random topics, and that any verse can be taken out of context to understand the author's intent.
- However, this is due to a lack of appreciation for the Quran's style.
- Let's look at the two pictures below:

Our creations

We measure and create beauty through symmetry to bring accuracy to patterns

Allah's Creations

Allah creates beauty through apparent randomness and repeated patterns, without measurement, yet in a perfect balance necessary for the object's harmony.

- The same way, the Quran exhibits apparent randomness, but its topics and verses are repeated in a perfect pattern within their own context, necessary to deliver the message in the most balanced way possible.
- There are no two verses that are exactly the same in intent or context. Each instance of a repeated theme or story provides a new angle, different details, or a unique lesson tailored to the specific context in which it appears.
- Instead of keeping every subject in one place, the Quran "sprinkles" related verses throughout different Surahs. Each occurrence connects naturally with the major theme of that Surah, like threads forming a complete tapestry.

Considerations when approaching the Quran

Style of the Quran

- To comprehend the style of the Quran's writing, the following must be appreciated.

Genre
- The Quran resembles (though not strictly) an oration or a sermon delivered by a powerful Orator.
- However, scholars of the Quran unanimously agree that it is difficult to determine the exact genre of the Quran.
- It has the beat, rhythm, and poise of poetry, yet it is not poetry.
- It has the simplicity and continuity found in prose, yet it is not prose.

Dialogues
- The Quran contains dialogues between real characters of the 7th-century Arabia, very similar to a book of dialogues, and God is the author of these dialogues.
- The speaker and the addressee in these dialogues are determined by the occasion and context (unlike in worldly books, where the author writes the names).

"We"
- In Arabic, this type of "We" is called the 'plural of someone who is exalting himself' – it is considered suitable for God but for human beings it is a sign of arrogance.

Rhymes
- The Quran's poetic style and rhythmic recitation are pleasing to the ears of every listener.
- The ending sound changes multiple times when the topic changes.

Stories
- The Quran narrates many real stories about past events.
- Some stories were repeated multiple times with different details depending on the context.

Similes
- The Quran also employs similes in certain places to explain specific facts or truths or to emphasize critical points in its message.

Unseen World
- The Quran has two types of verses: Muhkam & Mutashabihaat. The latter are verses that mention things beyond human knowledge and observation, or pertain to matters of the Hereafter or the unseen world.

Parallel Verses

- The Quran presents its message in various ways and in a variety of styles
- The same subject or story is repeated at multiple places with different details, and is relevant to the context in which it comes

Alif-Laam

Alif-Laam ٱل

The Definite Article
(Alif Laam of Ehad)

The Article of Genus
(Alif Laam of indicating a genus, a common entity)

- In the Arabic language, the article Alif Laam is used as a definite article (referring to something specific to a time and place) and also to indicate a common entity (a family of something) without being specific (for example, the word "man" may also refer to human beings, depending on the context).
- When the Quran uses terms such as Al-Mushrikun, Al-Yahud, and Al-Nasara, it refers to specific groups of people living in that time and place, not to every idolator, Jew, or Christian in the world.
- They were the direct addressees of the Quran; any instruction regarding them cannot be extended to those living around us.

Topic of the Quran

The Quran's central theme is the documentation of the account of Prophet Muhammad's warning mission (Indhar) to his people and the people around him that happened according to the Law of Conclusive Communication of the Truth

- The same court of justice that will be set up for every person on that day was set up for the nations of the Messengers in this world after the phase of Itmam al Hujjah.
- By the time of the Itmam al-Hujjah phase, the believers become distinct and separated from the disbelievers.
- The disbelievers were punished either through various natural calamities if the Messenger had fewer companions, or through wars (killed or subjugated) if there were enough companions, and if there was a place to migrate safely.
- It was due to the deliberate denial of the disbelievers.

- On the other hand, those who accepted the message and helped Messenger in his mission were rewarded – they either remained safe from the punishment or were given power over the rejectors and hence authority in the land.
- In this process, believers are tested and trained to purify their hearts and strengthen their faith in God.

So, when that which they recognized came to them, they disbelieved in it. So let the curse of Allah be on the disbelievers. (2:89)

- The punishment and humiliation inflicted upon the Messenger's nation was God's retribution carried out by God Himself, in which the Messenger and his companions were nothing but divine weapons.
- The purpose of this practice is to remind humanity about the Day of Judgment and the accountability on that day, based on the knowledge that we have been given and the actions that follow that knowledge.

God's law of *Itmam al Hujjah*

- The *Qanoon Itmam al-Hujjah* (the Conclusive Communication for the Truth) is a divine principle that governs the application and scope of certain Quranic instructions, particularly those relating to divine punishment and Jihad.
- It significantly affects the understanding of which instructions were specific to the time of the Prophet Muhammad and his direct addressees, versus those that are universally applicable today.
- Several instructions in the Quran concerning Jihad and the treatment of idolaters in the Arabian Peninsula were context-specific, meant to implement this divine law at that particular time. These directives are therefore not perpetual mandates for all Muslims at all times.
- The law is summarized in the picture below:

Warning (Indhar)

Announcement of Messengerhood and initial warning to specific people around the Prophet

Through Natural calamities and disasters
(Examples: Prophet Nuh, Lut, Shoaib, Saleh .....)

At the hands of Messengers and their companions through Wars
(Examples: Prophet Musa (after Firaun), and Muhammad)

General Warning (Indhar-e-Aam)

General warning to the people in that area and around that area

Punishment (Azaab)

Punishment at the hands of Messenger and his companions and/or Angels

The Polytheists were killed, and the People of the Book were overpowered and forced to pay tax (Jizyah)

Completion of Arguments (Itmam-al-Hujjah)

Arguments are completed and evidence is presented in its concrete and undeniable form

Migration and Disassociation

If possible, Messenger and his people migrate to another land and completely disassociate themselves from people who rejected the message

In the case of Prophet Muhammad, God separated non-believers from believers at this stage as per His Law. He announced in the Quran that all associations must be severed.

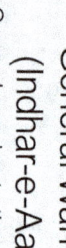

Characters of the Quran

يَا أَيُّهَا الَّذِينَ آمَنُوا كُلُوا مِنْ طَيِّبَاتِ مَا رَزَقْنَاكُمْ

O you who believe! Eat of the lawful things that We have provided you with (Baqarah:172)

يَا أَيُّهَا النَّبِيُّ إِنَّا أَرْسَلْنَاكَ شَاهِدًا وَمُبَشِّرًا وَنَذِيرًا

O Prophet, verily, We have sent you as a witness, and a bearer of glad tidings, and a warner (Ahzab:45)

إِذَا جَاءَكَ الْمُنَافِقُونَ قَالُوا نَشْهَدُ إِنَّكَ لَرَسُولُ اللَّهِ

When the hypocrites come to you, [O Muhammad], they say, "We testify that you are the Messenger of Allah." (Munafiqoon:71)

يَا أَهْلَ الْكِتَابِ لِمَ تَلْبِسُونَ الْحَقَّ بِالْبَاطِلِ

O People of the Book: "Why do you conceal truth with falsehood (Aal-e-Imran:71)

إِنَّ الشَّيْطَانَ لِلْإِنْسَانِ عَدُوٌّ مُبِينٌ

Indeed, Satan is an open enemy of man (Yusuf:5)

نَزَلَ بِهِ الرُّوحُ الْأَمِينُ

Which is brought down by the Rooh Al Ameen (Gabriel) (Shuara:193)

وَ إِنْ أَحَدٌ مِّنَ الْمُشْرِكِينَ اسْتَجَارَكَ فَأَجِرْهُ حَتَّى يَسْمَعَ كَلَمَ اللَّهِ

And if anyone of the Mushrikun seeks your protection, then grant him protection, so that he may hear the Word of Allah (the Quran) (Tawbah:06)

Oaths in the Quran

- In the Quran, God Almighty has sworn by Himself and by many of His creations to affirm a claim-statement.

- Scholars of the Quran have debated the nature, significance, and wisdom behind these oaths – some have referred to them as Mutashabihaat, whose meaning is known only to God.

- Three main questions have been raised (some critics of the Quran have raised them as objections) by almost every careful reader of the Quranic text, as the human reason inspires them.

    - Oaths are taken to emphasize and register the truth of one's statement by invoking someone who is a higher being, nobler and more respected than the oath-taker. Oaths are conventionally sworn by taking the name of sacred objects. However, in the Quran, God swears by ordinary and insignificant things on many occasions. It does not match God's exalted position.

    - God has taken oaths to affirm fundamental Islamic beliefs, such as monotheism, the Day of Judgment, and prophethood. To non-believers, these beliefs cannot be imposed by the mere sanctity of an oath unless they are established independently for them first. In other words, the oaths appear to be a fruitless insistence only.

    - Islam has taught believers not to swear by anything other than the Glorious God, but God has taken oaths of cities, fruits, the sun, and the moon.

- Components: In a Quranic oath, the object sworn by is called the _Muqsam Bihi_, and the statement or truth for which the oath is taken is known as the _Muqsam Alayh_. These two components come after the letter of Oath, which is Wow. و

Muqsam Bihi	This is the entity or thing by which the oath is sworn.
Muqsam Alayh	This is the statement or the truth that is being emphasized by the oath.

وَ التِّينِ وَ الزَّيْتُونِ وَ طُوْرِ سِيْنِيْنَ وَ هٰذَا الْبَلَدِ الْاَمِيْنِ	Muqsam Bihi (Swear by)
لَقَدْ خَلَقْنَا الْاِنْسَانَ فِيْ اَحْسَنِ تَقْوِيْمٍ ثُمَّ رَدَدْنٰهُ اَسْفَلَ سٰفِلِيْنَ	Muqsam Alayh (Swear for)

Relationship between Swear by and Swear for

- If oaths are taken merely for emphasis, then they fail to address the question of the relationship between the Swear by and Swear for – for example, Quran 68:1-2, 100:1-6, 103:1-2.
- One of the greatest Islamic scholars of the 20th century, Imam Hamid Uddin Farahi, considers these oaths as evidence (something bearing witness) presented by God to establish a fact, not just an emphasis.
- Swear-by furnishes evidence or becomes a witness for Swear for.
- Linguistically, the particles of the oath are ba', waw, and ta'.
- Oaths are an instrument of Quranic logic and reasoning, and there is no reason to emphasize the greatness of the Swear by (it can be the sun or the moon or fighting horses, etc).
- There are multiple types of oaths (or Swear by) in the Quran:

Phenomenal Oath	Historical Oath
Multiple phenomena of nature are sworn by	Cites one or more events from the past
وَالذَّٰرِيَٰتِ ذَرْوًا	وَ التِّينِ وَ الزَّيْتُونِ
By the wind that carries dust particles	By the figs and the olives (Where Jesus was born)

Experiential Oath	Conjugate Oath
Certain aspect of human experience is presented as evidence	One member of a pair is discussed, and the other member is cited as evidence
وَ لَآ أُقْسِمُ بِالنَّفْسِ اللَّوَّامَةِ	وَ الشَّمْسِ وَ ضُحَٰهَا
I swear by the soul that rebukes	By the Sun and its brightness

Quran explains itself

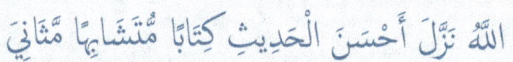

God has revealed the best discourse whose verses resemble one another and whose surahs occur in pairs. (39:23)

We have explained this in the Quran in multiple ways, so that they take heed (17:41)

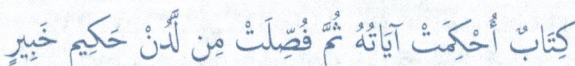

This is a Book whose verses were first concise, then explained by Him, who is wise and all-knowing. (11:1)

- The Quran presents its message in various ways and styles. As a result, it has become unparalleled among other works in its ability to explain its own verses.
- The same topic appears in various surahs with different details – this is not mere repetition.
- The background, context, and details vary across different places for the same incident.
- In some places, the description is concise, and the matter is only alluded to, and in other places, the details of that matter are revealed.
- At one point, a word is unclear, but at another point, its usage provides a hint of how it was used in the first place.
- The emphasis and perspective on the same event differ from place to place.

Generic and Specific Verses

- When reading the Quran, the general and specific verses should be differentiated.
- There are many places in the Quran where the words are general; however, the context clearly indicates that something specific is meant.
- An example is shown below:

- For example, the Quran uses the word An'naas (people), but it does not refer to all people in the world; often, it does not even refer to all the people of Arabia: it refers to a group among them. ← النَّاس
- It uses the expression Alad Deeni Kullihi (over all the religions), and it does not refer to all religions of the world ← عَلَى الدِّيْنِ كُلِّهِ
- It refers to Al-Mushrikun (the polytheists), but they do not refer to all those who are guilty of polytheism ← المُشْرِكُوْن
- Similarly, the words Min Ahl al Kitaab (And from these People of the Book) do not refer to all the People of the Book of the world ← مِنْ أَهْلِ الْكِتَابِ
- It mentions the word Insaan (the man), but it does not refer to mankind, but a group of people ← الإِنْسَان

Importance of the Context

وَ اعْتَصِمُوْا بِحَبْلِ اللهِ جَمِيْعًا وَّ لَا تَفَرَّقُوْا

And hold firmly to the rope of Allah (the Quran) all together and do not become divided (3:103)

- Turning to the Quran to resolve all disagreements is possible only when its verdict is clear and unambiguous.
- There is a general misunderstanding that the verses of the Quran have multiple meanings, and it is evident that there are many interpretations of every verse (some even contradictory to one another).
- If a difference of opinion arises in the interpretation of a discourse, the most satisfactory way to resolve this is through the context and coherence of the discourse.
- Many differences of opinion have arisen in understanding Islam due to disregard for the context of a verse. If this context is kept in consideration, one will find that on most occasions, only one interpretation is possible (in that context).
- What makes the Quran a document having one definite meaning and which resolves all differences of interpretation is the CONTEXT of the verse.

الْقُرْآنُ لَا يَحْتَمِلُ إِلَّا تَأْوِيْلاً وَاحِداً

"There is no possibility of more than one interpretation in the Quran." (a famous quote of Iman Hamid Uddin Farahi, a Quran Scholar)

The meaning of a word

The meaning of a word is determined:

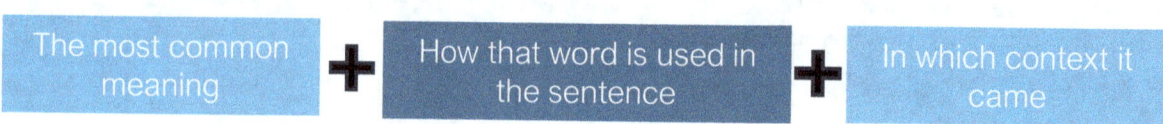

Look at this example:

> ## What does Tiger imply here?
>
> Tipu Sultan, the Tiger of Mysore, was the Indian Muslim ruler of the Kingdom of Mysore and was considered a brave leader.

- In this example, the writer has written this sentence to convey a specific message or meaning.
- To convey a message with specific meaning, a three-step process is required:
  - **Analyze Common Usages:** Investigate both the literal and figurative applications of a key word (e.g., "Tiger"). The determination of its intended nature will be informed by the subsequent two steps.
  - **Contextualize Usage:** Ascertain how the word is employed within the specific sentence or phrase, and identify the message it aims to communicate in that context.
  - **Understand Broader Context:** Analyze the surrounding text or statement to fully comprehend the environment in which the sentence or phrase appears.
- Following this comprehensive analysis, it becomes evident that the term "Tiger" is utilized figuratively to commend the renowned bravery of a prominent figure, such as Tipu Sultan.

The meaning of a word: Example

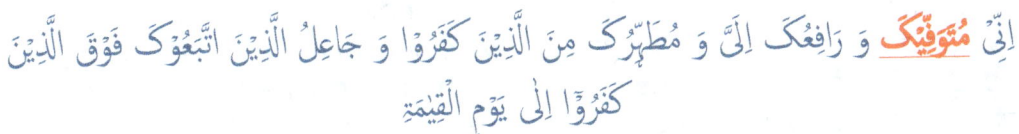

اِنّی مُتَوَفّیْکَ وَ رَافِعُکَ اِلَیَّ وَ مُطَهّرُکَ مِنَ الَّذِیْنَ کَفَرُوْا وَ جَاعِلُ الَّذِیْنَ اتَّبَعُوْکَ فَوْقَ الَّذِیْنَ کَفَرُوْا اِلٰی یَوْمِ الْقِیٰمَةِ

At that time, God said: "Jesus, I have <u>decided to give you death</u> and lift you to Myself. I shall purify you from those who have disbelieved in you and grant your followers supremacy over these disbelievers until the Day of Judgement.

Step #1: The most common meaning

The word "*Mutawaffa*" is used in the Quran multiple times to mean death. This is the most popular meaning of this word.

Step #2: How that word is used in the sentence **+**

Allah is telling Jesus what his plan is for him step by step. Raising will occur after he dies

Step #3: In which context it came

Allah has made such a decision because the Jews have decided to kill him, and Allah's practice is that He does not allow anyone to overpower Messengers

---

Some scholars of the Quran have taken the meaning of *Mutawaffa* as "take someone to yourself," which does not fit well in the sentence

Hazf (Omission) in the Quran

- *Hazf* (Omission) in the Quran is very common, as it was common in the language at the time the Quran was revealed.
- In the Quran, *Hazf* (omission) is a significant symbolic and linguistic device used to convey subtle and deeper meanings, achieve eloquence, and avoid redundancy. It is a recognized feature within the science of Arabic rhetoric known as *'ilm al-ma'ani'* (the science of meanings).
- In Hazf, when a sentence is spoken, certain words are omitted, either because they are quite obvious and people will understand the full sentence, or to leave a deeper impression of the meaning.
- We also do that in our language, but it's not as common as in Arabic in the Quran.
- A few examples in our language are given below before the Quran's examples:

> "John can play the guitar, and Mary [can play] the piano.
> "One person gave me a book, and another [person gave me] a CD."
> "If you don't stop talking ill about me (silence)."

وَ مَا مِنْ دَآبَّةٍ فِى الْأَرْضِ وَ لَا طَآئِرٍ يَطِيرُ بِجَنَاحَيْهِ اِلَّا أُمَمٌ اَمْثَالُكُمْ

[Do you not see that] all the beasts that roam on their legs on the earth and all the birds that soar on both their wings [in the sky] are all communities like your own. (6:38)

- A little deliberation shows that in the above verse, a suppression of <u>parallel phrases</u> has occurred. Because of the presence of the expression on the earth in the first part of the sentence, there is a suppression of its parallel expression in the sky in the second part (which is understood).

اَمَّنْ هُوَ قَانِتٌ اٰنَآءَ الَّيْلِ سَاجِدًا وَّ قَآئِمًا يَّحْذَرُ الْاٰخِرَةَ وَ يَرْجُوا رَحْمَةَ رَبِّهٖ قُلْ هَلْ يَسْتَوِى الَّذِيْنَ يَعْلَمُوْنَ وَ الَّذِيْنَ لَا يَعْلَمُوْنَ

Will those who, during the night, prostrate at times and at times stand humbly, fear the Hereafter and hope for their Lord's mercy, and [those who have forgotten Him while relying on their associates] ever become equal? Ask them: Can those who know and those who do not ever be the same? (39:9)

- The part in red in the sentence is actually suppressed. It is evident from the emphasis in the speaker's later words, where He said, "those who know and those who do not." Obviously, God is first compared with those who know and, second (omitted), with those who do not.

Parentheses in the Quran

- There are many places in the Quran where a comment is inserted (text in parentheses without actual brackets) by God – these sentences are called Parenthetical Sentences.
- There are two types:
    - Parenthetical sentences – comment on the previous sentence
    - Insertion – added to carry the conversation forward

Examples of Parenthetical Sentences

Then when she delivered the child, she said: "Lord, I have given birth to a daughter" – and God well knew of what she had delivered – and [said:] "That boy would not have been like this girl. And I have named her Mary, and I give her and her progeny in your refuge from Satan, the Accursed One." (3:36)

And if they break their oath after their pledge and find blame in your religion, wage war against these leaders of disbelief – their words and promises are baseless – so that they abstain. (9:12)

Recall when Luqman, while counselling his son, had said: "Son! Do not associate partners with God. In reality, polytheism is a great injustice – We have counselled a human being about his parents also. His mother kept him in her womb, tolerating woe after woe, and [after birth] it took two years for his weaning. [We have counselled him:] "Be grateful to Me and to your parents [and remember that ultimately] to Me is the return. But if they force you to associate someone with Me about whom you have no proof, do not obey them. However, treat them kindly in this world and follow the way of those who turn to Me. Then you will have to return to Me alone. Then I shall inform you of what you have been doing." – Son! The fact is that if a deed is equal to even the grain of a mustard seed ...... (31:13-15)

> As a parent, Luqman did not consider it right to discuss his rights and the sacrifices that parents make, so God inserted this into his talk.

Many verses in the Quran address the Prophet. Why do some of them not apply to us anymore?

Does the Quran also address us? Find two verses in the Quran where the Quran is addressing us?

Chapter 5

Examples from the Quran

This chapter discusses examples from the Quran in which the principles of understanding we have learned are applied.

Importance of Context

- First, look at examples where context makes a big difference in understanding the verse.
- In some places, it even impacts the rulings of Shariah.

فَلَا أُقْسِمُ بِمَوَاقِعِ النُّجُومِ ۞ وَ إِنَّهُ لَقَسَمٌ لَّوْ تَعْلَمُونَ عَظِيمٌ ۞ إِنَّهُ لَقُرْآنٌ كَرِيمٌ

فِي كِتَابٍ مَّكْنُونٍ ۞ لَّا يَمَسُّهُ إِلَّا الْمُطَهَّرُونَ ۞ تَنْزِيلٌ مِّن رَّبِّ الْعَالَمِينَ

[They deny the Quran.] So no! [This has not been inspired by some devil.] I present as a witness the abodes where stars fall, and if you understand, this is surely a great witness. Undoubtedly, this is a glorious Quran in a protected book. None touches it except the pure (angels); it has been revealed by the Lord of the Universe. (Surah Waqiah:75-80)

This verse has been used to make Wudu obligatory for reading the Quran because, according to some Quran interpreters, it speaks to the state of purity required to touch the Quran. However, the context suggests that Allah SWT is referring to the sanctity of this book and its protection from the devils. This verse does not address the conditions under which humans may touch this book.

Note: *Out of respect, one may decide always to read the Quran in the state of Wudu. That's a personal decision, but not the instruction of the Quran.*

فَإِذَا انسَلَخَ الْأَشْهُرُ الْحُرُمُ فَاقْتُلُوا الْمُشْرِكِينَ حَيْثُ وَجَدتُّمُوهُمْ وَ خُذُوهُمْ وَ احْصُرُوهُمْ وَ اقْعُدُوا لَهُمْ كُلَّ مَرْصَدٍ ۚ

فَإِن تَابُوا وَ أَقَامُوا الصَّلَاةَ وَ آتَوُا الزَّكَاةَ فَخَلُّوا سَبِيلَهُمْ ۚ إِنَّ اللَّهَ غَفُورٌ رَّحِيمٌ

After this [declaration on the day of the great Hajj], when the sacred months have passed, kill these Idolaters wherever you find them, and for this purpose, capture them and besiege them, and lie in wait for them in every ambush. Then, if they repent and diligently pray and pay Zakah, leave them alone. Surely, God is Merciful (Surah Taubah:5)

This verse is called "the verse of the sword" and has been used to fight non-Muslims. It is famously used by groups fighting in different parts of the world. However, the context of the Quran, and specifically of Surah Taubah, clearly suggests that these verses are not generic but instead give instructions to Muslims regarding a specific group they were fighting. This is the announcement of God's punishment for those people.

Importance of Context and Addressee

- Surah Ad-Duha is a perfect example of considering context and the addressee when reading a Surah, and of how literature like the Quran speaks coherently within its text.
- Examples like these dispel the idea that the Quran is a collection of random verses, each conveying a message, and that there is no need to read a Surah as a unit.

وَ الضُّحٰی وَ الَّیْلِ اِذَا سَجٰی ۙ مَا وَدَّعَکَ رَبُّکَ وَ مَا قَلٰی ۙ

وَ لَلْاٰخِرَةُ خَیْرٌ لَّکَ مِنَ الْاُوْلٰی ؕ وَ لَسَوْفَ یُعْطِیْکَ رَبُّکَ فَتَرْضٰی ؕ

اَلَمْ یَجِدْکَ یَتِیْمًا فَاٰوٰی ۪ وَ وَجَدَکَ ضَآلًّا فَهَدٰی ۪ وَ وَجَدَکَ عَآئِلًا فَاَغْنٰی ؕ

فَاَمَّا الْیَتِیْمَ فَلَا تَقْهَرْ ؕ وَ اَمَّا السَّآئِلَ فَلَا تَنْهَرْ ؕ وَ اَمَّا بِنِعْمَةِ رَبِّکَ فَحَدِّثْ

Support
> The day bears witness when it brightens, and the night also when it becomes peaceful [that the joy and sorrow are part of life], so, neither has your Lord abandoned you nor is he displeased with you. The days to come shall be much better for you than these initial ones, [O Prophet!] And your Lord will soon give you so much that you shall be well-pleased.

Favors
> Is it not a fact that He found you an orphan and thus sheltered you? Found you searching for guidance, hence guided you? And found you in need, so [gave you such contentment of the heart that it] enriched you?

Advice
> So, treat not now the orphan with harshness and scold not the one who asks, and keep proclaiming the favor of guidance the Lord has given you.

(Surah Ad Duha)

Favors	Advice
Sheltered the Prophet when he was an orphan	→ Do not treat orphans with harshness
Guided him when he was searching for guidance	→ Do not reprimand the one who is asking you questions for guidance
Gave him the content of the heart and a deeper understanding of religion when he was in need	→ Spread the blessings of knowledge by sharing it with others, and do not hide it

Parallel Verses

- As in other literature, when a reader wants to conclude a specific topic in the Quran, they should read the entire Quran and examine various passages related to that topic before concluding. These passages are called parallel verses.

- Below is an example of parallel verses.

وَ اِذْ قُلْنَا لِلْمَلٰٓئِكَةِ اسْجُدُوْا لِاٰدَمَ فَسَجَدُوْٓا اِلَّآ اِبْلِيْسَ ۗ اَبٰى وَ اسْتَكْبَرَ ۗ وَكَانَ مِنَ الْكٰفِرِيْنَ

And [to understand the trial of human beings in Our scheme] also narrate the incident when We asked the angels to bow down to Adam; then all of them bowed down except Iblis. He refused and showed arrogance and, in this manner, became among the rejecters. (Surah Baqarah:34)

- According to this verse, it seems that Iblis was among the Angels

وَ اِذْ قُلْنَا لِلْمَلٰٓئِكَةِ اسْجُدُوْا لِاٰدَمَ فَسَجَدُوْٓا اِلَّآ اِبْلِيْسَ ۗ كَانَ مِنَ الْجِنِّ فَفَسَقَ عَنْ اَمْرِ رَبِّهٖ

Remember when We directed the angels: "Prostrate before Adam." They prostrated except Iblis. He was among the Jinn. So, he evaded the directive of his Lord. (Surah Kahf:50)

- Looking at all the verses of the Quran related to this incident, it will be clear that the order to prostrate before Adam was given to both Angels and Jinns, and it was Iblis from among the Jinns who refused.

- In Arabic, the dominant group is sometimes addressed, including the other smaller groups.

The Quran is the Authority

Jabir reports that once Umar brought a book to the Prophet, which he acquired from the people of the book (the Jews), and said: 'O Rasulullah! I have a good book from the people of the book.' The Prophet became angry and said, "Are you reckless, O son of Khattab?! By Allah! I have brought it (religion) to you in a bright and clear state. It shouldn't be that you end up denying the truth they tell or believing the falsehood they tell. By oath of Allah! If Musa were alive today, he would have no option but to follow me.' (Masnad Ahmad and many other books)

إِنَّا أَنْزَلْنَا التَّوْرَاةَ فِيهَا هُدًى وَنُورٌ	وَكَيْفَ يُحَكِّمُونَكَ وَعِنْدَهُمُ التَّوْرَاةُ فِيهَا حُكْمُ اللَّهِ
Indeed, We sent down the Torah, which was guidance and light. (5:46)	But how do they come to you for judgment while they have the Torah, which has the judgment of Allah (about this matter)? (5:44)

Similes / Metaphors – Disbelievers

- In the Quran, metaphors are an essential linguistic feature that convey complex, abstract concepts in a way that is relatable to human understanding. Understanding these figurative expressions within the broader context of the Quran's message and the classical Arabic language, rather than taking them strictly literally, is very important. The verses of Surah Al-Baqarah are an excellent example.

Surah Baqarah Verses 6-7 & 17-18

The Behavior of Disbelievers (Rejectors)

اِنَّ الَّذِيۡنَ كَفَرُوۡا سَوَآءٌ عَلَيۡهِمۡ ءَاَنۡذَرۡتَهُمۡ اَمۡ لَمۡ تُنۡذِرۡهُمۡ لَا يُؤۡمِنُوۡنَ

خَتَمَ اللهُ عَلَىٰ قُلُوۡبِهِمۡ وَ عَلَىٰ سَمۡعِهِمۡ وَ عَلَىٰٓ اَبۡصَارِهِمۡ غِشَاوَةٌ وَّ لَهُمۡ عَذَابٌ عَظِيۡمٌ

On the other hand, people who have decided to reject this Book, it is the same to them whether you warn them or not; they will not believe. God has now set a seal on their hearts and on their ears [per His law], and on their eyes is a veil, and [on the Day of Judgement] a great torment awaits them.

The Metaphor Used For Rejectors' Behavior

مَثَلُهُمۡ كَمَثَلِ الَّذِى اسۡتَوۡقَدَ نَارًا ۚ فَلَمَّآ اَضَآءَتۡ مَا حَوۡلَهُ ذَهَبَ اللهُ

بِنُوۡرِهِمۡ وَ تَرَكَهُمۡ فِىۡ ظُلُمٰتٍ لَّا يُبۡصِرُوۡنَ صُمٌّ بُكۡمٌ عُمۡىٌ فَهُمۡ لَا يَرۡجِعُوۡنَ

Their example is like that of a person who kindled a large fire [in a dark night]; then, when the fire lit up the surroundings, God took away the ability to see for those for whom the fire had been kindled and left them in darkness, so that they could not see anything. Deaf, dumb, and blind; hence, they shall now never return.

- In the above example, the behavior of the rejectors and the consequences they faced are described metaphorically as people whose ability to see is taken away (because of their behavior) after someone (Prophet Muhammad) lit the fire, and the surroundings became bright.
- In the next verse, God used another example of hypocrites, describing their behavior and consequences metaphorically as people walking in heavy rain with lightning. They walk a little bit, but then wait when it becomes too dark. This represents their attitude of indecision.

Similes / Metaphors for Hypocrites

Example of the attitude of the hypocrites

Surah Baqarah Verses 8-10 & 19-20

The Behavior of the Hypocrites

وَ مِنَ النَّاسِ مَنْ يَّقُوْلُ اٰمَنَّا بِاللّٰهِ وَ بِالْيَوْمِ الْاٰخِرِ وَ مَا هُمْ بِمُؤْمِنِيْنَ

يُخٰدِعُوْنَ اللّٰهَ وَ الَّذِيْنَ اٰمَنُوْا وَ مَا يَخْدَعُوْنَ اِلَّآ اَنْفُسَهُمْ وَ مَا يَشْعُرُوْنَ

فِيْ قُلُوْبِهِمْ مَّرَضٌ ۙ فَزَادَهُمُ اللّٰهُ مَرَضًا ۚ وَ لَهُمْ عَذَابٌ اَلِيْمٌ ۢ بِمَا كَانُوْا يَكْذِبُوْنَ

And among these people are those [Hypocrites] who say: "We have professed faith in God and in the Last Day," whereas they do not have faith in any of these things. They want to deceive both God and the believers, and in reality, they are only fooling themselves, but realize it not! In their hearts was the ailment [of jealousy]; so, God has now further increased this ailment of theirs. And because they have been lying, there is a grievous penalty for them.

The Metaphor Used for the Hypocrites' Behavior

اَوْ كَصَيِّبٍ مِّنَ السَّمَآءِ فِيْهِ ظُلُمٰتٌ وَّ رَعْدٌ وَّ بَرْقٌ ۚ يَجْعَلُوْنَ اَصَابِعَهُمْ فِيْ

اٰذَانِهِمْ مِّنَ الصَّوَاعِقِ حَذَرَ الْمَوْتِ ۘ وَ اللّٰهُ مُحِيْطٌ بِالْكٰفِرِيْنَ

يَكَادُ الْبَرْقُ يَخْطَفُ اَبْصَارَهُمْ ۗ كُلَّمَآ اَضَآءَ لَهُمْ مَّشَوْا فِيْهِ ۙ وَ اِذَآ اَظْلَمَ عَلَيْهِمْ

قَامُوْا ۗ وَ لَوْ شَآءَ اللّٰهُ لَذَهَبَ بِسَمْعِهِمْ وَ اَبْصَارِهِمْ ۗ اِنَّ اللّٰهَ عَلٰى كُلِّ شَيْءٍ قَدِيْرٌ

Or is it such that it is raining; in it are dark clouds, and thunder and lightning also. They are trying to insert their fingers in their ears from the fear of death because of lightning, whereas God has encompassed such rejecters from all sides. The lightning snatches away their sight; when it lights up on them, they walk a little in it, and when darkness descends upon them, they stand still. If God willed, He could have also taken away their hearing and sight. Indeed, God has power over all things.

Insertion in the middle to complete the topic

- In the Quran, it is very common for God to insert His own statements in the middle of a verse when He wants to emphasize something or reveal what is hidden in other people's intent or statements. One example is presented here:

وَ لَقَدْ اٰتَيْنَا لُقْمٰنَ الْحِكْمَةَ اَنِ اشْكُرْ لِلّٰهِ ۚ وَ مَنْ يَّشْكُرْ فَاِنَّمَا يَشْكُرُ لِنَفْسِهٖ ۚ وَ مَنْ كَفَرَ فَاِنَّ اللّٰهَ غَنِيٌّ حَمِيْدٌ

وَ اِذْ قَالَ لُقْمٰنُ لِابْنِهٖ وَ هُوَ يَعِظُهٗ يٰبُنَيَّ لَا تُشْرِكْ بِاللّٰهِ ۗ اِنَّ الشِّرْكَ لَظُلْمٌ عَظِيْمٌ

وَ وَصَّيْنَا الْاِنْسَانَ بِوَالِدَيْهِ حَمَلَتْهُ اُمُّهٗ وَهْنًا عَلٰى وَهْنٍ وَّ فِصٰلُهٗ فِيْ عَامَيْنِ اَنِ اشْكُرْ لِيْ وَ لِوَالِدَيْكَ ۗ اِلَيَّ الْمَصِيْرُ

وَ اِنْ جَاهَدٰكَ عَلٰى اَنْ تُشْرِكَ بِيْ مَا لَيْسَ لَكَ بِهٖ عِلْمٌ ۙ فَلَا تُطِعْهُمَا وَ صَاحِبْهُمَا فِي الدُّنْيَا

مَعْرُوْفًا ۖ وَّ اتَّبِعْ سَبِيْلَ مَنْ اَنَابَ اِلَيَّ ۚ ثُمَّ اِلَيَّ مَرْجِعُكُمْ فَاُنَبِّئُكُمْ بِمَا كُنْتُمْ تَعْمَلُوْنَ

يٰبُنَيَّ اِنَّهَآ اِنْ تَكُ مِثْقَالَ ...

We also gave this wisdom to Luqman and directed: "Be grateful to God" – and he who is grateful will be grateful for himself, and he who is ungrateful, God does not care about him because God is self-sufficient; He has praiseworthy attributes. Recall when Luqman, while counseling his son, had said: "Son! Do not associate partners with God. In reality, polytheism is a great injustice." [There is no doubt that] We have also counseled a human being about his parents. His mother kept him in her womb, tolerating distress after distress, and [after birth] it took two years for his weaning. [We have counseled him:] "Be grateful to Me and to your parents [and remember that ultimately] to Me is the return. But if they force you to associate someone with Me about whom you have no proof, do not obey them. However, treat them kindly in this world and follow the way of those who turn to Me. Then you will have to return to Me alone. Then I shall inform you of what you have been doing." [Luqman had said:] "Son! The fact is that if a deed is equal to even the grain ...... (Surah Luqman: 12-16)

- Green – Allah inserted this entire section to complete the topic and the message that He wanted to convey.
- In many places in the Quran, Allah reminds people of the rights of parents right after His rights.
- In this conversation, Luqman talked about Allah's right to be worshipped alone, but he felt shy about talking about his own rights, being a parent himself.
- Allah inserted these verses in the middle as He wanted to reemphasize the rights of parents for two reasons:
  - Honor Luqman, as he skipped advising his son on his own rights
  - Complete the topic of great advice given by a great wise man
- When we read the inserted verses, it is clear that they cannot be Luqman's statement.

Unseen World

- Almost all of the verses related to the unseen world come under "*Mutashabihaat*". These are the verses about which there is no ambiguity in the meaning of the words and concepts used, but we do not understand their reality. The believers are asked to take these verses at face value and avoid delving into them for their reality.

Surah Muhammad Verse 15

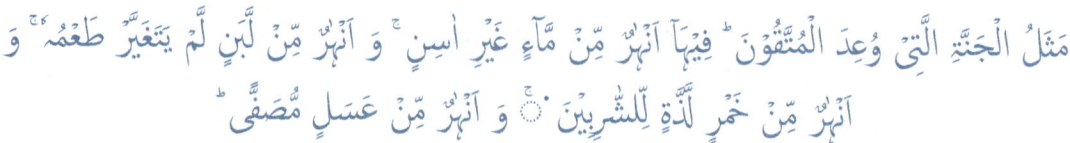

The example of Paradise, which the God-fearing have been promised, is that in it are streams of water that are pure, and in it are streams of milk whose taste shall not change in the slightest, and streams of wine which shall be sheer bliss for those who drink (no intoxication), and streams of honey which shall be absolutely transparent.

- For example, in verse 15 of Surah Muhammad, we know exactly what it means by water, milk, streams, honey, etc, but we cannot imagine what the stream of honey or milk would look like.
- Let's look at another verse in Surah Yunus.

Indeed, your Lord is the God Who created the heavens and the earth in six days. Then He settled Himself on His throne while governing affairs. (Yunus:3)

- In the above verses, there are two places that we can understand very well in terms of the words used and their meanings.
    - Heavens and Earth are created in 6 days (we understand the concept of creation).
    - God settled Himself on a Throne after the creation was done.
- However, we can never understand the true nature of the time it took to create heaven and earth, because the word *Yaum* is also used in Arabic for periods. The amount of time *Yaum* implies here is not known.
- Similarly, we don't know the nature of God settling on a throne. This is entirely beyond our imagination because we cannot comprehend the nature of God.

The Oaths

- In the Quran, there is a relationship between oaths and what follows the oaths.
- There are places in the Quran where God swears by Himself. In these places, God wants us to pay attention because something significant has been stated.
- In other places, God takes an oath of something else. In those places, God wants to present that thing as a witness to the claim that God is making after the oath.
- We will look at both examples.

فَلَا وَ رَبِّكَ لَا يُؤْمِنُونَ حَتَّى يُحَكِّمُوكَ فِيمَا شَجَرَ بَيْنَهُمْ ثُمَّ لَا يَجِدُوا فِيٓ أَنْفُسِهِمْ حَرَجًا

مِّمَّا قَضَيْتَ وَ يُسَلِّمُوا تَسْلِيمًا

But no, [O Messenger!] By your Lord! These people shall never be true believers until they accept you as the arbitrator in their disputes. Then, whatever decision you give, they must not feel any uneasiness in their hearts and submit to it wholeheartedly. (Nisaa:65)

- In the above verse, God is swearing by Himself to make a critical point about the believers' attitude towards the Prophet of the time. When a Prophet is among people, and they believe in him, then when he makes a decision among them for any dispute, they have no choice but to accept him. This is because God's messenger's decision is actually God's decision.

وَ الْمُرْسَلَٰتِ عُرْفًا   فَالْعَٰصِفَٰتِ عَصْفًا وَّ النَّٰشِرَٰتِ نَشْرًا   فَالْفَٰرِقَٰتِ فَرْقًا   فَالْمُلْقِيَٰتِ ذِكْرًا   عُذْرًا أَوْ نُذْرًا

إِنَّمَا تُوعَدُونَ لَوَاقِعٌ

These winds, whose reins are let loose, then viciously blow dust all over. These winds, which scatter the clouds, then settle affairs separately, then infuse the hearts with a reminder to leave no justification for some and to warn others, bear witness that the torment which you are being promised is bound to come. (Mursalat)

- God presented the entire scenery of nature and the complete control He has over the wind and clouds, as a symbol of the Almighty's absolute authority and of His reward and punishment. In other words, the control over these winds is a testimony to that control that He will have on the Day of Judgment, so be careful.

Hazf (Omission)

- *Hazf* (Omission) is a literary device commonly used in the Quran. Some examples are shown here, along with how *Hazf* can be opened to understand the whole meaning.

وَ مَا تَفْعَلُوا مِنْ خَيْرٍ فَإِنَّ اللهَ كَانَ بِهِ عَلِيمًا

[Remember] that any other act of virtue that you do, [you shall definitely get its reward] because it will remain in the knowledge of God. (4:127)

- What's in red isn't available in Arabic. The translator has to open it (or add it) to complete the sentence.

وَ لَهُ مَا سَكَنَ فِى الَّيْلِ وَ النَّهَارِ ۚ وَ هُوَ السَّمِيعُ الْعَلِيمُ

In reality, whatever is stationed in the night [or moves in the day] is under His control alone. And He hears all and knows all. (6:13)

- Again, what's in red isn't available in Arabic. The translator has to open it (or add it) to complete the sentence. The word "*sakan* (peaceful)" is compatible with "*Lail* (night)" only. There must be another verb for the "*An-Nahaar* (day)" which should be moving (opposite of peaceful).

وَ لَوْ اَنَّ قُرْاٰنًا سُيِّرَتْ بِهِ الْجِبَالُ اَوْ قُطِّعَتْ بِهِ الْاَرْضُ اَوْ كُلِّمَ بِهِ الْمَوْتٰى ۚ بَلْ لِّلّٰهِ الْاَمْرُ جَمِيعًا

In reality, had there been a Quran through which the mountains could be set in motion, or the earth be rent asunder, or the dead could talk because of it, [would they have accepted faith?] No, this is not your job [to show signs to them;] in fact, all authority belongs to God. (13:31)

- Again, what's in red isn't available in Arabic. The translator has to open it (or add it) to complete the sentence.
- God started the statement with a condition, "had there been...", but the result or the consequence of that condition is omitted.

Chapter 6

Topic 1: Living faith in God

This chapter discusses examples from the Quran that guide us on the type of faith we should have in God: living faith. The examples also show us how to build that relationship with God.

Surah Aaraf: Verse 172-174

وَ اِذۡ اَخَذَ رَبُّكَ مِنۡۢ بَنِیۡۤ اٰدَمَ مِنۡ ظُهُوۡرِهِمۡ ذُرِّیَّتَهُمۡ وَ اَشۡهَدَهُمۡ عَلٰۤی اَنۡفُسِهِمۡ

اَلَسۡتُ بِرَبِّكُمۡ ؕ قَالُوۡا بَلٰی ۛ شَهِدۡنَا ۛ اَنۡ تَقُوۡلُوۡا یَوۡمَ الۡقِیٰمَةِ اِنَّا كُنَّا عَنۡ هٰذَا غٰفِلِیۡنَ

اَوۡ تَقُوۡلُوۡۤا اِنَّمَاۤ اَشۡرَكَ اٰبَآؤُنَا مِنۡ قَبۡلُ وَ كُنَّا ذُرِّیَّةً مِّنۡۢ بَعۡدِهِمۡ ۚ اَفَتُهۡلِكُنَا

بِمَا فَعَلَ الۡمُبۡطِلُوۡنَ وَ كَذٰلِكَ نُفَصِّلُ الۡاٰیٰتِ وَ لَعَلَّهُمۡ یَرۡجِعُوۡنَ

[O Prophet!] Remind them of that time, too, when your Lord had brought forth from the loins of Adam's children their progeny and had made them testify to themselves. [He had asked:] "Am I not your Lord?" They replied: "Yes, [You alone are our Lord.] We bear witness to it." We did this so you don't say on the Day of Judgement: "*We had no knowledge of this*," or present this excuse: "*Our forefathers had already adopted polytheism and we later became their children*; then, will You destroy us on account of what these wrongdoers did?" In this way, We explain Our revelations so that people are left with no excuse to deny the truth and so that they may return to the right path.

- These verses are famously known as the verses of "the Pledge of **Alast**" عَهدُ الۡأَلۡسُتِ

- The Quran presents different arguments regarding God and monotheism. These verses followed the Quran's initial argument, based on incidents of God punishing nations on Earth, which reflect God's worldly retribution.

- Now the Quraysh are reminded of the pledge by which all mankind will be held accountable to God on the Day of Judgment.

- No one will be able to present the excuse that the message of a Prophet did not reach him/her or that he/she grew up in an environment of polytheism and disbelief, so he/she couldn't confess to God's existence and the concept of monotheism.

- These verses suggest that God's knowledge is innate to human beings, and no external source, like the Prophet's message, is required for that.

Belief in a Higher Power

- The words used in the verses suggest that it happened to the entire humanity.
- The incident of the Pledge caused the internal recognition of a Supreme Power (God) to be stamped on the human's heart and ingrained in the soul.
- The incident is erased from memory so that this life can be a trial.
- Just as we are born from a mother's womb, and the memory fades, the ingrained knowledge of a mother's presence remains. This is why a child, when introduced to their mother, instinctively moves toward her—a primal recognition that supersedes conscious memory.
- Similarly, the concept of God is never a 'strange' concept for any human being and always appears to answer a natural need within him/her.
- That concept of God may be a mythological god or a supernatural force, but it exists.
- According to the Quran, this inner testimony is so indisputable that God will hold the person accountable for His Lordship even when they are completely unaware of God's messenger and his teachings.
- However, this matter remains between the person and God.
- Two excuses that a person can put forward that won't be accepted because of this innate knowledge:
    - We did not know about that.
    - We grew up in an environment of atheism or polytheism
- In the Quran, when God talks about Polytheism, He calls it "gods that people have named or created" because there is no basis for it in nature.

What is the significance of the word "living" in the living faith in God?

Surah Anfal: Verse 2-4

اِنَّمَا الْمُؤْمِنُوْنَ الَّذِيْنَ اِذَا ذُكِرَ اللّٰهُ وَجِلَتْ قُلُوْبُهُمْ وَ اِذَا تُلِيَتْ عَلَيْهِمْ اٰيٰتُهٗ زَادَتْهُمْ

اِيْمَانًا وَّ عَلٰى رَبِّهِمْ يَتَوَكَّلُوْنَ الَّذِيْنَ يُقِيْمُوْنَ الصَّلٰوةَ وَ مِمَّا رَزَقْنٰهُمْ يُنْفِقُوْنَ

اُولٰٓئِكَ هُمُ الْمُؤْمِنُوْنَ حَقًّا لَهُمْ دَرَجٰتٌ عِنْدَ رَبِّهِمْ وَ مَغْفِرَةٌ وَّ رِزْقٌ كَرِيْمٌ

[Bear in mind that] believers are those whose hearts are filled with awe when God is mentioned to them, and when His verses are recited in front of them, they (verses) strengthen and increase their faith and, in every matter, they put their trust in their Lord. Those who are consistent in prayers and spend [in good things] from what We have given them. Such are the true believers. For them are higher ranks before their Lord, forgiveness, and a very honorable sustenance.

- These verses came right after the answer given to the Muslims about the spoils of war – after the Battle of Badr.
- When Muslims captured many spoils of war in the Battle of Badr, a dispute arose over them, as everyone wanted a share.
- Before Islam in Arabia, the winning fighters used to get the spoils of war solely.
- God told them in the Quran that since He helps the Muslims in these wars (through angels), it is solely the right of God and His Messenger.
- God reminded them of the objective behind fighting these wars: is it to gain temporary worldly gains, or to please God, which is deeply rooted in their belief in God (that they claim), and the real gain will be in the Hereafter.
- In that context, God told them the features and the attitude that believers should have, because otherwise, it would merely be a verbal claim.

Attributes of Believers

Heart is full of God's Awe	• They are God-conscious all the time. • Inside their hearts, they sense the profound significance of a command from God. • When they are reminded of the true objective of their life and actions, they surrender their wishes and desires.
Faith Increases	• When the verses of the Quran are recited, they hear them as if God is speaking directly to them, and this increases their faith in God – they realize that the situation they are in is a trial and that God is testing them. • If a person strives to shape their conduct to the commands of God, which may go against his/her personal opinions and inclinations, then as a result of this attitude, their faith in God increases.
Reliance on God	• In difficult situations, even when they feel things are going against their personal interests and inclinations, their trust in God is not shaken. • They strongly believe that this trial period is going to be temporary and ultimately, God will give them success, which He has promised.
Pray and Charitable	• The tools required to maintain such an attitude are Prayer and spending money on others for the sake of God. • These two actions build the foundation of faith. • Without this foundation, nothing mentioned above would be possible.

Reward for the Believers

God promises three rewards in these verses:

- **Higher Ranks:** These people will be rewarded in higher ranks on the Day of Judgment – the ranks of Paradise are not just for anyone who claims to be a believer.
- **Forgiveness:** Even the most devoted believer lapses. As human beings, we cannot be free from all our mistakes, shortcomings, and weaknesses. Out of His infinite mercy, however, God will overlook the shortcomings of these believers on the Day of Judgment – without this mercy, no one can make it to Paradise.
- **Dignified Provisions:** They will be given sustenance (anything a person has in this world, including food, shelter, family, etc.) with the honor of someone rightfully earning it after making an effort.

Concept of Reliance on Allah (Tawakkul)

قُلْ لَّنْ يُّصِيْبَنَآ اِلَّا مَا كَتَبَ اللّٰهُ لَنَا ۚ هُوَ مَوْلٰىنَا وَ عَلَى اللّٰهِ فَلْيَتَوَكَّلِ الْمُؤْمِنُوْنَ

Tell them (O Muhammad), "Never will we face calamity except by what Allah has already written for us; He is our protector (guardian) and the believers must rely upon Allah alone (Surah Tawbah # 51)

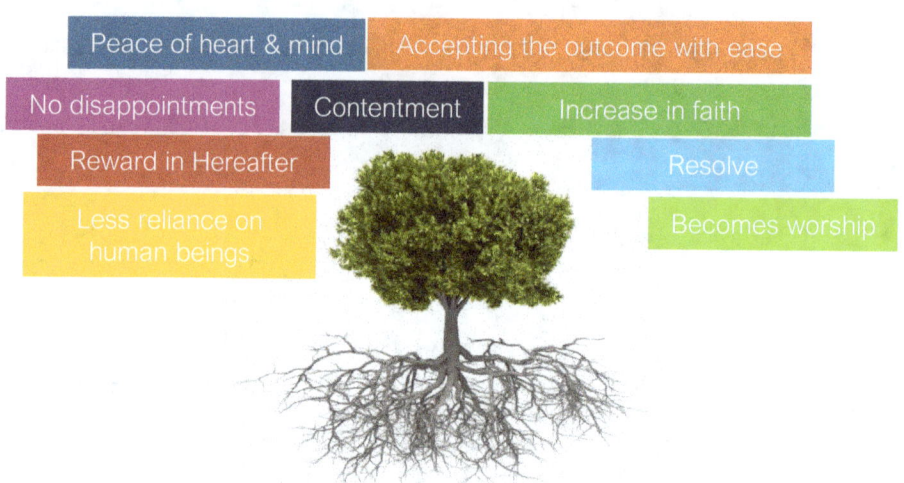

Fruits of Tawakkul

- Tawakkul means that after taking all the necessary means in a task at hand to achieve the desired outcome, in the end, you leave the matter in the hands of Allah, whether the outcome is favorable or not.

- It is a leap of faith into that very unknown after making the necessary efforts.

- It directly relates to your Faith in Allah and how well you know Allah. To know Allah is to know and acknowledge His attributes.

- Hence, it is also an act of submission to the Master and becomes a form of worship.

- It is an acknowledgment that the outcome of your effort was in full control of Allah, and He is fully aware of it.

What do you understand from this Hadith?

It is reported like this:
The Prophet saw a camel wandering outside Masjid Al-Nabawi, which was not tied. The Prophet asked the man," Why don't you tie the camel?". The man said, "I have trust in Allah." The Prophet remarked, *"Tie your camel and then trust in Allah"*

Sunan al-Tirmidhi #2517 (Hasan)

Surah Aal-e-Imran: Verse 190-191

اِنَّ فِیْ خَلْقِ السَّمٰوٰتِ وَ الْاَرْضِ وَ اخْتِلَافِ الَّیْلِ وَ النَّهَارِ لَاٰیٰتٍ لِّاُولِی الْاَلْبَابِ

الَّذِیْنَ یَذْکُرُوْنَ اللهَ قِیٰمًا وَّ قُعُوْدًا وَّ عَلٰی جُنُوْبِهِمْ وَ یَتَفَکَّرُوْنَ فِیْ خَلْقِ

السَّمٰوٰتِ وَ الْاَرْضِ ۚ رَبَّنَا مَا خَلَقْتَ هٰذَا بَاطِلًا ۚ سُبْحٰنَکَ فَقِنَا عَذَابَ النَّارِ

In reality, in the creation of the heavens and the earth and in the alternation of night and day, there are many signs for the people of insight; for those who remember God day and night, whether standing, sitting, or lying down on their sides and keep reflecting (pondering) on the creation of the heavens and the earth. [Their prayer is always:] "Lord! You have not created all this without a purpose. You are free from all weaknesses (you are above this that you do anything which is purposeless); so, save us from the torment of the Fire.

- A few verses before these verses (183-185), the disbelievers (especially the People of the Book) asked for specific signs from God to believe that Prophet Muhammad is His chosen Prophet.

- This was a fairly consistent request from the disbelievers, who sought excuses for not believing in the messenger.

- Historically, Jews have been given all kinds of signs from God, but they still disbelieved and even killed the Prophets of God if their teachings were not according to their desires and wishes.

- They were again asking for the same types of signs (of physical nature).

- There was nothing wrong in asking for a sign if Prophet Muhammad was not presenting the Quran to them. But in the case of the revelation of the Quran, no other sign was required.

- The Quran's literary majesty, coherence, power to reform hearts, and its predictions about people, places, and events stand as a divine proof or sign beyond human capacity.

Signs are all around us

Human Nature	Birth	Conscience	Feelings

Eco System	Earth is for living	Complex Universe

Life is perfectly created for test	History	Good and Evil

Death	Purpose	Human bond

- The Quran is full of verses that talk about the signs around us – they are with us all the time.
- We must look around and continuously reflect on the creations around us, and conclude that a perfect Creator and Designer is behind all this.
- When people examine the order of the universe closely, the harmony within it, despite its complexity, and how seemingly opposite things complement each other, it becomes clear to them that there is deep wisdom and intelligence behind it.
- They conclude:
  - If this universe were not created purposefully, then it could not simply end without a result – humans do not create anything without a purpose, not even a needle.
  - If the day comes after night, rain comes after drought, spring comes after fall, good times come after bad times ..... then another life/world should come after this world because it appears incomplete.
  - This universe cannot be an accident – calling it an accident is a very shallow conclusion.
  - A world that is complete in every respect must be created, where people are held accountable for their actions – good people are rewarded, and bad people are punished for their misdeeds.

Who is intelligent in the sight of God?

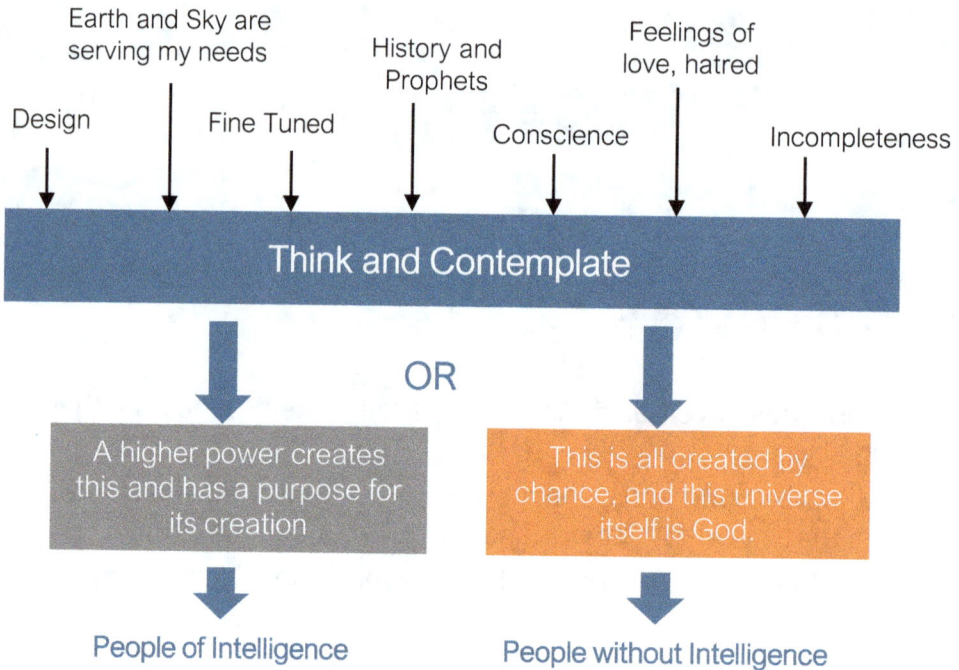

An intelligent person who has concluded that this world is created for a purpose behind it and there will be another world created after this world to recompense people for what they have done must ask this:

$$\text{سُبْحٰنَكَ فَقِنَا عَذَابَ النَّارِ}$$

You are free from all weaknesses (you are above this that you do anything which is purposeless); so, save us from the torment of the Fire

Why doesn't Allah show Himself to us so everyone can believe in Him and can go to Heaven?

Surah Nur: Verse 35

اَللّٰهُ نُوْرُ السَّمٰوٰتِ وَ الْاَرْضِ ۗ مَثَلُ نُوْرِهٖ كَمِشْكٰوةٍ فِيْهَا مِصْبَاحٌ ۗ اَلْمِصْبَاحُ فِيْ زُجَاجَةٍ ۗ اَلزُّجَاجَةُ كَاَنَّهَا كَوْكَبٌ دُرِّيٌّ يُّوْقَدُ مِنْ شَجَرَةٍ مُّبٰرَكَةٍ زَيْتُوْنَةٍ لَّا شَرْقِيَّةٍ وَّ لَا غَرْبِيَّةٍ ۙ يَّكَادُ زَيْتُهَا يُضِيْٓءُ وَ لَوْ لَمْ تَمْسَسْهُ نَارٌ ۗ نُوْرٌ عَلٰى نُوْرٍ ۗ يَهْدِى اللّٰهُ لِنُوْرِهٖ مَنْ يَّشَآءُ ۗ وَ يَضْرِبُ اللّٰهُ الْاَمْثَالَ لِلنَّاسِ ۗ وَ اللّٰهُ بِكُلِّ شَىْءٍ عَلِيْمٌ

[The parable is that] God is the light of the heavens and the earth. [In the heart of a person,] the example of this light of His is as if a niche (special place) has a lamp. The lamp is in a crystal. The crystal is as if it were a shining star. It is lit up by oil from a lush olive tree that is neither eastern nor western. Its oil is [so transparent] as if it will light up even without fire touching it. Light upon light. God grants this light of His guidance to whomsoever He wills. God mentions these parables to guide people, and God is aware of everything

- Right before these verses, God gave very detailed instructions about the etiquette of gender mixing.
- The instructions were given in the light of an incident called "the incident of slander," in which the hypocrites of Medinah made a scandal out of an event that happened with Aisha (RA), the wife of Prophet Muhammad.
- The rumors of the scandal were spread in such a way that many of the weaker. Muslims of Medinah also believed in it, and it caused great pain to Prophet Muhammad.
- In this background, God talked about true faith in God and how people can benefit from the Quran and the Messenger, using a simile.
- These verses present the parable of belief and disbelief, illustrating how faith shines from within and without, and how disbelief creates darkness for those who reject it.

God is the Light of this Universe

- A niche is a special place where a lamp is housed.

Meaning: It refers to the heart of a person, which houses the lamp that lights everything.

- The lamp lights up the house when it is kept at a higher place.

Meaning: If the fire of God's faith is lit in that place, then the inner and the outer self of a person lights up, and the person can see everything clearly.

- The lamp is enclosed in a crystal, which protects it from external influences (such as wind or rain) without altering its light or brightness.

Meaning: When the heart is lit with the firm belief in God, then no philosophy or –ism would influence it and cause any deviations from it.

- The lamp is lit with oil from the trees in the center of the garden. These trees are greener and produce the best burning oil.

Meaning: This belief originates from an internal need and a natural desire for God, as evident in the world around us for thousands of years – it is not a man-made phenomenon.

- Light upon light.

Meaning: The light of faith (through the Quran and the Messenger) sits on top of the light of human nature – it's like thirst (internal) meets the water (external).

Summary: Although God's light of guidance shines universally, only those whose hearts are pure and sincerely seeking the truth are able to receive it. Just as not every eye can see even when light is present, not every soul perceives the truth even when revelation is before it. This divine light is both offered and filtered — offered to all through revelation and reason, but received only by those who cleanse their hearts of arrogance, prejudice, and hypocrisy. Thus, the verse concludes by emphasizing that guidance is a divine gift bestowed upon those who align their inner selves with sincerity and humility, making them worthy of being illuminated by God's "light upon light."

God is the Light of this Universe

- A person who does not believe in God sees this world as deficient, nonsensical, full of agony, injustice, and unanswered questions.

- That person has no way of getting the answers to some of the questions, which only God can provide satisfactorily.

- That person lives in darkness and wanders in search of answers from different philosophies and isms because the questions are critical.

- As soon as the person believes in one True God, everything lights up, all questions are answered, and things start making sense.

- However, a person will only benefit from the faith in the form of the Quran and the Messenger when he/she appreciate the guidance already provided in nature (a sound and untainted heart).

Sunnah of God – Guidance and Error

Only if you cherish the inner guidance

- One aspect of trial in this life is to adhere to the straight path and not to go astray

- This guidance towards one Lord and His path is an inner guidance fortified by the signs in the heavens and the earth around him, once the person attains intellectual maturity

- If the person values and treasures this 'inner' guidance and acts towards it, God increases in him/her the desire for guidance, and faith continues to settle in his heart

- Though in the Quran, the guidance is conditioned with the Will of God, it is actually this law that prevails (it's an expression that God's laws will prevail)

- Angels and righteous people help the person in further guidance if he/she continue to value the guidance and remain grateful and steadfast

If you neglect/evade the inner guidance

- On the other hand, a person may evade or neglect inner guidance, refuse to use intellect, and deliberately deviate from the truth.

- God shows His signs and warnings both inside and outside as reminders.

- If the person persists in defiance and shows no sign of turning back, God then leaves Him to wander in the darkness of error and misguidance.

- In Quranic terms, that person commits "*zulm*" (injustice) to himself.

- Persistence increases stubbornness and selfishness, and that person is deprived of the ability to think and understand in the proper manner.

- Satan and his agents support this person in everything he does.

- If he is even mischievous and spreads corruption as a result, then God finally seals his heart for any guidance.

Examples: Increase in the faith of a believer

اَمْ حَسِبْتَ اَنَّ اَصْحٰبَ الْكَهْفِ وَ الرَّقِيْمِ ۙ كَانُوْا مِنْ اٰيٰتِنَا عَجَبًا

اِذْ اَوَى الْفِتْيَةُ اِلَى الْكَهْفِ فَقَالُوْا رَبَّنَا اٰتِنَا مِنْ لَّدُنْكَ رَحْمَةً وَّ هَيِّئْ لَنَا مِنْ اَمْرِنَا رَشَدًا

فَضَرَبْنَا عَلٰى اٰذَانِهِمْ فِى الْكَهْفِ سِنِيْنَ عَدَدًا ۙ ثُمَّ بَعَثْنٰهُمْ لِنَعْلَمَ اَىُّ الْحِزْبَيْنِ اَحْصٰى لِمَا لَبِثُوْا اَمَدًا

نَحْنُ نَقُصُّ عَلَيْكَ نَبَاَهُمْ بِالْحَقِّ ۚ اِنَّهُمْ فِتْيَةٌ اٰمَنُوْا بِرَبِّهِمْ وَ زِدْنٰهُمْ هُدًى

وَّ رَبَطْنَا عَلٰى قُلُوْبِهِمْ اِذْ قَامُوْا فَقَالُوْا رَبُّنَا رَبُّ السَّمٰوٰتِ وَ الْاَرْضِ

لَنْ نَّدْعُوَا۟ مِنْ دُوْنِهٖٓ اِلٰهًا لَّقَدْ قُلْنَآ اِذًا شَطَطًا

Do you think the people of the cave and Raqim were an extraordinary sign from among Our many signs? At the time when those youth took refuge in the cave, then prayed [to their Lord:] "Our Lord! Bless us with mercy from Yourself, and in this matter of Ours, provide us the guidance." At this, We calmed them to sleep for many years in the cave. Then We woke them up to see which of the two groups had correctly counted the period of their stay (in the cave). We relate to your anecdote in truth. They were a few youngsters who professed faith in their Lord, and We increased them in their guidance and strengthened their hearts at that time when they [campaigned in favor of monotheism] and declared: "Our Lord is He Who is the Lord of the heavens and the earth. We shall not call upon anyone except Him as God; if we do this, we will say what is far from the truth. (Surah Kahf: 9-14)

اَلَّذِيْنَ قَالَ لَهُمُ النَّاسُ اِنَّ النَّاسَ قَدْ جَمَعُوْا لَكُمْ فَاخْشَوْهُمْ فَزَادَهُمْ اِيْمَانًا ۖ وَّ قَالُوْا حَسْبُنَا اللّٰهُ وَ نِعْمَ الْوَكِيْلُ

These are those people who, when told by the people: "The enemy has mustered a great force against you: so, fear it," grew more in their faith [on hearing this] and replied: "God is all-sufficient for us, and He is the best disposer of the affairs" (Surah Aal-e-Imran: 173)

Given the numerous signs around us, why don't millions believe in God?

Hadith

The Sweetness of Faith

عن أَنَسٍ عن النبي صلى الله عليه وسلم قال ثَلَاثٌ من كُنَّ فيه وَجَدَ حَلَاوَةَ الْإِيمَانِ أَنْ
يَكُونَ الله وَرَسُولُهُ أَحَبَّ إِليه مِمَّا سِوَاهُمَا وَأَنْ يُحِبَّ الْمَرْءَ لَا يُحِبُّهُ إلا لِلَّهِ وَأَنْ يَكْرَهَ أَنْ يَعُودَ
في الْكُفْرِ كما يَكْرَهُ أَنْ يُقْذَفَ في النَّارِ

Anas ibn Malik reported that the Prophet said: "A person who has three qualities will acquire the sweetness of faith: "God and His Messenger become dearer to him/her than the rest; he/she loves people only because of God; he/she dislikes returning to disbelief the way he/she dislikes being cast into Hell." Sahih Al Bukhari, vol. 1, 14, (no. 16)

- When the command of God is known, a person surrenders their will to it.
- The focus of life, even when dealing with the people in this world, should be the Hereafter, which purifies their hearts from all ill feelings.
- Deviation from God's path is greatly disliked.

The Real Criteria Before God

عن أَبِي هُرَيْرَةَ قال قال رسول اللَّهِ صلى الله عليه وسلم إِنَّ اللَّهَ لَا يَنْظُرُ إِلى صُوَرِكُمْ وَأَمْوَالِكُمْ
وَلَكِنْ يَنْظُرُ إِلى قُلُوبِكُمْ وَأَعْمَالِكُمْ

Abu Hurairah stated that God's Messenger said: "Indeed, God does not look at your appearance and wealth; He, in fact, looks at your hearts and deeds." Sahih Muslim vol. 4, 1987, (no. 2564)

- Your reward with God depends on your intention and what follows from it.
- Sincere efforts made in the path of God are much appreciated.
- A dollar spent in the path of God when you are poor has more worth than $1,000 spent when you are rich.
- Showing off in front of people is considered minor shirk, especially when it involves religious acts.

Bible

Condemnation of Polytheism

And God said: I am the Lord, your God who took you out of the land of Egypt, out of the prison house. You are to have no other gods but me. You are not to make an image or picture of anything in heaven or on the earth or in the waters under the earth: You may not go down on your faces before them or give them worship: for I, the Lord, your God, am a God who will not give His honor to another; **(Exodus, 20:1-4)**

Faith is the Foremost

Do not have the thought that I have come to send peace on the earth; I came not to send peace but a sword. For I have come to put a man against his father, and the daughter against her mother, and the daughter-in-law against her mother-in-law: And a man will be hated by those of his house. He who has more love for his father or mother than for me is not good enough for me; he who has more love for his son or daughter than for me is not good enough. And he who does not take his cross (ready to sacrifice his life) and come after me is not good enough for me. He who wants to keep his life will have it taken from him, and he who gives up his life because of me will have it returned to him. **(Matthew, 10:34-39)**

Faith defines our actions. Pick a few life situations and compare what you would do when you have faith in God and when you don't. The teacher can also assign the life situations to students.

Chapter 7

Topic 2: Merciful God

This chapter introduces God in the Quran and shows that Mercy is His overriding attribute in dealing with this universe and with us.

Surah Al Baqarah: Verse 255

اَللّٰهُ لَا اِلٰهَ اِلَّا هُوَ اَلْحَىُّ الْقَيُّوْمُ ۚ لَا تَأْخُذُهٗ سِنَةٌ وَّ لَا نَوْمٌ ۚ لَهٗ مَا فِى السَّمٰوٰتِ وَ مَا فِى الْاَرْضِ ۗ مَنْ ذَا الَّذِىْ يَشْفَعُ عِنْدَهٗٓ اِلَّا بِاِذْنِهٖ ۚ يَعْلَمُ مَا بَيْنَ اَيْدِيْهِمْ وَ مَا خَلْفَهُمْ ۚ وَ لَا يُحِيْطُوْنَ بِشَىْءٍ مِّنْ عِلْمِهٖٓ اِلَّا بِمَا شَآءَ ۚ وَسِعَ كُرْسِيُّهُ السَّمٰوٰتِ وَ الْاَرْضَ ۚ وَ لَا يَئُوْدُهٗ حِفْظُهُمَا ۚ وَ هُوَ الْعَلِىُّ

Allah, there is no other deity but He, the Living, the Sustainer. Neither slumber nor sleep overtakes Him. All that is in the heavens and the earth belongs to Him. Who can intercede with Him for someone except by His permission? He knows what lies before them and what is after them, and without His will, they cannot grasp any part of His knowledge. His dominion prevails in the heavens and the earth, and their protection does not fatigue Him, and He is the Exalted, the Great One.

- This verse is also called "the Verse of the Throne (*Ayat-ul-Kursi*)," which describes the Lord of the Universe in unparalleled terms.
- The verses before these verses encourage Muslims to spend in the path of Allah, especially for fighting the wars against disbelievers at that time.
- The Quran calls that charity (spending in the path of Allah) a 'goodly loan' given to Allah, which He would return with plenty more.
- However, the condition is that it must be spent for the sake of Allah with pure intentions.
- In this discussion, Allah reminded them that they should spend in Allah's path before a Day when there will be no buying or selling, and this hoarded wealth will not help them.
- Allah reminded them that this wealth is a gift from Him, not a right.
- Allah also warned those who cherish this false notion that on that Day, somehow, they will be able to secure salvation through friendship, association, or intercession.
- On that day, the only thing that will help them in their salvation is their good deeds done for the sake of Allah, and they will be dealing with a Powerful Allah whose attributes are described in the next verse.

Who is our Lord?

- There is no doubt that we are created beings, and this universe was created. For the Creator, there are only two possibilities

Universe has a Creator	OR	Universe is the Creator

- In ISLAM, we believe that the universe has a Creator, and we are going to learn about the attributes of that Creator as introduced in *Ayat-ul-Kursi*.

Allah	His name is Allah (Al-ILah) because He is "The Lord"
No other god	He is alone and does not need another god because of His attributes presented in the verse. No one shares these attributes. Also, God did not appoint anyone to share these attributes. Anyone who claims or elevates this status must prove that God appointed him to be so. In reality, whoever does so fabricates the whole lie
Ever-Living	He is ever-living and gives life to others, while none of the other gods that people worship are living. There was no time, and will never be, when He was not living.
Self-Subsisting	He exists of His own accord and is instrumental in keeping others living. His existence does not depend on anything, but everything depends on Him for its existence.
No slumber, no sleep	This statement completely negates all forms of sleep. The implication is that Allah is aware of everything and is free from any distraction that might impair His awareness. This negates any imperfection or weakness (such as sleep overtaking a person, which is a weakness) associated with Allah. There is a famous Biblical statement that God created the heavens and the earth in six days and that on the seventh day He rested (Genesis, chapters 1 & 2).
The Sole Owner	To God belongs the heavens and the earth and everything therein. No one shares anything with God in governance, either of the heavens or the earth. Any conceivable being other than God would necessarily be a part of the universe and thus belong to, and be a subject of, God rather than His partner and equal. God is beyond this Universe that we see.

Who is our Lord?

Intercession	Who can intercede for someone before Him without His permission when no one shares His dominion? This refutes the idea that saints, angels, or other beings are so influential with God that their wishes would be granted if they were to ask Him for something. They are being told that, far from anyone having the power to impose his will on God, none, not even the greatest Prophets and the angels, will dare utter one word in the majestic court of the Lord unless they are expressly permitted to do so.
All-Knowing	When Allah is fully aware of the past and future of a person and when no one can even grasp this knowledge about the past and future without His permission, then on what basis shall a person intercede for someone? Will anyone intercede to increase the knowledge of God?
Authority	Allah's sovereignty (Authority) is unlimited (has no bounds), and He is Omnipotent. This power and authority are described with the word "Throne." He not only created this Universe but also continued to govern it. Since only He possesses all the knowledge of the heavens and the earth, no one can comprehend the order and design of this Universe and manage it properly. He takes care of all the affairs of this Universe, and it does not cause any fatigue to Him. Note that in Philosophy, people believe in the First Cause (Deism), who started everything, but now He is "uninterested and uninvolved"

- This verse is a great reminder for all of us that what kind of God we believe in – plays an important role in our faith in Him.
- When we are asked to follow the guidance given by Him (which is good for us), we should listen and obey instead of finding excuses because we should realize who we are dealing with – the Lord of the Worlds with these attributes.
- It warns those who take others as His associates or partners.
- It rejects any notion that someone from this world would be able to help on that Day in front of Allah – even if that person is a Prophet – unless Allah permits that person.
- It reaffirms our belief and gives us hope that when we are in difficulty, we should ask for help, knowing that we are reaching out to someone with these attributes.

Why does God have to be perfect? What is wrong with an imperfect God?

Surah Al Raad: Verse 1-4

الٓمٓرٰ ۚ تِلْكَ اٰيٰتُ الْكِتٰبِ ۗ وَ الَّذِیْۤ اُنْزِلَ اِلَیْکَ مِنْ رَّبِّکَ الْحَقُّ وَ لٰکِنَّ اَکْثَرَ النَّاسِ لَا یُؤْمِنُوْنَ

اَللّٰهُ الَّذِیْ رَفَعَ السَّمٰوٰتِ بِغَیْرِ عَمَدٍ تَرَوْنَهَا ثُمَّ اسْتَوٰی عَلَی الْعَرْشِ وَ سَخَّرَ الشَّمْسَ وَ الْقَمَرَ ؕ

کُلٌّ یَّجْرِیْ لِاَجَلٍ مُّسَمًّی ؕ یُدَبِّرُ الْاَمْرَ یُفَصِّلُ الْاٰیٰتِ لَعَلَّکُمْ بِلِقَآءِ رَبِّکُمْ تُوْقِنُوْنَ

وَ هُوَ الَّذِیْ مَدَّ الْاَرْضَ وَ جَعَلَ فِیْهَا رَوَاسِیَ وَ اَنْهٰرًا ؕ وَ مِنْ کُلِّ الثَّمَرٰتِ جَعَلَ فِیْهَا

زَوْجَیْنِ اثْنَیْنِ یُغْشِی الَّیْلَ النَّهَارَ ؕ اِنَّ فِیْ ذٰلِکَ لَاٰیٰتٍ لِّقَوْمٍ یَّتَفَکَّرُوْنَ

وَ فِی الْاَرْضِ قِطَعٌ مُّتَجٰوِرٰتٌ وَّ جَنّٰتٌ مِّنْ اَعْنَابٍ وَّ زَرْعٌ وَّ نَخِیْلٌ صِنْوَانٌ وَّ غَیْرُ صِنْوَانٍ یُّسْقٰی

بِمَآءٍ وَّاحِدٍ ۟ وَ نُفَضِّلُ بَعْضَهَا عَلٰی بَعْضٍ فِی الْاُکُلِ ؕ اِنَّ فِیْ ذٰلِکَ لَاٰیٰتٍ لِّقَوْمٍ یَّعْقِلُوْنَ

Alif Lam Mim Raa. These are the verses of this Book. And what has been revealed to you from your Lord is the truth, yet most people do not believe it. It is God who raised the heavens without visible pillars. He then ascended to the throne and made the sun and the moon subservient [to Him], each pursuing a path till an appointed time. He governs the Universe and makes simple His signs so that you may have confidence in meeting your Lord. It is He who spread out the earth and placed firmly upon it mountains and rivers, and He created pairs among all types of fruits. He covers the night over the day. Indeed, there are signs in this for those who deliberate. And on earth, there are adjacent pieces of land: vineyards, cultivated land, and palm trees [with] single [stems] and twin ones. All are nourished by the same water (next to each other), yet some are more productive than others. Indeed, there are signs in this for people who use their intellect.

- This is the beginning of Surah Al Raad, where Allah reiterated that these verses (or in other words, this Quran) are revealed by Allah and are the complete Truth.
- These verses describe the creations and wonders of the same Lord who inspired the revelation of these verses.
- The creations and beauty in them demonstrate that if you see a perfect design and wisdom in these creations, you can easily understand the wisdom in this Book as well.
- An Ever-Wise God only produces wisdom.
- There are many verses in the Quran where Allah describes His creations and wonders in detail, inviting people to reflect on them.
- These creations can only come from a Merciful God who allowed us to enjoy the variety in His creation.

Allah's Mercy

- People often complain, why did Allah not provide a very visible sign or a miracle for them to believe in Him.
- Allah gave miracles of a physical nature to His previous Prophets, but He gave a timeless miracle to Prophet Muhammad:

  Quran – a living miracle that can be witnessed by anyone, regardless of time and place
  & The Signs of Nature around us – that we can easily understand now due to science; how complicated, sophisticated, and miraculous this universe and life in it is

- People with sound minds and intent ponder both and conclude that a Creator exists in this world, having created everything.
- This is purely out of His Mercy that He gave us these signs to come to the correct conclusion and did not leave us in the dark.

The Results of Mercy

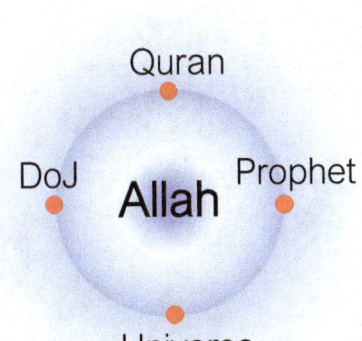

Quran is a Miracle and a Mercy

- The Quran is the message for everyone.
- A book saved in its original form for humanity to get guidance until the Day of Judgment.
- God's attributes, His dealings, and His awareness are known through the Quran.
- The Quran is NOT like any other book whose one copy is produced, and then copies of that copy are made to preserve it. The prophet, his companions, and generations after them adopt unusual means of memorization and verbal transmission to preserve it.
- The Quran is the only book on earth whose content, reading, and pronunciation are protected and transmitted as it is.
- In 1400 years, the world underwent tremendous changes; ideologies, thoughts, philosophies, and theories were presented, rejected, and forgotten, but the Quran has firmly stood the test of time.
- The world, despite its astounding scientific and academic discoveries, has failed to present a better alternative to the views and answers presented in the Quran.

This Universe is Miraculously Merciful

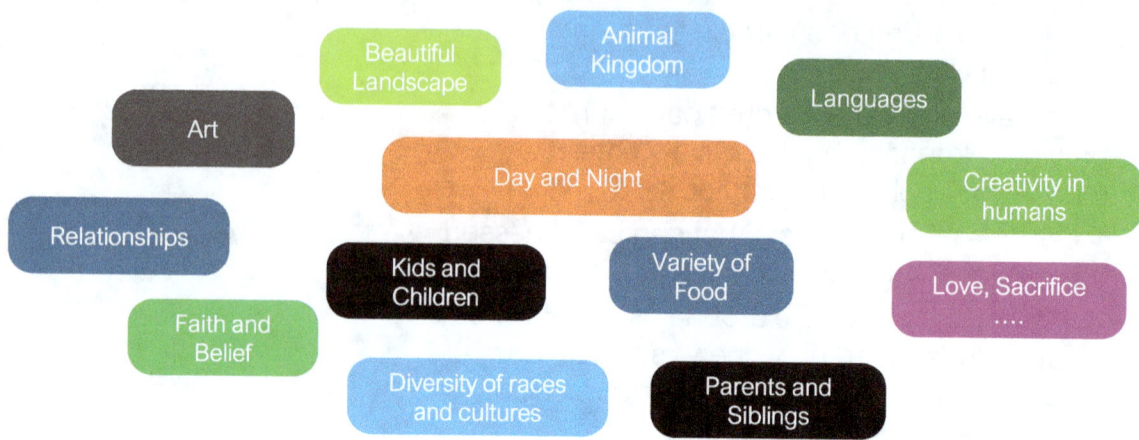

- Look around and reflect on the creations around you, and you will conclude that a perfect Creator and Designer is behind all this.
- When people examine the order of the universe — its harmony despite its complexity — and how seemingly opposite things complement each other, it becomes clear that there is deep wisdom and intelligence behind it.
- The existence of opposing forces, such as good and evil, health and sickness, provides believers with an opportunity to recognize God's limitless power. By creating both extremes, God demonstrates His omnipotence and gives humanity a reason to be grateful for the gifts He bestows.
- God placed a portion of His mercy in creation, causing creatures to show compassion toward one another. A mother animal, for example, lifts her hoof to avoid hurting her young. This mutual mercy is an indicator of a greater divine mercy that pervades all existence.
- The coherence and precise laws of the cosmos, such as the fact that planets remain in their orbits, testify to a single, sovereign Creator, not a multitude of clashing deities. The Qur'an states that if there were other gods, the heavens and earth would be in total chaos
- The rhythmic, never-ending cycle of day and night is a sign for people of understanding. This consistent, dependable system, along with the sun and moon orbiting their own paths, points to a purposeful design.

Surah Nahl: Verses 10-18

- Similar examples from the Quran are presented in the next few pages.

هُوَ الَّذِىٓ اَنْزَلَ مِنَ السَّمَآءِ مَآءً لَّكُمْ مِّنْهُ شَرَابٌ وَّ مِنْهُ شَجَرٌ فِيْهِ تُسِيْمُوْنَ. يُنْبِتُ لَكُمْ بِهِ الزَّرْعَ وَ الزَّيْتُوْنَ وَ النَّخِيْلَ وَ الْاَعْنَابَ وَ مِنْ كُلِّ الثَّمَرٰتِ ۗ اِنَّ فِىْ ذٰلِكَ لَاٰيَةً لِّقَوْمٍ يَّتَفَكَّرُوْنَ. وَ سَخَّرَ لَكُمُ الَّيْلَ وَ النَّهَارَ ۙ وَ الشَّمْسَ وَ الْقَمَرَ ۗ وَ النُّجُوْمُ مُسَخَّرٰتٌۢ بِاَمْرِهٖ ۗ اِنَّ فِىْ ذٰلِكَ لَاٰيٰتٍ لِّقَوْمٍ يَّعْقِلُوْنَ. وَ مَا ذَرَاَ لَكُمْ فِى الْاَرْضِ مُخْتَلِفًا اَلْوَانُهٗ ۗ اِنَّ فِىْ ذٰلِكَ لَاٰيَةً لِّقَوْمٍ يَّذَّكَّرُوْنَ. وَ هُوَ الَّذِىْ سَخَّرَ الْبَحْرَ لِتَاْكُلُوْا مِنْهُ لَحْمًا طَرِيًّا وَّ تَسْتَخْرِجُوْا مِنْهُ حِلْيَةً تَلْبَسُوْنَهَا ۚ وَ تَرَى الْفُلْكَ مَوَاخِرَ فِيْهِ وَ لِتَبْتَغُوْا مِنْ فَضْلِهٖ وَ لَعَلَّكُمْ تَشْكُرُوْنَ. وَ اَلْقٰى فِى الْاَرْضِ رَوَاسِىَ اَنْ تَمِيْدَ بِكُمْ وَ اَنْهٰرًا وَّ سُبُلًا لَّعَلَّكُمْ تَهْتَدُوْنَ. وَ عَلٰمٰتٍ ۗ وَ بِالنَّجْمِ هُمْ يَهْتَدُوْنَ. اَفَمَنْ يَّخْلُقُ كَمَنْ لَّا يَخْلُقُ ۗ اَفَلَا تَذَكَّرُوْنَ. وَ اِنْ تَعُدُّوْا نِعْمَةَ اللّٰهِ لَا تُحْصُوْهَا ۗ اِنَّ اللّٰهَ لَغَفُوْرٌ رَّحِيْمٌ.

He sent down water from the heavens from which you drink and from which spring forth the pasture on which your cattle feed. And from it, He brings forth corn, olives, dates, grapes, and fruits of all kinds. Indeed, there is a great sign in this for those who reflect. And He put the night, the day, the sun, and the moon into your service, and the stars too are of service at His behest. Indeed, there are signs in this for those who deliberate. And, in the earth, in which He has spread various things for you. Indeed, there is a great sign in this for those who pay attention. It is He who put the sea to your service so that you may eat fresh meat from it and take out from it ornaments to wear. And observe the ships cutting across their course through it [so that you can travel by it] and seek His bounty so that you may become grateful. And He set the mountains upon the earth lest it should move away with you, rivers and roads, so that you can find your way and other landmarks. And by the stars, too, are they guided. Is He, then, Who has created, like him who cannot create? Do you not think? If you count God's blessings, you will not be able to enlist all of them. God indeed is Forgiving and Merciful.

Surah Nahl: Verses 65-70

وَ اللهُ اَنْزَلَ مِنَ السَّمَاءِ مَاءً فَاَحْيَا بِهِ الْاَرْضَ بَعْدَ مَوْتِهَا ۚ اِنَّ فِيْ ذٰلِكَ لَاٰيَةً لِّقَوْمٍ يَّسْمَعُوْنَ ۝ وَ
اِنَّ لَكُمْ فِي الْاَنْعَامِ لَعِبْرَةً ۚ نُسْقِيْكُمْ مِّمَّا فِيْ بُطُوْنِهٖ مِنْۢ بَيْنِ فَرْثٍ وَّ دَمٍ لَّبَنًا خَالِصًا سَآئِغًا لِّلشّٰرِبِيْنَ ۝ وَ
مِنْ ثَمَرٰتِ النَّخِيْلِ وَ الْاَعْنَابِ تَتَّخِذُوْنَ مِنْهُ سَكَرًا وَّ رِزْقًا حَسَنًا ۚ اِنَّ فِيْ ذٰلِكَ لَاٰيَةً لِّقَوْمٍ
يَّعْقِلُوْنَ ۝ وَ اَوْحٰى رَبُّكَ اِلَى النَّحْلِ اَنِ اتَّخِذِيْ مِنَ الْجِبَالِ بُيُوْتًا وَّ مِنَ الشَّجَرِ وَ مِمَّا يَعْرِشُوْنَ ۝ ثُمَّ
كُلِيْ مِنْ كُلِّ الثَّمَرٰتِ فَاسْلُكِيْ سُبُلَ رَبِّكِ ذُلُلًا ۚ يَخْرُجُ مِنْۢ بُطُوْنِهَا شَرَابٌ مُّخْتَلِفٌ اَلْوَانُهٗ فِيْهِ شِفَآءٌ
لِّلنَّاسِ ۚ اِنَّ فِيْ ذٰلِكَ لَاٰيَةً لِّقَوْمٍ يَّتَفَكَّرُوْنَ ۝ وَ اللهُ خَلَقَكُمْ ثُمَّ يَتَوَفّٰىكُمْ ۝ وَ مِنْكُمْ مَّنْ يُّرَدُّ اِلٰٓى
اَرْذَلِ الْعُمُرِ لِكَيْ لَا يَعْلَمَ بَعْدَ عِلْمٍ شَيْئًا ۚ اِنَّ اللهَ عَلِيْمٌ قَدِيْرٌ ۝

And it is God Who sent down water from the heavens; thus, He enlivened the earth from it after its death. Indeed, there is a great sign in this for those who hear. And in your cattle, too, there is a great lesson. We provide pure milk between the guts and blood in their bellies, which is very pleasant for those who drink it. And [provide you nutrition] from the fruits of the palm and the vine; you make <u>intoxicants</u> from them and <u>good wholesome food</u>. Indeed, this is a great sign for those who use their intellect. And your Lord inspired the honey bee, saying: "Make your hives in the mountains, trees, and roofs built by people. Then feed on every kind of fruit and follow the trodden paths of your Lord." From its belly comes forth a fluid of different colors; it also carries cures for people. Indeed, there is a great sign in this for those who reflect. It is God Who created you, and then it is only He Who makes you die; some He returns to abject old age when they no longer know all that they once knew. God, indeed, is Knowledgeable and Powerful.

Surah Rum: Verses 21-25

وَ مِنْ اٰیٰتِهٖۤ اَنْ خَلَقَ لَكُمْ مِّنْ اَنْفُسِكُمْ اَزْوَاجًا لِّتَسْكُنُوْۤا اِلَیْهَا وَ جَعَلَ بَیْنَكُمْ مَّوَدَّةً وَّ رَحْمَةً ؕ اِنَّ فِیْ ذٰلِكَ لَاٰیٰتٍ لِّقَوْمٍ یَّتَفَكَّرُوْنَ ؕ وَ مِنْ اٰیٰتِهٖ خَلْقُ السَّمٰوٰتِ وَ الْاَرْضِ وَ اخْتِلَافُ اَلْسِنَتِكُمْ وَ اَلْوَانِكُمْ ؕ اِنَّ فِیْ ذٰلِكَ لَاٰیٰتٍ لِّلْعٰلِمِیْنَ ؕ وَ مِنْ اٰیٰتِهٖ مَنَامُكُمْ بِالَّیْلِ وَ النَّهَارِ وَ ابْتِغَآؤُكُمْ مِّنْ فَضْلِهٖ ؕ اِنَّ فِیْ ذٰلِكَ لَاٰیٰتٍ لِّقَوْمٍ یَّسْمَعُوْنَ ؕ وَ مِنْ اٰیٰتِهٖ یُرِیْكُمُ الْبَرْقَ خَوْفًا وَّ طَمَعًا وَّ یُنَزِّلُ مِنَ السَّمَآءِ مَآءً فَیُحْیٖ بِهِ الْاَرْضَ بَعْدَ مَوْتِهَا ؕ اِنَّ فِیْ ذٰلِكَ لَاٰیٰتٍ لِّقَوْمٍ یَّعْقِلُوْنَ ؕ وَ مِنْ اٰیٰتِهٖۤ اَنْ تَقُوْمَ السَّمَآءُ وَ الْاَرْضُ بِاَمْرِهٖ ؕ ثُمَّ اِذَا دَعَاكُمْ دَعْوَةً ۖ مِّنَ الْاَرْضِ ۖ اِذَاۤ اَنْتُمْ تَخْرُجُوْنَ ؕ

And among His signs are that He has created spouses for you from your species so that you may receive comfort from them, and [for this] He has created love and mercy among you. Indeed, there are many signs in this for those who reflect. And among His signs are the creation of the heavens and the earth and the variety of your languages and colors (among people). Indeed, there are signs in this for people of knowledge. And among His signs is your sleeping in the night, seeking His bounty by day. Indeed, there are signs in this for those who lend ears. And among His signs are that He shows you lightning which creates both fear and hope, and He sends down water from the sky and through it enlivens the land after its death. Indeed, there are signs in this for those who use their intellect. And among His signs are that the heavens and the earth stand firm at His bidding. And when He calls you just once to come out of the earth (that Day), you will spontaneously come out.

Why does the Quran mention so much of the natural world around us to pay attention to?

Surah Zumr: Verse 53

قُلْ يَٰعِبَادِىَ الَّذِينَ اَسْرَفُوا عَلَىٰ اَنْفُسِهِمْ لَا تَقْنَطُوا مِنْ رَّحْمَةِ اللهِ ۚ اِنَّ اللهَ يَغْفِرُ الذُّنُوبَ جَمِيعًا ۚ اِنَّهُ هُوَ الْغَفُورُ الرَّحِيمُ

Tell them: My servants, who have been unjust to their souls, do not lose hope in God's Mercy. God shall forgive all sins. Undoubtedly, He is very Forgiving, Ever-Merciful.

- Right before these verses, Allah talked about people engaged in polytheistic beliefs and, as a result, used to display strange behavior.
- When a calamity strikes them, they call Allah as if they only worship Him.
- And other times, when Allah shows them His favors, they brag, "I have attained this because of my knowledge and wisdom."
- Allah told them that this was selfish behavior. Whatever good they receive is from Allah, not because they deserve it, but because this is a trial for them.
- At this moment, Allah warned them that for these people who have been unjust to their souls, the evil consequences of their deeds would soon come before them, and they would not be able to defeat Allah.
- Similarly, the Idolaters were warned that the back door they had opened to polytheism and intercession would not save them; on the contrary, it would only facilitate their destruction.
- To give people hope, Allah revealed the verses of Mercy and Forgiveness.

Connecting with Allah Alone

- One of the most significant factors that leads people to polytheism and innovation in religion is when they lose hope in Allah and have wrong judgments about him.
- This can be witnessed in many Asian cultures where people pray before a shrine, asking dead saints for help when they think Allah is not responding to their prayers.
- They do not trust Allah's mercy, forgiveness, and compassion.
- They create hypothetical deities who are Allah's favorites to find immediate relief.
- By worshipping them, people hope that these intermediaries will intercede on their behalf before Allah and secure their forgiveness.
- This verse addresses those people who have "wronged their souls" by sinning and indulging in polytheism and should not seek the support of others and lose hope in Allah's mercy.
- They should seek His Mercy and forgiveness from Him alone.
- He is very forgiving and merciful, and He forgives the sins of His servants who turn to Him with sincerity.

How do we think of Allah?

- How Allah will deal with us if we are sincere and repentant depends on how we think of Allah. This is a critical factor in Islamic beliefs.
- In moments of despair, a believer should think positively of Allah.
- If we believe that Allah is Kind, Merciful, Compassionate, and All-Knowing, All-Hearing, then there is no reason to lose hope in times of despair.
- Recognize that this is a temporary test from Allah.

Islam's Approach

- In Islam, Allah is approachable to all His creations.
- This is unlike other religions, in which a religious leader must approach God.
- Whether Allah fulfills our needs or prayers entirely depends on whether that is good for us in this world and the Hereafter.
- We think we know everything, but we don't know what is hidden from us.
- A believer's attitude should be:
  - Do what is necessary by taking the necessary means
  - Make dua to Allah
  - Leave the results in His Hands

"I am as My servant expects Me to be"

Hadith Qudsi

Strange are the ways of a believer, for it is good in every affair of his, and this is not the case with anyone else except for a believer, for if he has an occasion of delight, he thanks (God). Thus, there is a good for him in it. If he gets into trouble and shows resignation (and endures it patiently), there is good for him in it as well. (Sahih Muslim #2999)

Surah Aal e Imran: Verses 133-136

وَسَارِعُوٓا اِلٰى مَغْفِرَةٍ مِّنْ رَّبِّكُمْ وَ جَنَّةٍ عَرْضُهَا السَّمٰوٰتُ وَ الْاَرْضُ ۙ اُعِدَّتْ لِلْمُتَّقِيْنَ

الَّذِيْنَ يُنْفِقُوْنَ فِى السَّرَّآءِ وَ الضَّرَّآءِ وَ الْكٰظِمِيْنَ الْغَيْظَ وَ الْعَافِيْنَ عَنِ النَّاسِ ۗ وَ اللّٰهُ يُحِبُّ الْمُحْسِنِيْنَ

وَ الَّذِيْنَ اِذَا فَعَلُوْا فَاحِشَةً اَوْ ظَلَمُوٓا اَنْفُسَهُمْ ذَكَرُوا اللّٰهَ فَاسْتَغْفَرُوْا لِذُنُوْبِهِمْ ۗ وَ مَنْ

يَّغْفِرُ الذُّنُوْبَ اِلَّا اللّٰهُ ۙ وَ لَمْ يُصِرُّوْا عَلٰى مَا فَعَلُوْا وَ هُمْ يَعْلَمُوْنَ

اُولٰٓئِكَ جَزَآؤُهُمْ مَّغْفِرَةٌ مِّنْ رَّبِّهِمْ وَ جَنّٰتٌ تَجْرِىْ مِنْ

تَحْتِهَا الْاَنْهٰرُ خٰلِدِيْنَ فِيْهَا ۗ وَ نِعْمَ اَجْرُ الْعٰمِلِيْنَ

And hurry towards the forgiveness of your Lord and to Paradise which is as vast as the heavens and the earth, prepared for the righteous who spend in all circumstances whether they are in ease or in hardship and [even if they encounter any harm from those upon whom they spend,] they curb their anger and forgive people – [These are people who are best in their deeds] and God befriends those people who are best in their deeds and such are they that if they commit an immoral act or do something evil to themselves, remember God and seek forgiveness for their sins – and who but God can forgive sins – and do not deliberately persist in what they have done. These shall be rewarded with forgiveness from their Lord and orchards beneath which streams will flow. They shall dwell there forever. And what a grand reward this is for those who do righteous deeds.

- Right before these verses, Allah talked about the people involved in the business of usury or interest.
- Primarily, the Jews of Medina were involved in it.
- It was easy for those with extra wealth to lend and earn money on it.
- The goal was to hoard as much money as possible.
- Before these verses, Allah also spoke about people not spending their wealth in His path, and all their efforts were directed towards hoarding money.
- Allah reminded them that the field in which they should compete is doing good and earning the pleasure and forgiveness of their Lord.
- Compete to get the highest places in Paradise, which is vast and much larger than the heavens and the earth – the maximum you can get in this world is not even close to what you will get in the Hereafter.

Who will earn the Mercy of Allah?

1. They spend their wealth on other people and in the path of Allah in all circumstances, whether in ease or hardship.

2. Spending money with others and on the path of Allah is one of the most challenging aspects of human nature.

3. They swallow their anger and forgive people – especially those with whom they have spent their wealth, and they, in return, hurt their feelings.

4. They forgive people in general and let go of their mistakes

5. If they commit immorality or injustice to themselves (by committing sins), they immediately remember Him, return to Him, repent, and ask for forgiveness from Allah.

6. They do not deliberately persist in committing wrong – even when repeated, it is done because of their inherent human weaknesses.

What will they get?

- Forgiveness from Allah for all the shortcomings they had in their lives.
- They will get paradise. A place that has been specially prepared for people who fear their Lord
- Despite this vastness, a person can 'buy' Paradise by spending in the way of Allah, not to mention that this vastness of Paradise is only a parable. Its actual expanse is beyond our imagination.
- The vastness of Paradise is especially emphasized due to the mindset that people had about the earnings through usury or interest (money multiplies itself)
- Paradise's pleasures will not cease - it's a promise from Allah.

يَوْمَ تُبَدَّلُ الْأَرْضُ غَيْرَ الْأَرْضِ وَ السَّمٰوٰتُ وَ بَرَزُوْا لِلّٰهِ الْوَاحِدِ الْقَهَّارِ

Remember the day when this earth will be replaced by another and this sky too, and everyone [alone and helpless] will set off towards God, the One and Mighty.
(Surah Ibrahim: 48)

Hadith

God's Graciousness

عن أبي هُرَيْرَةَ قال قال رسول اللَّهِ صلى الله عليه وسلم من هَمَّ بِحَسَنَةٍ فلم يَعْمَلْهَا كُتِبَتْ له حَسَنَةً وَمَنْ هَمَّ بِحَسَنَةٍ فَعَمِلَهَا كُتِبَتْ له عَشْرًا إلى سبعمائة ضِعْفٍ وَمَنْ هَمَّ بِسَيِّئَةٍ فلم يَعْمَلْهَا لم تُكْتَبْ وَإِنْ عَمِلَهَا كُتِبَتْ

Abu Hurairah stated that God's Messenger said: "A person who resolved to do a virtue but could not do it, its reward will be written down for him; a person who resolved to do a virtue and was able to do it, its reward ranging from ten to seven hundred times [the weight of the virtue] will be written down for him and a person who attempted to do an evil and was not able to do it, it is not written [in his account], and if he does it, it is written as one evil deed in his account." (Sahih Muslim #130)

Who would go to Hell after this?

Asserting a Supplication

عن أبي هُرَيْرَةَ قال قال النبي صلى الله عليه وسلم لَا يَقُولَنَّ أحدكم اللهم اغْفِرْ لي إن شِئْتَ اللهم ارْحَمْنِي إن شِئْتَ لِيَعْزِمْ في الدُّعَاءِ فان اللَّهَ صَانِعٌ ما شَاءَ لَا مُكْرِهَ له

Abu Hurairah stated that the Prophet said: "When any of you supplicates, he should not say: 'God! If You want, forgive me; if You want, have mercy on me.' He should assert himself while asking God because God will do what He wants. No one can force Him." (Sahih Muslim #2679)

Bible

God's love for those who repent

Now all the tax collectors and sinners came near to listen to him. And the Pharisees and scribes were angry, saying, This man gives approval to sinners and takes food with them. And he made a story for them, saying, What man of you, having a hundred sheep, if one of them gets loose and goes away, will not let the ninety-nine be in the wasteland by themselves, and go after the wandering one, till he sees where it is? And when he has got it again, he takes it in his arms with joy. And when he returns to his house, he sends for his neighbors and friends, saying, Be happy with me, for I have returned my sheep which had gone away. I tell you that even so, there will be more joy in heaven when one sinner has turned away from his wrongdoing than for ninety-nine good men who do not need a change of heart. Or what woman, having ten bits of silver, if one bit has gone from her hands, will not get a light and go through her house, searching with care till she sees it? And when she has it again, she gathers her friends and neighbors together, saying, 'Be happy with me, for I have found the bit of silver that had gone from me.' Even so, I tell you, there is joy among the angels of God when one sinner is turned away from his wrongdoing. (Luke, 15:1-10)

Select a few verses from the Quran that talk about God, His attributes, and His dealings with us, and write your impression about God from those verses

Remember!

Our relationship with Allah should NOT be tied to worldly benefits like our relationship with our parents. He is our Creator. That is more than enough to worship Him.

Chapter 8

Topic 3: Purpose of the Quran

This chapter discusses the Quran's purpose of revelation and preservation as described by the Quran.

A Common Misconception

- There is a common misconception among Muslims about the Quran, and that is: *"The Quran covers every aspect of our life and has the solution for everything. It gives us complete systems in various domains like the economy and politics."*
- This is a wrong statement about the Quran, as understood from the Quran itself.
- The Quran provides the moral and ethical principles for all of life's affairs, but does not contain a complete, ready-made system for anything, such as an economic or political system.
- It can be said that the Quran provides guidance and principles on <u>the moral aspects</u> of everything that touches human life.
- Once the moral principles are understood, then these specific systems are left to collective human reasoning and must be tailored to the needs of a particular time and place.
- For example, the divine guidance in economics, known as "Economic Shariah," provides moral principles about financial dealings. For example, it prohibits interest, specifies the laws of inheritance, and forbade cheating or causing harm in financial dealings. Now, it is up to modern Muslim scholars and economists to build flexible economic systems suited to their time and place, grounded in these core principles.

Why is it important to know what the purpose of the Quran is?

Surah Al Baqarah: Verse 213

كَانَ النَّاسُ أُمَّةً وَّاحِدَةً ۖ فَبَعَثَ اللهُ النَّبِيِّنَ مُبَشِّرِينَ وَ مُنْذِرِينَ وَ أَنْزَلَ مَعَهُمُ الْكِتٰبَ بِالْحَقِّ لِيَحْكُمَ
بَيْنَ النَّاسِ فِيمَا اخْتَلَفُوا فِيهِ ۚ وَ مَا اخْتَلَفَ فِيهِ إِلَّا الَّذِينَ أُوتُوهُ مِنْ بَعْدِ مَا جَآءَتْهُمُ الْبَيِّنٰتُ بَغْيًا
بَيْنَهُمْ ۖ فَهَدَى اللهُ الَّذِينَ اٰمَنُوا لِمَا اخْتَلَفُوا فِيهِ مِنَ الْحَقِّ بِإِذْنِهِ ۗ وَ اللهُ يَهْدِى مَنْ يَّشَآءُ إِلٰى
صِرَاطٍ مُّسْتَقِيمٍ

[They present differences among people as a pretext for their hypocrisy. They should know that] mankind was just a single community. Then [differences arose between them. So,] God sent forth prophets as bearers of glad tidings, and as warners, and with them, He sent down His Book as the decisive truth so that it may settle the differences among people. Only they differed in it to whom it was given after very clear signs had come to them because of spite for one another. Then, for these people, who believed [in the Quran], God guided them by His grace about the truth in which they were differing (before), and God guides whomsoever He intends [according to His law] to the straight path.

- The verses before this verse talked about the attitude of the disbelievers, including polytheists and hypocrites, who tried to give the impression that the difference of opinion in matters of faith and religion is perfectly fine.
- The hypocrites among the Jews adopted a non-partisan approach in the matter of the struggle between Muslims and disbelievers (although they were helping disbelievers secretly).
- They argued that the matter of Truth and falsehood is not so black-and-white that they should side with anyone – they will remain neutral.
- Allah told them that knowing the background of revelations and knowing that Prophet Muhammad is a true Messenger, they cannot remain neutral – in the matter of Truth and falsehood, one must make up their mind, as staying quiet means approving the falsehood.
- They were also making fun of the Muslims when it came to completely surrendering in front of Allah and His Messenger.
- Allah told them the history of humanity and the purpose of Messengers and the Book that was sent with them – giving Muslims a glad tiding that now they have a Book that will clarify the differences.

History of Guidance

- Since the beginning of humanity, people have been of one faith: Islam.
- Over time, differences arose among them.
- Allah continued to send the Prophets and the Books to them to keep them in that true faith.

- People did not create differences because the guidance was unclear or because they had no one to guide them; rather, it was due to rivalries and hatred among different groups.
- Allah gave them very clear guidance in matters of religion.
- Allah gave glad tidings to the Muslims that they now have the Final Guidance and a guide among them, and that they should use this Book for every matter of conflict and continue to support the Prophet.
- Even if they had differences earlier, they should be resolved now.
- Allah guides those who are ready to surrender in front of Allah and His Messenger.
- In this context, the real purpose of the Prophets and Books is clearly stated.

Messenger	Their job was to give glad tidings to those who believed in him and his message, and to warn those who rejected him.
Books	Act as the final authority on all matters of religion and become a judge in matters where there are differences

- The guidance for which Books are used as a Judge must always be religious (this includes moral guidance also).
- Regarding religion, the Quran <u>must</u> serve as the Judge among its followers on any matter on which people differ. All efforts must be made to understand the Quran rather than to bring evidence from outside it to understand its text. Sometimes the Quran leaves the details for readers to obtain from other sources, but what is already stated in the Quran should not be understood in light of those sources.
- Once a Book is considered divine, all religious dogmas, concepts, and interpretations presented by humans must be examined in light of that Book.

Surah Al Furqan: Verse 1

> تَبٰرَكَ الَّذِىۡ نَزَّلَ الۡفُرۡقَانَ عَلٰى عَبۡدِهٖ لِيَكُوۡنَ لِلۡعٰلَمِيۡنَ نَذِيۡرَا
>
> Very exalted and benevolent is the being who has revealed this Furqan to His servant so that it can warn the people of the world.

- Surah Al Furqan and Surah Ash Shuaraa make a pair.
- Both Surahs present a series of evidence for the prophethood of the Prophet Muhammad, the Truth of the Quran, and a warning against rejecting both.
- Allah responded in these two Surahs to the objections raised by the Quraysh and their allies.
- This verse is the beginning of Surah Al Furqan.

Quran is the Criterion – Al Furqan

- Allah called the Quran a Criterion – a Book that separates Truth from falsehood
- The Quran also used the word "the Scale" (Al Mizan) to refer to itself.
- The Quran is the Scale and the Criterion by which every matter of religion must be weighed and compared against.
- It is the supreme authority over all other religious texts.
- The text of the Quran is univocal. The meaning conveyed by each word is definitive. Whatever it intends to say, it says with full certainty, and there is no ambiguity about it.
- If a directive is given in the Quran, no external source, including the Prophet, can change it even slightly – his role is to deliver it and explain it if a question arises. The Prophet has mentioned that multiple times, and those statements are recorded in the Quran.

> وَ اِذَا تُتۡلٰى عَلَيۡهِمۡ اٰيَاتُنَا بَيِّنٰتٍ قَالَ الَّذِيۡنَ لَا يَرۡجُوۡنَ لِقَآءَنَا ائۡتِ بِقُرۡاٰنٍ غَيۡرِ هٰذَآ اَوۡ بَدِّلۡهُ قُلۡ مَا يَكُوۡنُ لِىۡ
>
> اَنۡ اُبَدِّلَهٗ مِنۡ تِلۡقَآئِ نَفۡسِىۡ اِنۡ اَتَّبِعُ اِلَّا مَا يُوۡحٰى اِلَىَّ اِنِّىۡ اَخَافُ اِنۡ عَصَيۡتُ رَبِّىۡ عَذَابَ يَوۡمٍ عَظِيۡمٍ

But their situation too is the same [O Prophet] that when Our clear revelations are recited before them, then those who do not have fear of meeting Us, say: "Bring another Quran instead of this or change it." Say: [This is God's word;] what right do I have to change it myself? I only follow the revelation that is sent to me. If I disobey my Lord, I fear the punishment of a horrible day.

The Quran is a Warner for the entire humanity

- The Quran is revealed in Makkah, but it is not just a warning for the people of Makkah and its direct addressees. Since they were the direct addressees of it, they faced the consequences of rejecting it because of the Messenger among them.
- Its message is directed toward the entire humanity, and in that sense, it becomes a warning for the entire world
- That is the only reason the Quran was protected, and the chain of prophethood has ceased

وَ أُوحِيَ اِلَيَّ هٰذَا الْقُرْاٰنُ لِاُنْذِرَكُمْ بِهٖ وَ مَنْ بَلَغَ

And this Quran has been revealed to me that I may warn you through it and all those also whom it will reach (Surah Anaam:19)

- The message of its warning is very simple and covers the following aspects:
  - There is a Creator of this Universe, and only He should be worshiped. The Quran warns against polytheism and idolatry, which are considered the gravest sins in the sight of God.
  - He has sent many Messengers before, and the life of the last Messenger is protected in the Quran.
  - Death is imminent, and everyone shall taste it.
  - A day will come when people are held responsible for their actions, so be careful. As a warner, it alerts people that they will be held accountable for their deeds and will face either divine reward or punishment. This serves as a powerful motivator for believers to lead a life of piety and goodness.
  - The Quran recounts the stories of past civilizations that were destroyed for rejecting God's messengers and guidance. These narratives serve as cautionary tales for later generations, highlighting the dangers of arrogance, disbelief, and injustice.

Quran is a Mercy from God

- While the Quran is a warner for humanity, it is also a Mercy from God.
- Allah said in the Quran that His Mercy prevails over His anger, and the Quran is evidence of that, as He preserved His final guidance in the form of a Book we can always refer to.
- It provides guidance and clarity in matters of religion, serving as a divine source of reassurance for believers.

وَ نُنَزِّلُ مِنَ الْقُرْآنِ مَا هُوَ شِفَاءٌ وَّ رَحْمَةٌ لِّلْمُؤْمِنِينَ

We are revealing in this Quran that which is a cure (for the diseases of the hearts) and a Mercy for the believers (Surah Bani Israel:82)

- Those who make the Quran their guide and their book of law are favored with the blessings of Allah and are cured of all their mental, psychological, moral, and cultural diseases.
- It offers a remedy for despair by reminding people not to lose hope in God's mercy, even after they have made mistakes.
- It balances the mention of punishment with the overarching theme of God's mercy, helping believers cope with hardship.
- By reminding people that they are all children of the same origin, it also encourages compassion and discourages division based on cultural or tribal differences.

Because one of the names of the Quran is a "reminder" and a "warner", the critics of Islam say that the style of the Quran is threatening. Why did Allah adopt the style of warning in the Quran in the first place?

Surah Baqarah: Verse 185

شَهْرُ رَمَضَانَ الَّذِىٓ أُنزِلَ فِيهِ الْقُرْآنُ هُدًى لِّلنَّاسِ وَ بَيِّنْتٍ مِّنَ الْهُدَى وَ الْفُرْقَانِ

It is the month of Ramadan in which the Quran was revealed as a book supplied with guidance for mankind and in the form of extremely clear arguments, which, by their nature, are guidance and also a means of distinguishing right from wrong.

- Right before this verse, Allah spoke about fasting as a form of worship.
- He told us that fasting is prescribed for us (the followers of Prophet Muhammad) as it was prescribed before us (the followers of other prophets like Ibrahim, Musa, Isa, and others).
- In those verses, the purpose of fasting was also described: to become God-conscious.
- The Quran is also one of the primary sources of guidance for a person who is God-conscious, as Allah mentioned in the third verse of Surah Baqarah (guidance for the God-conscious).
- The verse related to Ramadan ties everything together and explains why Allah chose Ramadan for fasting: it is also the month of the Quran.
- Allah stressed three aspects related to the Quran:
  - Complete guidance for humanity (in the matter of religion).
  - It provides clear evidence and arguments that serve as a guide.
  - This clear evidence and arguments separate Truth from falsehood.
- Clear evidence and arguments show that these verses clarify any confusion about religion and the message that Allah conveys through the Quran.
- Allah again called the Quran a Criterion (Al Furqan), a Book that separates Truth from falsehood.
- The Quran is not just a collection of dos and don'ts, but it is a treasure full of guidance that will be there until the Day of Judgment.
- If a person is sincerely seeking guidance, this Book provides it.
- Fasting is a form of worship that embodies total submission and manifests our deep gratitude to Allah for giving us this guidance through the Quran.
- One of the greatest blessings of Allah is our intellect, but if revelation does not guide it, it can lead to corruption in society and foster artificial ideas with extreme positions.

The Quran and Ramadan

- Ramadan is celebrated as the month in which the Quran was revealed, emphasizing the connection between fasting and frequent recitation of the holy book.

- The recitation of it and the understanding we gain from the Quran in this month bring great spiritual reward, as the Prophet Muhammad taught.

- Early Muslim scholars and communities dedicated themselves almost exclusively to reading, studying, and acting upon the Quran during Ramadan, sometimes completing its recitation multiple times in the month.

- The early generations not only recited and studied the Quran but also preserved and developed the Arabic language as a means of serving and understanding it.

- The Quran was a source of strength and upliftment, shaping the manners and ethics of the early Muslim community.

- Experiences of community cohesion and youth development are sometimes also centered on Quranic recitation and study during Ramadan.

- However, many Muslims today have distanced themselves from the Quran, leading to spiritual and social challenges. Ramadan provides an excellent opportunity to reconnect with the Quran.

- The Quran holds a transformative power, creating a unique worldview and ethical system that deeply influences communities that engage with it.

- Muslims are encouraged to read, study, and live by the Quran; reduce distractions from modern media; and foster group study circles focused on understanding the Quran.

- The Prophet Muhammad embodied the Quran in his character, serving as the model to follow, especially during Ramadan, the "blessed month of the Quran".

In Surah Baqarah, verse 2, Allah states that the Quran is guidance for those who fear God, whereas in this verse He declares it guidance for all humanity. Is there a contradiction?

Surah Ibrahim: Verse 1

الٓرۚ كِتَـٰبٌ أَنزَلۡنَـٰهُ إِلَيۡكَ لِتُخۡرِجَ ٱلنَّاسَ مِنَ ٱلظُّلُمَـٰتِ إِلَى ٱلنُّورِ ۛ بِإِذۡنِ رَبِّهِمۡ إِلَىٰ صِرَٰطِ ٱلۡعَزِيزِ ٱلۡحَمِيدِ

This is Surah Alif Lam Ra. This is the Book We have revealed to you so that you may bring out people from darkness into the Light with the permission of their Lord to the path of the God Who is powerful and has all praiseworthy attributes.

- Surah Ibrahim and Al Hijr form a pair.
- Both Surahs address the warning to the disbelievers and the glad tidings to the believers.
- Before discussing the message of warning and glad tidings, Allah told them what kind of Book the Quran is and why it presents its arguments with such clarity.
- Before this Surah, in Surah Al Rad, Allah concluded by stating that He is closing in on the disbelievers, and their fate will soon be announced.

Quran directs us to the straight path

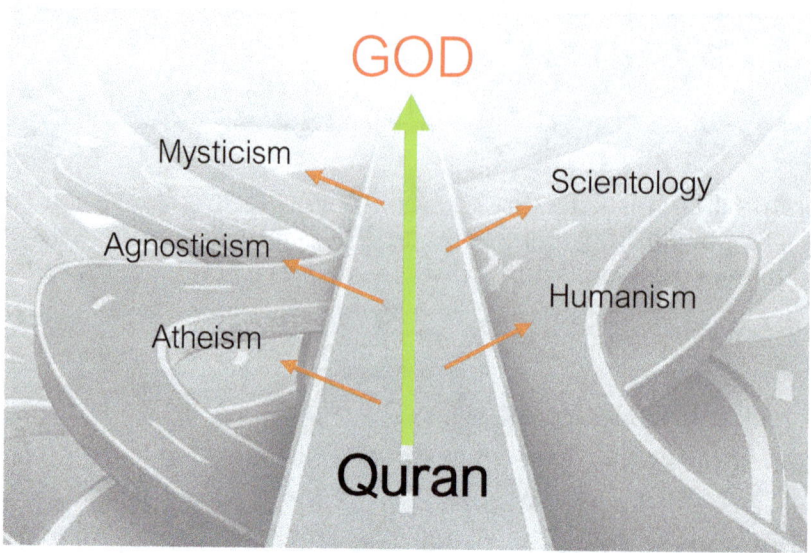

- The plural is used for darkness, and the singular is used for light because there are many darknesses (deviations) when the light of the Quran is missing.
- The straight path towards which the Quran guides is only one.
- The Quran directs us to that straight path and takes people out of the darknesses in which they may be wandering.
- The Quran describes any guidance not from God as "darkness" because it leads to religious error, ignorance, and moral chaos. People either get the wrong answers to their questions or find no answer at all.
- Atheism is a good example of darkness. People have no answers to many critical questions, such as how life began, what the purpose of this life is, and why we have a universal understanding of fundamental good and evil.
- In contrast, God's guidance is portrayed as a single, unifying "light" that illuminates the path to truth, righteousness, and order. Most of the time, these deviations concern matters of faith and belief.
- Light is a metaphor for knowledge and truth, while darkness represents the absence of this knowledge. Seeking truth solely through limited human intellect or worldly desires leaves a person in ignorance.
- Prophet Muhammad was tasked with doing the same, with the help of the Quran, to remove ignorance of the faith and actions.
- However, the guidance will be given only in accordance with the law or with Allah's permission (to those who strive for it without bias).

Surah Saad: Verse 29

كِتَابٌ اَنْزَلْنَاهُ اِلَيْكَ مُبَارَكٌ لِّيَدَّبَّرُوْٓا اٰيٰتِهٖ وَ لِيَتَذَكَّرَ اُولُوا الْاَلْبَابِ

It is a blessed book which We have revealed to you [O Prophet] so that people would ponder over its verses and so that those endowed with intellect are reminded by it.

- In this particular group of verses where this verse appears, Allah argued that the Day of Judgment is inevitable, and the criminals who were opposing the Prophet would see their results.
- In that context, Allah argued that, given the inevitability of the Day of Judgment, one can conclude that this world is not created purposelessly.
- It is emphasized that if the Day of Judgement does not come about, it would mean that this world is a place of evil with no purpose, and its creator is a game-maker who created it for his amusement; there is no distinction between good and evil in it. Such statements obviously can be given by those who have decided to accept everything except the Hereafter, however indisputable the arguments in its favor may be.
- Both arguments provide evidence that on that Day, the criminals and the righteous could not be treated equally.
- In this context, Allah reminded people that if they pondered the verses of the Quran, they could easily reach this conclusion.

The verses of the Quran are for pondering over them

- A book like the Quran, which claims to be authored by God, cannot be read without paying attention to the following:
  - The choice of words and how sentences are put together in the form of verses
  - Their placement in a Surah
  - The relationship between them
  - The relationship of the verses with the main message
  - Deep thinking is required when solving complex issues related to religion
  - Looking at other man-made philosophies and theories in its light
  - The overall theme of a Surah and its relationship with the Surahs next to it
  - Description of human nature and the tendencies it has when it comes to relationships with God and other human beings
- God equated just the reading of the Quran with no understanding to the hearts that are locked for any receiving any truth or guidance.
- The Quran should be read for guidance by deeply pondering its verses – recommended to be read with a translation at all times.

اَفَلَا يَتَدَبَّرُوْنَ الْقُرْاٰنَ اَمْ عَلٰى قُلُوْبٍ اَقْفَالُهَا

Then, do they not reflect on the Quran, or are their hearts locked? (lost the ability to ponder) (Surah Muhammad:24)

Reading the Quran for blessings only

- Reading the Quran can bring blessings; however, the primary purpose is to seek guidance and understand its message.
- Culturally, Muslims consider the Quran a blessed Book, respected and used for: seeking blessings in the home/business, prayers for the dead, blessings for the newlywed, relief from misfortune, etc.
- Reciting the Quran without understanding its message distracts from the Quran's real purpose and forces people to rely only on a Scholar's understanding of the religion, right or wrong.

Hadith

Attentiveness in Reading the Quran

عن جُنْدَبِ بن عبد اللَّهِ الْبَجَلِيِّ قال قال رسول اللَّهِ صلى الله عليه وسلم اقرؤوا الْقُرْآنَ ما
ائْتَلَفَتْ عليه قُلُوبُكُمْ فإذا اخْتَلَفْتُمْ فيه فَقُومُوا

Jundab ibn Abdullah stated that God's Messenger said: "Read the Quran as long as your hearts are inclined to it; when you feel disinterested in it, move away. (Sahih Muslim #2667)

- Read it as long as you want, pay attention to it, and ponder over it.
- For example, avoid playing the Quran recitation loudly in the background for "blessings" while busy in conversations.
- The Quran instructed us to listen to the Quran when it is recited to us.
- This hadith also discourages us from occasions, for example, gathering and reading the Quran to bless the dead, because, in such occasions, people try to finish as many Qurans as possible, which forces people to read it with no heart in it.

Prophet's character was the Quran

عن قتادة قُلْتُ لعائشة يَا أُمَّ الْمُؤْمِنِينَ أَنْبِيِينِي عَنْ خُلُقِ رَسُولِ اللَّهِ صَلَّى اللَّهُ عَلَيْهِ وَسَلَّمَ قَالَتْ
أَلَسْتَ تَقْرَأُ الْقُرْآنَ قُلْتُ بَلَى قَالَتْ فَإِنَّ خُلُقَ نَبِيِّ اللَّهِ صَلَّى اللَّهُ عَلَيْهِ وَسَلَّمَ كَانَ الْقُرْآنَ

Qatadah reported: I told Aisha, "O mother of the believers, tell me about the character of the Messenger of Allah, peace and blessings be upon him." Aisha said, "Have you not read the Quran?" I said, "Of course." Aisha said, "Verily, the character of the Prophet of Allah was the Quran." (Sahih Muslim #746)

- This is a great example of understanding the Quran.
- A person cannot become a walking Quran in their character unless they know which attributes the Quran expects of a believer.

Assignment

Take the example of Music and list various scholarly opinions after conducting thorough research about Music in the light of the Quran only. Why do you think there are so many opinions about it? Does the Quran explicitly prohibit music? Which verses are used for its prohibition?

Chapter 9

Topic 4: Parents in the Quran

This chapter discusses the rights of parents as mentioned in the Quran, right after the rights of God.

Surah Ahqaf: Verse 15-16

وَ وَصَّيۡنَا الۡاِنۡسَانَ بِوَالِدَيۡهِ اِحۡسٰنًا ۖ حَمَلَتۡهُ اُمُّهٗ كُرۡهًا وَّ وَضَعَتۡهُ كُرۡهًا ۖ وَ حَمۡلُهٗ وَ فِصٰلُهٗ ثَلٰثُوۡنَ شَهۡرًا ۖ حَتّٰٓى

اِذَا بَلَغَ اَشُدَّهٗ وَ بَلَغَ اَرۡبَعِيۡنَ سَنَةً ۙ قَالَ رَبِّ اَوۡزِعۡنِيۡٓ اَنۡ اَشۡكُرَ نِعۡمَتَكَ الَّتِيۡٓ اَنۡعَمۡتَ عَلَيَّ وَ عَلٰى

وَالِدَيَّ وَ اَنۡ اَعۡمَلَ صَالِحًا تَرۡضٰهُ وَ اَصۡلِحۡ لِيۡ فِيۡ ذُرِّيَّتِيۡ ۖ اِنِّيۡ تُبۡتُ اِلَيۡكَ وَ اِنِّيۡ مِنَ الۡمُسۡلِمِيۡنَ

اُولٰٓئِكَ الَّذِيۡنَ نَتَقَبَّلُ عَنۡهُمۡ اَحۡسَنَ مَا عَمِلُوۡا وَ نَتَجَاوَزُ عَنۡ سَيِّاٰتِهِمۡ فِيۡٓ اَصۡحٰبِ الۡجَنَّةِ ۖ

وَعۡدَ الصِّدۡقِ الَّذِيۡ كَانُوۡا يُوۡعَدُوۡنَ

[If you want to understand how people become good with age, then listen:] We have urged human beings to show kindness to their parents. With great difficulty, his mother carried him in her womb and, with great difficulty, delivered him, and his carrying and weaning took place in [almost] thirty months. Finally, after passing through all these stages, when a human fully matures and becomes forty years old, he prays: "God give me the urge to express gratitude for your favor which you did to my parents and me, and do those righteous deeds which please you. And also create kindness (and love) in my children toward me. I turn to you; indeed, I am from among the obedient." It is this group of people whose good deeds We shall accept from them and whose sins We shall overlook so that they be among the dwellers of Paradise. This is a true promise made to them.

- The verses before these two verses talk about two types of people whom Allah asked Prophet Muhammad to address:
  - People who have wronged themselves
  - People who are good in their deeds
- People who are good in their deeds constantly ask to be firm in their beliefs.
- Allah has promised them a good place in Paradise, where they will have no regrets about the past and no worries about the future.
- In the same context, Allah mentioned their behavior towards their parents and the attitude they have developed over time.

Why is there no verse in the Quran about children's rights and the parents' duties?

Being nice to parents, especially mothers

- In many places in the Quran, the rights of parents are described right after the belief in the oneness of Allah.
- The guidance about being nice to parents is given in our nature, but the Prophets of Allah took it to the next level for a Muslim.
- The entire paradigm of morality starts with "giving others their due rights," and it usually starts with the parents very early on.

- Allah has asked Muslims to keep excellence in their behavior towards parents, but He has primarily explained the reason why the mother is special.
- A mother carries the baby in her womb for 8-9 months, then provides the required care for her until the baby is old enough to walk and feed themselves.
- Many mothers go through a life-threatening situation at the time of the birth and immediately after that, which is a big sacrifice on her part.
- The mother is specially mentioned because they usually becomes a housewife, sacrifices their career, and, as a result, depends on other people for their survival.

A good believer

- A child develops an awareness of others' rights from their parents, which leads them to the next stage: the true giver, Allah.
- The same kind of love and care a person finds from His Lord is also given when they realize that these blessings are not coming from their parents, but from Allah.
- When a believer reaches a mature stage of their life, they can see the blessings of Allah all around them, which motivates them to be grateful to Allah.
- Recognizing the blessings of Allah and overcoming the mentality of "entitlement" is crucial for a believer to live with a sense of giving back to Allah and others, starting with parents.
- Not everyone recognizes this, so a believer asks for Allah's help.
- To show gratitude, a believer asks Allah to guide them to a life full of deeds that please Allah – the best way to repay (although we can never repay).

Surah Luqman: Verse 14-15

وَ وَصَّيْنَا الْإِنْسَانَ بِوَالِدَيْهِ ۚ حَمَلَتْهُ أُمُّهُ وَهْنًا عَلَى وَهْنٍ وَّ فِصَالُهُ فِى

عَامَيْنِ أَنِ اشْكُرْ لِى وَ لِوَالِدَيْكَ ۚ إِلَىَّ الْمَصِيرُ

وَ إِنْ جَاهَدَاكَ عَلَى أَنْ تُشْرِكَ بِى مَا لَيْسَ لَكَ بِهِ عِلْمٌ ۙ فَلَا

تُطِعْهُمَا وَ صَاحِبْهُمَا فِى الدُّنْيَا مَعْرُوفًا ۖ وَّ اتَّبِعْ سَبِيلَ مَنْ أَنَابَ إِلَىَّ ۚ

ثُمَّ إِلَىَّ مَرْجِعُكُمْ فَأُنَبِّئُكُمْ بِمَا كُنْتُمْ تَعْمَلُوْنَ

[There is no doubt that] We have also counseled a human being about his parents. His mother kept him in her womb, tolerating distress after distress, and [after birth] it took two years for his weaning. [We have counseled him:] "Be grateful to Me and to your parents [and remember that ultimately] to Me is the return. But if they force you to associate someone with Me about whom you have no proof, do not obey them. However, treat them kindly in this world and follow the way of those who turn to Me. Then you will have to return to Me alone. Then I shall inform you of what you have been doing."

- Interestingly, these verses came in the middle of the talk that Luqman had started with his son.
- He began his advice to his son with the concept of true monotheism, emphasizing the importance of not associating anyone or anything with Allah. Then he moved on to the Power of Allah and the reminder about the Day of Judgment.
- He overlooked the importance of parents' rights out of humility, as he was one of the child's parents.
- These verses are an insertion from Allah into Luqman's talk to emphasize that after worshiping Allah alone come the rights of parents – a common theme in the Quran.
- There is no doubt that among human beings, the foremost right is that of the parents. This is because, after God, parents become the primary source of bringing a person into existence and raising them.

What does being kind to parents mean?

- Allah reiterated that He had repeatedly advised people about their parents, and since this is the occasion, He is doing so again.
- Here again, Allah emphasized the role of a mother in a child's birth and what is immediately required after the birth.
- Allah did not talk about the birth here, but it is obvious.
- The attention and affection of the father are also no less important in the upbringing of a child, yet the labor a mother undergoes in various phases of pregnancy, childbirth, and suckling is unmatched.
- Being kind means having an attitude of respect and kindness towards them – even when there is disagreement.
- A believer's priority is to obey Allah alone. Obedience to other people falls under that obedience. Allah never asked people to obey their parents unconditionally.
- Even in the extreme case of Shirk, Allah did not allow believers to be rude and disrespectful to their parents.

> Ali reported: The Prophet said, "There is no obedience to anyone if it is disobedience to Allah. Verily, obedience is only in good conduct." (Sahih Al Bukhari #6830)

- There is a common misconception in some cultures that being kind to parents includes unconditional obedience in all aspects of life if they insist on something. This is not correct in light of the Quran and the teachings of the Prophet Muhammad.
- Once a child comes of age, parents do not have the right to dictate personal choices, such as career or marriage. While a child should be respectful and seek a middle ground, the final decision rests with the child, not the parents.
- A child is not accountable to God for the unjustified displeasure of parents. The focus remains on treating them well, within one's capacity, even if their kindness was lacking.

The sense of Accountability

- Allah reminded the believers multiple times in these verses of a fact we often forget when dealing with others: we will ultimately be returned to Allah.
- This message of living with a sense of accountability is for both parents and children.
- The best way to focus on the return to Allah is to get out of the mentality of entitlement and be grateful to Allah and the people around us.
- The best way to pay back is not just with words, but also with actions.

- Allah reminded us that if parents took undue advantage of their rights given to them by Allah, then they would be questioned by Allah (for example, pushing their children to do things that Allah does not sanction).
- The same accountability applies to children as well. They may escape any retribution for their ill behavior toward their parents in this world, but they should know that this is a temporary life, and ultimately, Allah will question them on the Day of Judgment.
- This sense of return and accountability keeps a check on our actions, especially related to our relationships.

Surah Bani Israel: Verse 23-24

وَ قَضٰى رَبُّكَ اَلَّا تَعْبُدُوْۤا اِلَّاۤ اِیَّاهُ وَ بِالْوَالِدَیْنِ اِحْسَانًا ؕ اِمَّا یَبْلُغَنَّ عِنْدَکَ الْکِبَرَ

اَحَدُهُمَاۤ اَوْ کِلٰهُمَا فَلَا تَقُلْ لَّهُمَاۤ اُفٍّ وَّ لَا تَنْهَرْهُمَا وَ قُلْ لَّهُمَا قَوْلًا کَرِیْمًا

وَ اخْفِضْ لَهُمَا جَنَاحَ الذُّلِّ مِنَ الرَّحْمَةِ وَ قُلْ رَّبِّ ارْحَمْهُمَا کَمَا رَبَّیٰنِیْ صَغِیْرًا

رَبُّکُمْ اَعْلَمُ بِمَا فِیْ نُفُوْسِکُمْ ؕ اِنْ تَکُوْنُوْا صٰلِحِیْنَ فَاِنَّهٗ کَانَ لِلْاَوَّابِیْنَ غَفُوْرًا

Your Lord has enjoined you to worship none but Him and to treat your parents excellently. If either or both of them attain old age, show them no sign of impatience, nor scold them while answering; speak to them with respect and softness, lower arms of tenderness on them (like birds), and keep praying: "Lord! Be merciful to them who nursed me [with love and tenderness] in childhood." [People!] Your Lord fully knows what is in your hearts. If you remain righteous, He forgives those who turn to Him.

- A few verses before the start of this section, God talked about the role of the Quran and how it guides people to the straight path.

اِنَّ هٰذَا الْقُرْاٰنَ یَهْدِیْ لِلَّتِیْ هِیَ اَقْوَمُ وَ یُبَشِّرُ الْمُؤْمِنِیْنَ

[People!] In reality, this Quran shows the way, which is straight and glad tidings to the believers (Bani Israel:9)

- The Quran presented the ten commandments in these verses 22-39, and the verses under study are the beginning of those verses.
- This is the straight path (verses 22-39) that the Quran guides us to.
- Being kind to parents is also one of the qualities needed to be on the straight path.

Parents in the old age

- These verses come right after the first commandment, which is to worship Allah alone – this is the second commandment in the order.
- The Quran again emphasized the importance of excellent behavior towards our parents.
- These verses specifically address the situation of growing old – there is a saying that a child and an elderly person are the same.

- A person should treat their parents with respect, so that they are not just respected outwardly but also from the heart.
- 'Uff' is a sign of annoyance – God wants us not even to show that sign.
- It is in old age that people regard their parents as a burden and forget their selflessness when they were young, unable to do anything.
- Just as parents hide and protect their children the way birds do, children, too, should provide that kind of protection to their parents under the wings of love and kindness.
- This prayer is a right of the parents over their children.
- This is a reminder to believers that, in the end, kindness towards their parents should stem from inner warmth and fondness, because Allah knows what's in their hearts.

Hadith

Importance of serving your old parents

عَنْ يَزِيدَ بن أبي حَبِيبٍ أَنَّ نَاعِمًا مولَى أُمِّ سَلَمَةَ حدثه أَنَّ عَبْدَ اللَّهِ بن عَمْرِو بن الْعَاصِ قال أَقْبَلَ رَجُلٌ إلى نَبِيّ اللَّهِ صلى الله عليه وسلم فقال أُبَايِعُكَ على الْهِجْرَةِ وَالْجِهَادِ أَبْتَغِي الْأَجْرَ من اللَّهِ قال فَهَلْ من وَالِدَيْكَ أَحَدٌ حَيٌّ قال نعم بَلْ كلاهما قال فَتَبْتَغِى الْأَجْرَ من اللَّهِ قال نعم قال فَارْجِعْ إلى وَالِدَيْكَ فَأَحْسِنْ صُحْبَتَهُمَا

Yazid ibn Abi Habib reported that Naim, the freed slave of Umm Salamah, reported to him that Abdullah ibn Amr ibn al-As said: "A person came to the Prophet of God and said: "I want to pledge allegiance to you for migration and Jihad seeking reward only from God." He replied: "Are any of your parents alive?" The person said, "Yes, both are alive." The Prophet further asked: "Do you want to seek reward from God?" He replied: "Yes." At this, the Prophet said: "Go back to your parents and treat them kindly." (Sahih Muslim #2549)

عَنْ أبيه عن أبي هُرَيْرَةَ عن النبي صلى الله عليه وسلم قال رَغِمَ أَنْفُ ثُمَّ رَغِمَ أَنْفُ ثُمَّ رَغِمَ أَنْفُ قِيلَ من يا رَسُولَ اللَّهِ قال من أَدْرَكَ أَبَوَيْهِ عِنْدَ الْكِبَرِ أَحَدَهُمَا أو كِلَيْهِمَا فلم يَدْخُلْ الْجَنَّةَ

Abu Hurairah reported that the Prophet said: "May he be disgraced; May he be disgraced; May he be disgraced." It was asked: "Who, O God's Messenger?" He said: "He who found either of his parents or both of them during their old age, but [still] did not enter Paradise [by serving them]." (Sahih Muslim #2551)

عن عبد اللَّهِ بن عُمَرَ أَنَّ النبي صلى الله عليه وسلم قال أَبَرُّ الْبِرِّ أَنْ يَصِلَ الرَّجُلُ وُدَّ أبيه

Abdullah ibn Umar reported that God's Prophet said: "The finest act of virtue is that a person should be kind to the loved ones of his father (or either parent)." (Sahih Muslim #2552)

Bible

Respect for parents

Give honor to your father and mother so that your life may be long in the land the Lord your God is giving you. (Exodus, 20:12)

Important Summary of the Topic

- Allah created the institution of marriage and family so we can help each other when it is needed most.
- Our parents nurture us when we can't feed or clean ourselves.
- Similarly, when they become old, they need our help the same way – remember their sacrifices when you were young.
- Among all your relationships, parents have the most rights over you – no one can replace them.
- Allah asked us to deal with them gently and with kindness, regardless of the situation.
- This does not mean we are asked to obey them blindly – however, even if we disagree with them on something, no sign of disrespect should be shown.
- Allah is pleased with the people who are gentle and kind to their parents, and they will be rewarded with a happier life in this world and paradise in the Hereafter.

How is our relationship with parents closely tied to our relationship with Allah?

Chapter 10

Topic 5: The life of this world

This chapter introduces how God and the Quran view the concept of life and the perspective we have as we live in this world.

Quran's Concept of Life

- We understand that life starts when we are born and ends when we die. However, in God's eyes, life is much more than that.

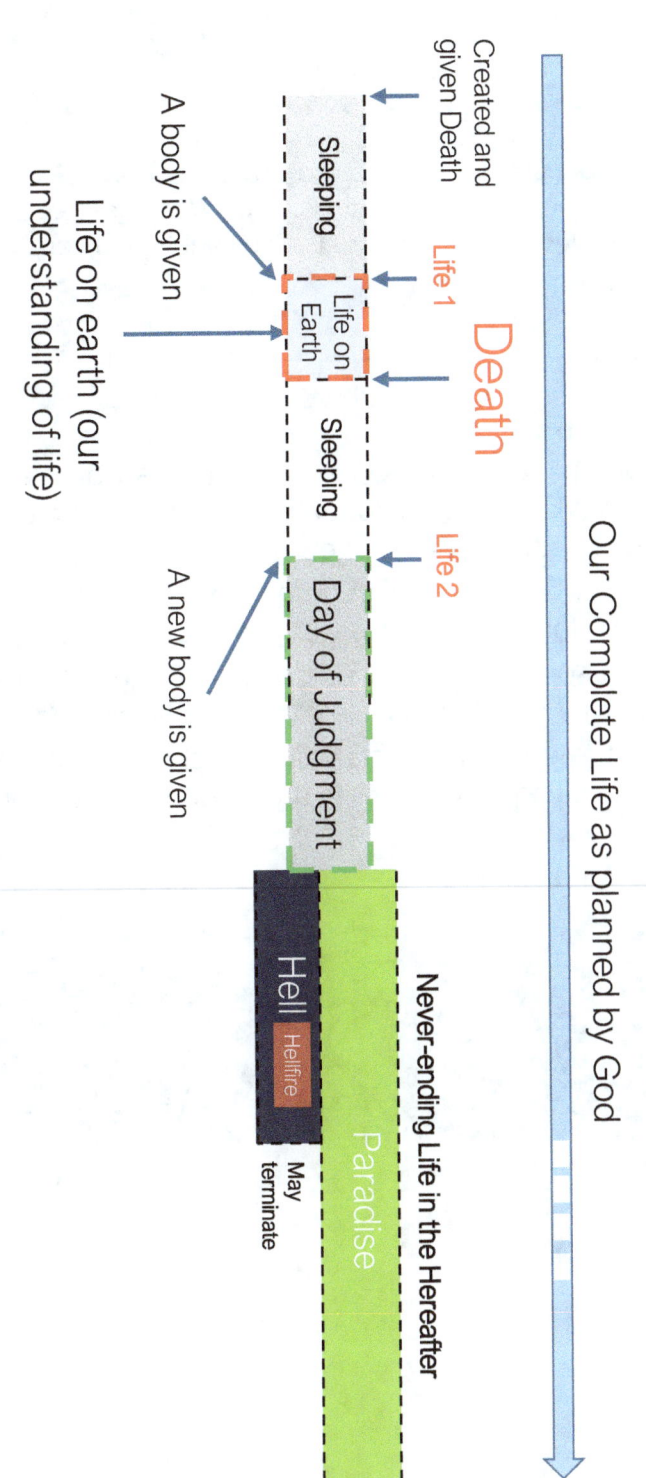

Surah Mulk: Verses 1-2

تَبٰرَكَ الَّذِىْ بِيَدِهِ الْمُلْكُ ۖ وَ هُوَ عَلٰى كُلِّ شَىْءٍ قَدِيْرُۙ

الَّذِىْ خَلَقَ الْمَوْتَ وَ الْحَيٰوةَ لِيَبْلُوَكُمْ اَيُّكُمْ اَحْسَنُ عَمَلًا ؕ وَ هُوَ الْعَزِيْزُ الْغَفُوْرُۙ ۟

Very Exalted and very Benevolent is the [Lord] in Whose hands is the dominion [of the world,] and He has power over all things. [He] Who <u>created death and life to test which of you does better deeds.</u> And He is also Mighty and Forgiving. (67:1-2)

- Surah Mulk and Surah Qalam form a pair. Surah Mulk warns about the Day of Judgment, and Surah Qalam talks about the punishment that is implemented on the nations who reject the Messenger.
- Surah Mulk explains why the Day of Judgment is the logical conclusion of the way and the reasons for which this life was created.
- It explains why a person cannot live life while remaining indifferent to the fact that one day they will be held responsible for their beliefs and actions.
- The surah presents evidence from this universe, showing how Allah's Mercy, Power, and ability to sustain life on Earth are evident in everything around us.

Tabaraka is a superlative from *Barakah*. *Barakah* encompasses the meanings of exaltation and greatness, abundance and plenty, and permanence and multiplicity of virtues and excellence

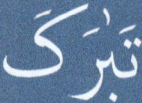

The World is a factory of life and death

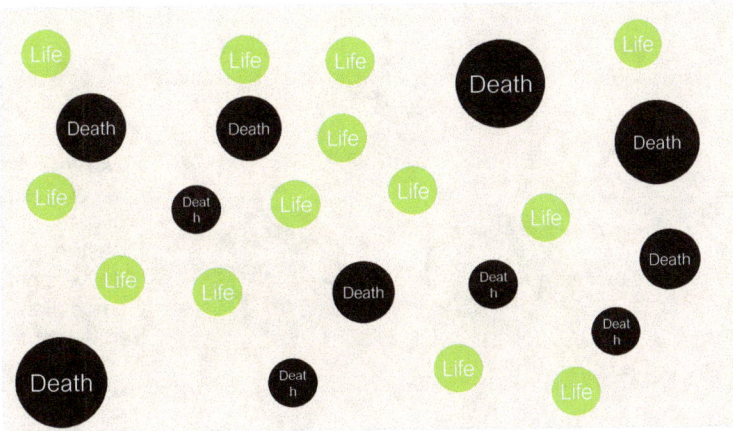

According to the World Bank, for every 1,000 people worldwide, an average of 7.748 people will die each year, and 19.349 will be born. That's a ratio of about 2.5 births for every death. (www.sciencefocus.com)

- Allah has introduced Himself in such a way that one cannot imagine for a second that this universe is purposeless: God is Exalted and Benevolent (generous); He owns the dominion of this universe; He controls everything.
- The above introduction also indicates that if He has allowed evil to exist, then it is merely for the reason of trial.
- If we were dead, then brought to life, and will be dead again before we are brought to life one more time, then this life cannot be without a purpose (it must be planned).
- Since this life is temporary and the purpose of this life on earth is to test people in their beliefs and actions, then death is nothing but a means to an end (the reasons might differ).
- The verses end with two of His qualities: He is Powerful, and He is Forgiving – Be mindful of His Powers when living in this world, but if you have made mistakes, then know that He is ready to forgive all the time.
- This world and life in it are perfectly designed for trials and tests. Happiness and grief, affluence and poverty, strength and weakness, abundance and scarcity, honor and disgrace …. live side by side.
- For the sake of this test, the Creator has given every human being an opportunity for action so that they may do good or evil in the world and practically show if they deserve an immortal life full of bliss and joy.

The impact of faith in going through the trials and tribulations

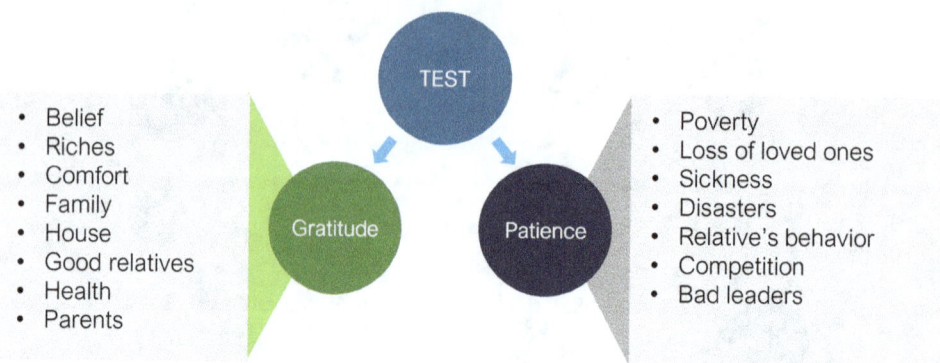

- Belief
- Riches
- Comfort
- Family
- House
- Good relatives
- Health
- Parents

TEST

Gratitude

Patience

- Poverty
- Loss of loved ones
- Sickness
- Disasters
- Relative's behavior
- Competition
- Bad leaders

- In the Quran, the trial is used for both situations—poverty and hardship, and affluence and ease.

- They do not represent in <u>any shape or form</u> your relationship with Allah.

- Allah has tested us with both, but in a different way.

- A firm faith in Allah, combined with a good understanding of the nature of this life, helps us succeed in this test with flying colors.

- Hardship is considered an easier test because difficulties in life keep you in check, and by nature, you always turn to a higher power for help

- In Surah Kahf, we learned that:

  - Allah gave an arrogant person one more garden so he could boast about his power and luck.

  - Allah took away the child of a couple (who would be grief-stricken for them in the future) whom He loved because of their righteousness.

- In a time of ease and affluence, faith in Allah with a good understanding of the nature of this life propels you to do good by sharing your blessings and keeps you in check for the Hereafter.

- This is one of the main concepts that most human beings do not understand properly, which has led to disbelief in God and the rise of Atheism.

How do non-believers cope with tough life situations?

Surah Zukhruf: Verses 31-32

وَ قَالُوْا لَوْ لَا نُزِّلَ هٰذَا الْقُرْاٰنُ عَلٰى رَجُلٍ مِّنَ الْقَرْيَتَيْنِ عَظِيْمٍ

اَهُمْ يَقْسِمُوْنَ رَحْمَتَ رَبِّكَ ۚ نَحْنُ قَسَمْنَا بَيْنَهُمْ مَّعِيْشَتَهُمْ فِى الْحَيٰوةِ الدُّنْيَا وَ رَفَعْنَا بَعْضَهُمْ

فَوْقَ بَعْضٍ دَرَجٰتٍ لِّيَتَّخِذَ بَعْضُهُمْ بَعْضًا سُخْرِيًّا ۚ وَ رَحْمَتُ رَبِّكَ خَيْرٌ مِّمَّا يَجْمَعُوْنَ

وَ لَوْ لَا اَنْ يَّكُوْنَ النَّاسُ اُمَّةً وَّاحِدَةً لَّجَعَلْنَا لِمَنْ يَّكْفُرُ بِالرَّحْمٰنِ

لِبُيُوْتِهِمْ سُقُفًا مِّنْ فِضَّةٍ وَّ مَعَارِجَ عَلَيْهَا يَظْهَرُوْنَ

وَ زُخْرُفًا ۚ وَ اِنْ كُلُّ ذٰلِكَ لَمَّا مَتَاعُ الْحَيٰوةِ الدُّنْيَا ۚ وَ

الْاٰخِرَةُ عِنْدَ رَبِّكَ لِلْمُتَّقِيْنَ

They say: "Why was the Quran not revealed to some prominent person in both cities [Makkah and Taif]?" Do they allocate the mercy of your Lord? It is We who have allocated among them the means of their livelihood in the life of this world and have allocated them in such a way that We have raised some status above others so that they can mutually serve each other. And better is your Lord's mercy than what they are amassing. [They should not show conceit on this.] Had it not been for the fear that all people will adopt the same way [and none will profess faith], We would have made of silver the roof of the houses of those who are disbelieving in God and the staircases too which they climb and the doors of their houses and their thrones on which they sit reclining on pillows; in fact, [not only of silver,] but of gold also. In reality, all these things are merely provisions of worldly life, and the Hereafter [O Prophet] before your Lord is only for those who fear God.

- Before these verses, Allah talked about their claim in which they said that if taking partners with Allah were a bad thing, He would have forcefully stopped us, but our forefathers have been engaged in this practice for centuries now.

- Allah responded to them by giving them examples from the past where affluent leadership refused to accept the message of Allah merely because of their arrogance and allegiance to their tribes and forefathers.

- Allah advised them that the practice of their forefathers is not a criterion for accepting or rejecting the truth.

- Allah pointed out to them that it's their affluence, influence in society, and leadership that have resulted in arrogance and their attitude of denial.

- Allah correctly diagnosed their issue because the Messenger's status in society was one of their major concerns in accepting the truth.

Allah is the best planner, and He does not need help

- Makkah and Taif were the two city centers where most of the wealthy and the leadership of Quraysh resided.
- The disbelievers' objection: "Why, for Messengerhood and revelation of the Quran, was not an influential person among the leaders of these two towns chosen?"
- Allah used this opportunity to tell them that if He had never asked them how to distribute blessings and wealth among people (depending on the test they would face), why would He ask them when choosing the Messenger among them?
- They thought that since wealth and leadership had remained among a few people in society, why would Allah give the honor of Messengership to a person who was an orphan and had no status in society?
- Among many excuses that the leaders of Quraysh had for not accepting the Prophet, this was another attempt to misguide their followers.
- It is important to note that Allah called the Quran and the Prophethood of Prophet Muhammad mercy in this verse.

Distribution of wealth

- Allah clearly rejected the notion that the wealth and worldly status gained by some people entitle them to a specific position with Allah.
- Allah decides our skills and talents; it is up to us whether we take advantage of them and polish them.

- This decision does not hinder our efforts to attain or gain something.
- If human beings do not interfere in this process out of greed, wealth is distributed so that people depend on each other, functioning like gears in a watch or machine.
- This distribution is ideally suited to testing gratitude and patience.
- This is mandatory for industries and professions to exist.
- Who will mow the lawn or build furniture if everyone is a wealthy banker?
- Looking at it this way, every trade is respectable because we depend on each other to survive.
- Allah advised that instead of competing for positions, people should compete in good deeds.

The value of this world in the sight of Allah

- The disbelievers were asking for the honor of Messengerhood and the revelation of the Quran, merely based on wealth or status in society.
- Allah told them that worldly wealth and status have no value in His sight.
- He could have given them more in this world if that's what they wanted alone.
- He told them that He could have given them so much that their houses' roofs and stairs would be made of gold and silver.
- But then an ordinary person around them would falsely assume that the more they disbelieve, the richer they get.
- Allah reminded people in these verses that the wealth of this world is nothing but play and amusement, but the real success is to earn a better life in the Hereafter, which will only be done by the people who are conscious of Allah.
- Elsewhere, the Quran states that the riches of this life are temporary and a deceptive form of enjoyment compared to the eternal and superior rewards of the Hereafter. This is a very common topic in the Quran.

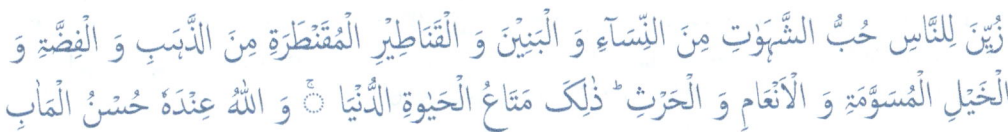

For those [who are deprived of this vision, the lures of the world] – women and sons, treasures of gold and silver, marked horses, cattle, and vegetation have been made very tempting. All this is just a provision of this life, and a nice abode is only with God. (3:14)

The Prophet passed through a market and came upon a dead one-eared goat, so he reached out and took its ear. Then he said, "Who would like to buy this for a dirham?" They said, "Why would we want it when it is worthless? What would we do with it?" He said, "Would you like to have it?" "No," they replied. He asked them that three times, and they said, "No, by Allah! If it were alive, it would have a defect, as it only has one ear. Why would we want it when it is dead?" The Prophet said, "By Allah, this world is lesser in value in the sight of Allah than this goat is to you." (*Aadaab al Mufrad #962*)

Surah Hadeed: Verses 20-21

اِعْلَمُوْٓا اَنَّمَا الْحَیٰوةُ الدُّنْیَا لَعِبٌ وَّ لَهْوٌ وَّ زِیْنَةٌ وَّ تَفَاخُرٌۢ بَیْنَكُمْ وَ تَكَاثُرٌ فِی الْاَمْوَالِ وَ الْاَوْلَادِ ؕ كَمَثَلِ غَیْثٍ اَعْجَبَ الْكُفَّارَ نَبَاتُهٗ ثُمَّ یَهِیْجُ فَتَرٰىهُ مُصْفَرًّا ثُمَّ یَكُوْنُ حُطَامًا ؕ وَ فِی الْاٰخِرَةِ عَذَابٌ شَدِیْدٌ ۙ وَّ مَغْفِرَةٌ مِّنَ اللّٰهِ وَ رِضْوَانٌ ؕ وَ مَا الْحَیٰوةُ الدُّنْیَآ اِلَّا مَتَاعُ الْغُرُوْرِ سَابِقُوْٓا اِلٰی مَغْفِرَةٍ مِّنْ رَّبِّكُمْ وَ جَنَّةٍ عَرْضُهَا كَعَرْضِ السَّمَآءِ وَ الْاَرْضِ ۙ اُعِدَّتْ لِلَّذِیْنَ اٰمَنُوْا بِاللّٰهِ وَ رُسُلِهٖ ؕ ذٰلِكَ فَضْلُ اللّٰهِ یُؤْتِیْهِ مَنْ یَّشَآءُ ؕ وَ اللّٰهُ ذُو الْفَضْلِ الْعَظِیْمِ

[Do not evade this spending and] bear in mind that the parable of the life of this world – a sport and entertainment, an embellishment and, in the matter of wealth and children, a mutual show off and a quest to outdo one another in them – is that of rain which produces a crop that lures the hearts of these disbelievers; then it blooms, and you see it turn yellowish orange, then [a calamity strikes, and it] turns into bits and pieces. [But they should bear in mind that after this] there is a grievous penalty in the Hereafter and the forgiveness of God and His pleasure. In reality, the life of this world is but a provision of deception. [For this reason,] strive fervently while outdoing one another towards the forgiveness of your Lord and for a Paradise as vast as the heavens and the earth. It has been prepared for those who genuinely believe in God and His messengers. Such is the grace of God: He bestows it on whomsoever He wills, and great is God's grace.

- The verses before these verses under study encourage Muslims to spend in the path of Allah, especially for the wars that Muslims were engaged in.
- The Quran appreciated those who were willing to spend on this cause.
- Allah called this type of charity "a goodly loan," promising to return it on the Day of Judgment after multiplying it hundreds of times.
- On this occasion, the hypocrites were creating doubts among Muslims by saying that this Prophet is saying new things and they have never fought in the name of religion – especially the Christians were misguiding them about the whole concept of war and spending wealth for it.
- In this environment, while the enemies of Islam were spreading confusion, Allah told Muslims to spend and the reality of the riches of this life.

Why did the Quran call children a trial for their parents?

A parable of this life and beauty in it

- To explain the reality of this life and the temporary nature of its attractions, Allah gave a parable.
- As human beings, we are all attracted to the following: luxuries and comforts, competition to get more riches, children, and wealth.
- When it rains, it produces lush green vegetation and makes an ungrateful farmer delighted (with no thanks to Allah).
- But over time (when the season changes, there is no rain, or a natural calamity strikes), the same vegetation withers, turns yellow, and crumbles away.
- In the same way, the life and luxuries of this world are going to entertain you for some time, but this is all temporary, and ultimately, either they are taken away from you, or you leave this world, and everything stays behind.
- A wise person should keep this reality of life in mind, but that's precisely what we forget all the time.
- We have examples around us of people who were millionaires, but ultimately they either lost everything or left this world without using any of that money.
- We have two choices in this world:

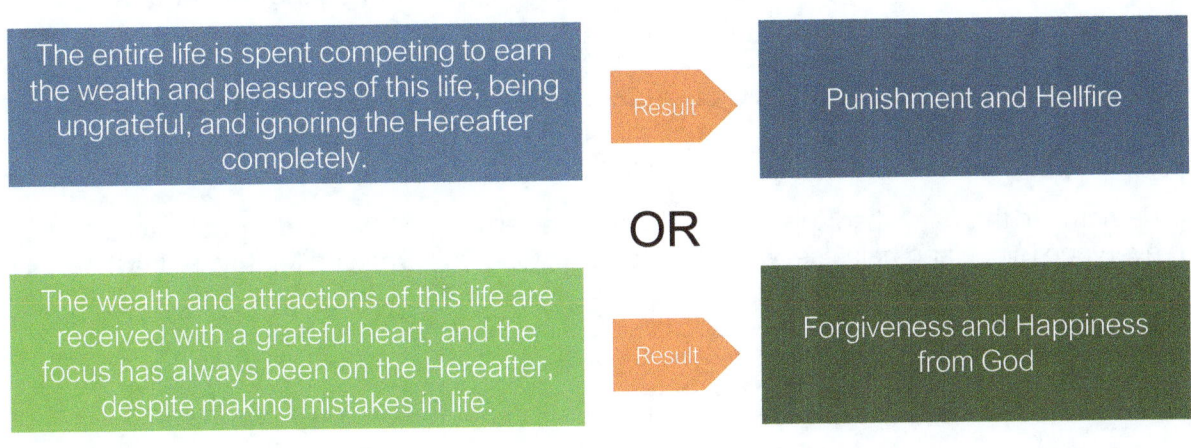

The real field of competition

- Instead of amassing wealth in rivalry, the real competition should be in earning the forgiveness of Allah and the pleasures of the Hereafter in the form of paradise.

- To give us an idea of comparison, Allah told us in these verses that the vastness of paradise will extend beyond this earth into the heavens – meaning there is no comparison between what one could own on this earth and what people would own in paradise.

- Allah told us that paradise is specially prepared for the believers who believe in Allah and His messenger (and perform righteous deeds).

- Allah will give this reward to anyone who follows the commands of Allah and lives a balanced life without ignoring their portion in this world.

- It would be a bad bargain if someone is satisfied with this world and completely ignores life in the Hereafter, which is going to be everlasting.

In various Ahadith, it is mentioned that the last person to enter paradise will receive an area ten times the size of the earth. That's what Allah mentions about the vastness of paradise in these verses.

- We can get some idea of the vastness of the heavens from this verse: knowing that the universe is huge compared to our earth, and that all that material will be used to prepare the heavens, it must be extremely vast.

يَوْمَ تُبَدَّلُ الْأَرْضُ غَيْرَ الْأَرْضِ وَ السَّمٰوٰتُ وَ بَرَزُوْا لِلّٰهِ الْوَاحِدِ الْقَهَّارِ

Remember the day when this earth will be replaced by another and this sky too, and everyone [alone and helpless] will set off towards God, the One and Mighty. (14:48)

Surah Munafiqun: Verses 9-11

يَا أَيُّهَا الَّذِينَ آمَنُوا لَا تُلْهِكُمْ أَمْوَالُكُمْ وَ لَا أَوْلَادُكُمْ عَنْ ذِكْرِ اللَّهِ ۚ وَ مَنْ يَفْعَلْ ذَٰلِكَ فَأُولَٰئِكَ هُمُ الْخَاسِرُونَ

وَ أَنْفِقُوا مِنْ مَّا رَزَقْنَاكُمْ مِّنْ قَبْلِ أَنْ يَّأْتِيَ أَحَدَكُمُ الْمَوْتُ فَيَقُولَ رَبِّ لَوْ لَا أَخَّرْتَنِيَ إِلَىٰ أَجَلٍ قَرِيبٍ

فَأَصَّدَّقَ وَ أَكُنْ مِّنَ الصَّالِحِينَ وَ لَنْ يُّؤَخِّرَ اللَّهُ نَفْسًا إِذَا جَاءَ أَجَلُهَا ۚ وَ اللَّهُ خَبِيرٌ بِمَا تَعْمَلُونَ

Believers! [Like these Hypocrites,] let neither your riches nor your children make you indifferent to remembering God, and [remember that] those who do this, it is they who will be the losers. Spend [for the cause of God] from what We have blessed you before death befalls any of you, then he [longingly] says: "Lord! Why did you not give me some more respite that I would have spent for Your cause, and if I had done so, today I would have been among the righteous?" Even though God will never give respite to a soul when its appointed time arrives, whatever you do is entirely in God's knowledge.

- The context and background of these verses are very similar to the verses of Surah Hadeed.
- The Surah Munafiqun (the hypocrites) was revealed to expose the hypocrites' behavior in Medinah.
- Allah exposed them so Muslims would be aware that these hypocrites were utterly lying when they displayed their sincerity toward Muslims.
- The best way to test their faith and sincerity is to ask them to spend their wealth in the path of Allah – they would never do that.
- The verses preceding these discussed the behavior of hypocrites regarding spending wealth in the path of Allah.
- The hypocrites were creating doubts among Muslims by saying that this Prophet was saying new things, and they had never fought in the name of religion, so why spend money?
- Allah has warned believers to avoid such an attitude so as not to be losers like them.
- The verses address the believers at that time, but the message applies to us as well.

How do we forget Allah?

- Allah mentioned the two things — children and wealth — in these verses that mostly keep adults from the remembrance of Allah.
- But in our lives, there is always something that keeps us from remembering Allah at different stages.
- Allah told the believers not to forget Allah; otherwise, they would be among the losers.

Toys, games, and fun

Education, sports, and fun

Job, dreams, and career

Wealth, house, and children

What would people wish at the time of their death

- Allah has asked the believers to spend from the wealth <u>given to them by Allah</u> in the first place.
- Allah asked the believers to spend money in the path of Allah when a need arose in the community.
- This was done to distinguish hypocrites from believers at that time.
- The hypocrites used to claim their belief, but as soon as they were asked to spend money in the path of Allah, their true faces were exposed.
- Allah told believers to spend their wealth before their death, when hoarders would request Allah to give them another chance to go back to this world and spend money and become righteous as a result.
- Allah told them that when a person's time of death approaches, nothing will help them go back – so take advantage of the life that they have been given.
- The people who procrastinate in such situations and think, "Insha'Allah, next time," have a warning in these verses.

Hadith

Focus on the Hereafter & the insignificance of this world

عَنْ أَبِي هُرَيْرَةَ قَالَ قَالَ رَسُولُ اللَّهِ صلى الله عليه وسلم الدُّنْيَا سِجْنُ الْمُؤْمِنِ وَجَنَّةُ الْكَافِرِ

Abu Hurairah stated that God's Messenger said: "This world is a prison for a believer and Paradise for a disbeliever." (Sahih Al Bukhari #2956)

أَنَسَ بن مَالِكٍ يقول قَالَ رَسُولُ اللَّهِ صلى الله عليه وسلم يَتْبَعُ الْمَيِّتَ ثَلَاثَةٌ فَيَرْجِعُ اثْنَانِ وَيَبْقَى وَاحِدٌ يَتْبَعُهُ أَهْلُهُ وَمَالُهُ وَعَمَلُهُ فَيَرْجِعُ أَهْلُهُ وَمَالُهُ وَيَبْقَى عَمَلُهُ

Anas ibn Malik reported that God's Messenger stated: "Three things follow a deceased [in his funeral procession], and two of them return, and one remains with him: his family, his wealth, and his deeds follow him; the family and wealth return, and he is left with the deeds [only]." (Sahih Al Bukhari #2960)

حَدَّثَنَا عَبْدُ الْعَزِيزِ بْنُ عَبْدِ اللهِ قَالَ: حَدَّثَنِي الدَّرَاوَرْدِيُّ، عَنْ جَعْفَرٍ، عَنْ أَبِيهِ، عَنْ جَابِرِ بْنِ عَبْدِ اللهِ، أَنَّ رَسُولَ اللهِ صلى الله عليه وسلم مَرَّ فِي السُّوقِ دَاخِلاً مِنْ بَعْضِ الْعَالِيَةِ وَالنَّاسُ كَنَفَيْهِ، فَمَرَّ بِجَدْيِ أَسَكَّ، فَتَنَاوَلَهُ فَأَخَذَ بِأُذُنِهِ ثُمَّ قَالَ: أَيُّكُمْ يُحِبُّ أَنَّ هَذَا لَهُ بِدِرْهَمٍ؟ فَقَالُوا: مَا نُحِبُّ أَنَّهُ لَنَا بِشَيْءٍ، وَمَا نَصْنَعُ بِهِ؟ قَالَ: أَتُحِبُّونَ أَنَّهُ لَكُمْ؟ قَالُوا: لاَ، قَالَ ذَلِكَ لَهُمْ ثَلاَثًا، فَقَالُوا: لاَ وَاللَّهِ، لَوْ كَانَ حَيًّا لَكَانَ عَيْبًا فِيهِ أَنَّهُ أَسَكُّ، وَالأَسَكُّ: الَّذِي لَيْسَ لَهُ أُذُنَانِ، فَكَيْفَ وَهُوَ مَيِّتٌ؟ قَالَ: فَوَاللَّهِ، لَلدُّنْيَا أَهْوَنُ عَلَى اللهِ مَنْ هَذَا عَلَيْكُمْ.

Jabir ibn Abdullah reported that the Messenger of Allah passed through a market, entering from a part of the high part of the city, and the people were on both sides of him. He passed by a dead one-eared goat, reached out, and took its ear. Then he said, "Who would like to buy this for a dirham?" They said, "Why would we want it when it is worthless? What would we do with it?" He said, "Would you like to have it?" "No," they replied. He asked them three times, and they said, "No, by Allah! It would have a defect if alive, as it only has one ear. Why would we want it when it is dead?" The Prophet said, "By Allah, this world is less in the sight of Allah than this goat is to you." (Al Adaab Al Mufrad # 962)

Bible

Life is more than food

Then Jesus said to his disciples: "Therefore I tell you, do not worry about your life, what you will eat; or about your body, what you will wear. Life is more than food, and the body is more than clothes. Consider the ravens: They do not sow or reap; they have no storeroom or barn, yet God feeds them. And how much more valuable you are than birds! Who of you, by worrying, can add a single hour to your life? Since you cannot do this very little thing, why do you worry about the rest? (Luke, 12:22-26)

Summary

- Living your life in this world is essential, but temporary.
- A believer's attitude towards this life should be balanced between this temporary life and the everlasting life in the Hereafter.
- While living our busy lives, we should never forget Allah.
- Spending in the path of Allah is the best way to test our faith in Him – if it is difficult for us, we need to revive it.
- Never compromise your Afterlife for this temporary life.
- Allah has given us tools to keep that balance:
  - Daily Salah
  - Quran
  - Mosque
  - Charitable work

Read Surah Qaaf with translation and write a quick summary of the topics discussed in the Surah.

Chapter 11

Topic 6: God's Scheme and Predestination

This chapter introduces the concept of Predestination and Qadr as described in the Quran. This is one of the most challenging topics.

Predestination and Free Will

- Predestination and free will are the most complex matters in religion, and many critics of religion use them to reject religion, arguing that, logically, both cannot be true at the same time.
- We will try to understand these concepts in the light of the Quran.

What is predetermined in our lives?

- Family, birthplace, features, talents, country, environments, etc., are all fixed.
- That is the playing field that God has chosen for us to test us.
- These 'factors' above will be considered when we are judged.
- Some of them may be impacting our moral judgments and will be considered in the final judgment.

What is Free Will?

- We are free in all those matters and cases involving our moral judgments. Otherwise, the test is meaningless. Few examples:
  - Accepting a religion or rejecting it
  - Helping a friend or not
  - Cheating a customer or not
  - Lying to your parents or not

Our Actions, Knowledge of God and His Will

- Our moral choices are not predetermined—God only knows, in His infinite knowledge, what we will choose as He transcends time. God is fully aware of all the possible options we can choose from.
- The strategies and plans that we make in our lives are key and always work, but sometimes God intervenes out of His infinite Wisdom and Grand Scheme, and also to test us.
- The concurrence of the outcome of our deed and God's Will is needed.
- **Example:** A farmer who does not do the requisites for his crops to grow will have nothing to reap. But if the farmer does everything he needs to reap the fruit, it still must concur with God's Will. If an Earthquake hits his field, it simply means that his and God's plans did not concur. This could be because it was required in the Grand Scheme of things and, at the same time, became a test for him.

Our choices and God's Knowledge

Video Games and Fate – Simple Example

- The modern world provides a better explanation of fate than at any other time. For example, the outcome of a popular computer game is predetermined, but at no point are our efforts and choices forced on us. There is a "space" in which we exercise our free will and make our own choices, but the programmer already knew the results of those choices.
- Let's take another example. Imagine God asked you to select one thing from the chart below.
- Assuming God knows your choice in advance, and He wrote down on paper what you chose.
- Your choice matches what God has written on the paper for you.
- The question is:

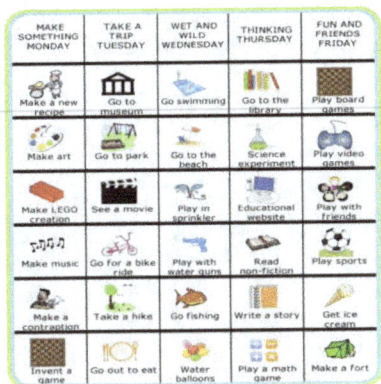

> **What influence did God have on your selection?**

> How do things that are predestined affect the execution of my free will and how will it influence my accountability in the Day of Judgment?

Surah Kahf: Verses 60-82

وَإِذْ قَالَ مُوسَىٰ لِفَتَىٰهُ لَآ أَبْرَحُ حَتَّىٰٓ أَبْلُغَ مَجْمَعَ ٱلْبَحْرَيْنِ أَوْ أَمْضِىَ حُقُبًا ٦٠

فَلَمَّا بَلَغَا مَجْمَعَ بَيْنِهِمَا نَسِيَا حُوتَهُمَا فَٱتَّخَذَ سَبِيلَهُۥ فِى ٱلْبَحْرِ سَرَبًا ٦١

فَلَمَّا جَاوَزَا قَالَ لِفَتَىٰهُ ءَاتِنَا غَدَآءَنَا لَقَدْ لَقِينَا مِن سَفَرِنَا هَٰذَا نَصَبًا ٦٢

قَالَ أَرَءَيْتَ إِذْ أَوَيْنَآ إِلَى ٱلصَّخْرَةِ فَإِنِّى نَسِيتُ ٱلْحُوتَ وَمَآ أَنسَىٰنِيهُ إِلَّا ٱلشَّيْطَٰنُ أَنْ أَذْكُرَهُ وَٱتَّخَذَ سَبِيلَهُۥ فِى ٱلْبَحْرِ عَجَبًا ٦٣

قَالَ ذَٰلِكَ مَا كُنَّا نَبْغِ ۚ فَٱرْتَدَّا عَلَىٰٓ ءَاثَارِهِمَا قَصَصًا ٦٤

فَوَجَدَا عَبْدًا مِّنْ عِبَادِنَآ ءَاتَيْنَٰهُ رَحْمَةً مِّنْ عِندِنَا وَعَلَّمْنَٰهُ مِن لَّدُنَّا عِلْمًا ٦٥

قَالَ لَهُۥ مُوسَىٰ هَلْ أَتَّبِعُكَ عَلَىٰٓ أَن تُعَلِّمَنِ مِمَّا عُلِّمْتَ رُشْدًا ٦٦

قَالَ إِنَّكَ لَن تَسْتَطِيعَ مَعِىَ صَبْرًا ٦٧

وَكَيْفَ تَصْبِرُ عَلَىٰ مَا لَمْ تُحِطْ بِهِۦ خُبْرًا ٦٨

قَالَ سَتَجِدُنِىٓ إِن شَآءَ ٱللَّهُ صَابِرًا وَلَآ أَعْصِى لَكَ أَمْرًا ٦٩

قَالَ فَإِنِ ٱتَّبَعْتَنِى فَلَا تَسْـَٔلْنِى عَن شَىْءٍ حَتَّىٰٓ أُحْدِثَ لَكَ مِنْهُ ذِكْرًا ٧٠

فَٱنطَلَقَا حَتَّىٰٓ إِذَا رَكِبَا فِى ٱلسَّفِينَةِ خَرَقَهَا ۖ قَالَ أَخَرَقْتَهَا لِتُغْرِقَ أَهْلَهَا لَقَدْ جِئْتَ شَيْئًا إِمْرًا ٧١

قَالَ أَلَمْ أَقُلْ إِنَّكَ لَن تَسْتَطِيعَ مَعِىَ صَبْرًا ٧٢

قَالَ لَا تُؤَاخِذْنِى بِمَا نَسِيتُ وَلَا تُرْهِقْنِى مِنْ أَمْرِى عُسْرًا ٧٣

فَٱنطَلَقَا حَتَّىٰٓ إِذَا لَقِيَا غُلَٰمًا فَقَتَلَهُۥ قَالَ أَقَتَلْتَ نَفْسًا زَكِيَّةً بِغَيْرِ نَفْسٍ لَّقَدْ جِئْتَ شَيْئًا نُّكْرًا ٧٤

۞ قَالَ أَلَمْ أَقُل لَّكَ إِنَّكَ لَن تَسْتَطِيعَ مَعِىَ صَبْرًا ٧٥

قَالَ إِن سَأَلْتُكَ عَن شَىْءٍ بَعْدَهَا فَلَا تُصَٰحِبْنِى ۖ قَدْ بَلَغْتَ مِن لَّدُنِّى عُذْرًا ٧٦

فَٱنطَلَقَا حَتَّىٰٓ إِذَآ أَتَيَآ أَهْلَ قَرْيَةٍ ٱسْتَطْعَمَآ أَهْلَهَا فَأَبَوْا أَن يُضَيِّفُوهُمَا فَوَجَدَا فِيهَا جِدَارًا يُرِيدُ أَن يَنقَضَّ فَأَقَامَهُۥ ۖ قَالَ لَوْ شِئْتَ لَتَّخَذْتَ عَلَيْهِ أَجْرًا ٧٧

قَالَ هَٰذَا فِرَاقُ بَيْنِى وَبَيْنِكَ ۚ سَأُنَبِّئُكَ بِتَأْوِيلِ مَا لَمْ تَسْتَطِع عَّلَيْهِ صَبْرًا ٧٨

أَمَّا ٱلسَّفِينَةُ فَكَانَتْ لِمَسَٰكِينَ يَعْمَلُونَ فِى ٱلْبَحْرِ فَأَرَدتُّ أَنْ أَعِيبَهَا وَكَانَ وَرَآءَهُم مَّلِكٌ يَأْخُذُ كُلَّ سَفِينَةٍ غَصْبًا ٧٩

وَأَمَّا ٱلْغُلَٰمُ فَكَانَ أَبَوَاهُ مُؤْمِنَيْنِ فَخَشِينَآ أَن يُرْهِقَهُمَا طُغْيَٰنًا وَكُفْرًا ٨٠

فَأَرَدْنَآ أَن يُبْدِلَهُمَا رَبُّهُمَا خَيْرًا مِّنْهُ زَكَوٰةً وَأَقْرَبَ رُحْمًا ٨١

وَأَمَّا ٱلْجِدَارُ فَكَانَ لِغُلَٰمَيْنِ يَتِيمَيْنِ فِى ٱلْمَدِينَةِ وَكَانَ تَحْتَهُۥ كَنزٌ لَّهُمَا وَكَانَ أَبُوهُمَا صَٰلِحًا فَأَرَادَ رَبُّكَ أَن يَبْلُغَآ أَشُدَّهُمَا وَيَسْتَخْرِجَا كَنزَهُمَا رَحْمَةً مِّن رَّبِّكَ ۚ وَمَا فَعَلْتُهُۥ عَنْ أَمْرِى ۚ ذَٰلِكَ تَأْوِيلُ مَا لَمْ تَسْطِع عَّلَيْهِ صَبْرًا ٨٢

Surah Kahf: Verses 60-82

When Moses said to his student: "I shall keep walking until I reach the place where two seas meet or keep walking for years in this way." So, when they reached the meeting place of the seas, they forgot their fish [fried for breakfast], and it went forth by tunneling towards the sea. Then, when they moved forward, Moses said to his student: "Bring our food now. We are very tired because of our journey." The student replied: "What should I say? When we were stationed near that large rock, at that time, I forgot the fish, and it was Satan who made me negligent of remembering it, and it strangely took to the sea." Moses said: "It was that very place we were searching for." Thus, they returned, tracing their footsteps. So, they found a servant from among Our servants whom We had specially blessed and had bestowed on him a special knowledge from Ourselves. Moses asked him: "If you allow me, I shall be your companion on the condition that you also teach me a little from the knowledge given to you?" He replied: "You will not be able to be patient with me, and how can you be patient at what is beyond your sphere of knowledge?" Moses said: "God willing, you will find me patient, and I shall not disobey you in any matter." He said: "Then if you have to accompany me, do not ask me about anything until I mention it myself." At last, both of them set off until when [at one place] they boarded a ship, that person made a hole. Moses said: "You have made a hole in it that you may drown all the ship's people? This is a bizarre thing that you have done!" He said: "Did I not say to you that you will not be able to exercise patience with me?" Moses said: "Do not hold me accountable for what I forgot, and please do not be very strict with me." Then both set off until they met a boy [on the way], and he killed that boy. Moses said: "You have harmed an innocent person even though he has not harmed anyone? This is a very terrible thing that you have done." He said, "Did I not say to you that you would not be able to exercise patience along with me?" Moses said: "If I ask you something after this, you may not keep me with you. You would have reached an excuse from me." At this, both journeyed on until they reached the city's inhabitants; they asked the people for food. But they were not hospitable. Then they saw a wall there that was about to fall. So, he restored it. Moses said: "If you wanted, you could have asked for some compensation (because they were rude)." He replied: "Now this is parting of ways between you and me. I shall now tell you the reality behind the acts on which you have not been able to exercise patience. In the case of the ship, it belonged to some poor people who would earn their living at sea. So, I intended to make it defective [because] there lived a king ahead who was snatching every ship. As for the boy, both his parents were people of faith. So, We feared that [after growing up] he may grieve them because of his rebelliousness and disbelief. Hence, we wanted their Lord to bless them with a child in his place, who is purer and more affectionate than he is. And the matter of the wall was that it belonged to two orphans. Beneath it was their treasure, and their father was a pious person. [It was he who had buried the treasure.] So, your Lord wanted them to reach maturity and take out their treasure. This happened because of your God's grace. And all that I did was not out of my own intention. This is the reality behind the acts on which you have not been able to show patience."

Background and Context

- Surah Kahf was revealed in response to the questions raised by the enemies of Islam, especially the Jews.

- This surah was revealed when the argumentation with the disbelievers was reaching its end, but at the same time, the persecution of Muslims was at its peak.

- Muslims were asking basic questions: why is this happening to us while we believe in Allah? When is this going to end? When will the help of Allah come?

- Through these verses, Allah showed Muslims that Allah has a way of working in this world, and what is happening right now may have a deeper meaning or reasons behind it that Muslims cannot understand, but it will become clear later.

- Both believers and disbelievers were told that if they concluded the seeming aspects of events, they would make a serious error in their deductions.

- Through these verses, Allah wanted to show the believers that if they strongly believe in Allah and His powers and are patient in this difficult situation, it will be good for them.

- Historians believe this incident occurred while Musa was still struggling with the Pharaoh over the freedom of the Children of Israel, and the situation was very difficult.

- The Quran called this person "a servant of God from among the servants."

- In the traditions of Prophet Muhammad, his name was mentioned as "Khidr".

- There would be a difference of opinion among scholars if Khidr were a prophet himself or an angel of God who appeared in the form of a man.

- The types of acts he performed made it quite likely that he was an angel, either visible only to Musa or appearing to him and others as a man.

- Musa was asked to spend some time with him to learn the wisdom behind Allah's acts.

- Khidr agreed to take him on a journey, with the promise that, regardless of what happened, Musa would not ask him any questions about the situation.

- Musa promised Khidr, despite Khidr's warning that he wouldn't be able to keep quiet on this journey.

The three incidents

While they were on the journey, they hired a ship to cross a river	**Khidr made a hole in a ship**	Musa got angry because the sailor helped them cross the river
They entered a village where children were playing	**Khidr killed an innocent boy**	Musa got angry because he was just an innocent young boy who did not harm anyone
They entered a village and asked for food which they refused to give	**Khidr rebuilt a falling wall in the town**	Musa asked Khidr to charge them for rebuilding because they were mean to them

Breaking the ship - Apparent	Reality
Musa and Khidr embarked on a ship, and the poor sailors were kind enough to give them a ride. Khidr, instead of thanking them, made a hole in their ship that damaged it and could cause people to drown—a terrible behavior.	A tyrant king was seizing sailors' ships by force, using them illegally. He was only interested in ships in good condition. Khidr made a hole that the poor sailors later patched, but the ship did not remain in good condition, and the king did not seize it.

Killing the boy - Apparent	Reality
Khidr killed an innocent boy in a neighborhood without any reason. It was a grave act of killing an innocent person, making Musa angry.	The boy's parents were righteous, and in Allah's knowledge, this boy grew up to be wicked, a big grief for the parents. Allah took the boy's life, and he died. Later, Allah gave the parents a righteous child who cared for them and was merciful to them.

Rebuilding the wall - Apparent	Reality
The people in the village were rude and did not provide them with food, so there was no reason to give them any favors. Khidr must have asked for food or something in exchange for rebuilding the house's wall. That makes perfect sense.	The house was owned by two orphan boys. Their father was righteous, leaving them some wealth buried next to the wall. The father wanted them for when they grew older. Not rebuilding the wall would have exposed the hidden wealth, and since the people of the town were greedy, they would have taken it

The conclusions we make in our daily lives

- The conclusions that we make in our daily lives are mostly based on what's apparent to us. Some examples are given below:

I am poor	It's unfair and definitely Allah is not happy with me
I am rich	My parents worked very hard, and definitely Allah is happy with use
The teen died in a car accident	Unfortunately, he/she used to drive recklessly
Abdullah lost his job	Because he was not hardworking and faced the results
I missed my flight	Because the airline sucks, I would never travel with them
I did not get a scholarship	It's unfair, people use connections to get scholarship
I could not marry this boy/girl	My friend must have said something bad about me

- There may be some truth to what we have concluded, but we are not sure exactly why things turned out the way they did.

What is the correct concept of relying on Allah (Tawakkul)?

Surah Hadeed: Verses 31-32

مَآ أَصَابَ مِنْ مُّصِيبَةٍ فِى الْأَرْضِ وَ لَا فِىٓ أَنْفُسِكُمْ إِلَّا فِى كِتٰبٍ مِّنْ قَبْلِ أَنْ نَّبْرَأَهَآ إِنَّ ذٰلِكَ عَلَى اللهِ يَسِيرٌ لِّكَيْلَا تَأْسَوْا عَلٰى مَا فَاتَكُمْ وَ لَا تَفْرَحُوا بِمَآ اٰتٰكُمْ وَ اللهُ لَا يُحِبُّ كُلَّ مُخْتَالٍ فَخُورٍ

[They do not spend in the way of God because they want to save it in case some calamity visits them. Remember that] there is no such calamity that visits you in the earth or in your persons that We have not written in a book before We bring it into existence. This is very easy for God. You have been made to understand this so that you may not grieve over what you lose, nor be proud of what God has blessed you with. And [remember that] God does not love the haughty and conceited at all.

- The subject of Surah Hadeed is to encourage Muslims to fight wars with the disbelievers and spend in the path of Allah, especially during the war when the resources are most needed.
- The disbelievers, especially the hypocrites, used to make excuses that we save money for bad times. If a calamity struck us, we should have our savings to deal with that calamity.
- However, their behavior was completely at odds with what they used to say.
- They were spendthrift in other areas like comfort, luxuries, lewdness, and illicit relationships.
- The only time they become stingy is when it comes to spending in the path of Allah.
- Allah told them and indirectly told Muslims that it is OK to have something saved for bad days, but if Allah asks for charity, then beware of your stinginess.
- It is Allah who has written in a Book what calamity is going to strike you (because of His knowledge), and it is only He who is going to save you from that.

Allah's Knowledge and our behavior

- Allah's knowledge transcends time and space – He knows what's going to happen in the future before it happens.
- A believer's attitude in both good and bad times must be based on this faith, and if Allah did not will it, it would not have happened in the first place.
- Since He allowed it to happen, He will also help us get out of this, because it's just a test, and Allah is watching my behavior in these circumstances.

A believer's attitude in bad times

- This is from Allah, and it was written for me.
- This life is temporary, and this problem is temporary. It will go away soon.
- If there is a need that requires me to spend in the path of Allah even in these times, I should do whatever I can, because it is highly rewarding.
- If I am patient and resolved to change the situation, Allah will help me come out.

A believer's attitude in good times

- This is from Allah, and it was written for me as it happens.
- This is purely a blessing from Allah; otherwise, I could not have achieved it or deserved this.
- Since Allah gave me this, and if there is a demand to spend in the path of Allah, I should not shy away from it.
- These blessings are a trust given to me, so I should share them with others.
- Allah does not like boastful and conceited people.

Our trust in Allah

- When there is a dire need for charity in the path of Allah, the saved wealth that we have becomes a test of our faith. This is the time when people react according to the level of faith and trust they have in Allah.
- A believer's reaction should be to show complete trust in Allah in these times, with the belief that Allah will pay this back multiple times, either in the Hereafter or both in this world and the Hereafter.
- Under normal circumstances, our response should be balanced – taking care of our and our family's needs first and then taking care of others' needs as much as we can.
- However, under abnormal circumstances, our response might be very different, with a feeling of empathy and sacrifice.
- A believer's response should be in accordance with his/her financial situation.

Hadith

Sickness brushes away the Sins of Believers

عن عبد اللهِ قال دَخَلْتُ على رسولِ اللهِ صلى الله عليه وسلم وهو يُوعَكُ
فَمَسِسْتُهُ بِيَدِي فقلت يا رَسُولَ اللهِ إِنَّكَ لَتُوعَكُ وَعْكًا
شَدِيدًا فقال رسولُ اللهِ صلى الله عليه وسلم أَجَلْ إِنِّي أُوعَكُ كما يُوعَكُ رَجُلانِ مِنْكُمْ
قال فقلت أَنَّ لك أَجْرَيْنِ فقال رسولُ اللهِ صلى الله عليه وسلم أَجَلْ ثُمَّ قال
رسولُ اللهِ صلى الله عليه وسلم ما من مُسْلِمٍ يُصِيبُهُ أَذًى من مَرَضٍ فما سِوَاهُ إلا حَطَّ
اللهُ بِهِ سَيِّئَاتِهِ كما تَحُطُّ الشَّجَرَةُ وَرَقَهَا

Abdullah ibn Masud reported: "I [once] visited God's Messenger while he had a fever. I touched him and said, ' O Messenger of God! You have a high fever.' At this, God's Messenger replied: 'Yes. I have a fever equivalent to two people among you.' I said, ' Is it because there is a double reward for you?' Thereupon, God's Messenger replied: 'Yes.' He then said: 'When a Muslim falls ill or is afflicted with some other [hardship], God sheds his minor sins the way a tree sheds its leaves.'" (Sahih Al Muslim 2571)

Trial and Patience

قال فَوَاللهِ ما ... أخبره أَنَّ رَسُولَ اللهِ صلى الله عليه وسلم ... أَنَّ عَمْرَو بن عَوْفٍ
الْفَقْرَ أَخْشَى عَلَيْكُمْ وَلَكِنِّي أَخْشَى عَلَيْكُمْ أَنْ تُبْسَطَ الدُّنْيَا عَلَيْكُمْ كما بُسِطَتْ على من
كان قَبْلَكُمْ فَتَنَافَسُوهَا كما تَنَافَسُوهَا وَتُهْلِكَكُمْ كما أَهْلَكَتْهُمْ

Amr ibn Awf reported that God's Messenger said: "... By God! It is not poverty which I fear for you; however, I fear that you be given abundance in wealth the way those before you were given; then you begin to compete with one another for them as they did, which may destroy you as it destroyed them." (Sahih Al Muslim #2961).

عن أبي هُرَيْرَةَ أَنَّ رَسُولَ اللهِ صلى الله عليه وسلم قال لِنِسْوَةٍ من الْأَنْصَارِ لَا يَمُوتُ لِإِحْدَاكُنَّ
ثَلَاثَةٌ من الْوَلَدِ فَتَحْتَسِبَهُ إلا دَخَلَتْ الْجَنَّةَ فقالت امْرَأَةٌ مِنْهُنَّ أو اثْنَيْنِ يا رَسُولَ اللَّهِ قال أو اثْنَيْنِ

Abu Hurairah stated that God's Messenger told a woman of the Ansar: "If any of you loses three children and she shows patience, hoping to get a reward, she will enter Paradise. A woman from amongst them said: "Even if they are two, O God's Messenger!" Thereupon, he replied: "Even if they are two." (Sahih Al Muslim #2632)

BIBLE

Taming the tongue and Helping Out

There are some whose uncontrolled talk is like the wounds of a sword, but the tongue of the wise makes one well again. (Proverbs 12:18)

If you see your brother's ox or sheep wandering, do not go by without helping, but take them back to your brother. If their owner is not near, or if you are not certain who he is, take the beast to your house and keep it till its owner comes in search of it, and then you are to give it back to him. Do the same with his ass, robe, or anything which has gone from your brother's keeping and that you have come across: do not keep it to yourself. (Deuteronomy, 22:1-3)

Are there some people born evil? If so, what's their fault?

Chapter 12

Topic 7: Great Advice in the Quran

This chapter discusses various pieces of advice mentioned in the Quran, given by God and by different people, including Satan, that we can all learn from.

Islam and Sincerity

- For a Muslim, sincerity is desired in every act.
- It is required in both relationships one has: with Allah and with other human beings.
- It is the sole criterion for accepting all good deeds for Allah. A deed, no matter how great in appearance, is rendered worthless if the intention behind it is not pure and aimed solely at seeking the pleasure of Allah.
- Similarly, it is paramount when advising someone—whether a friend, relative, leader, neighbor, or colleague.
- When someone asks you for a suggestion or advice, it burdens you. Because sincerity is required when giving advice.
- The ultimate display of your Islam is your sincerity toward everyone.

"الدِّينُ النَّصِيحَةُ." قُلْنَا: لِمَنْ؟ قَالَ: "لِلَّهِ، وَلِكِتَابِهِ، وَلِرَسُولِهِ، وَلِأَئِمَّةِ الْمُسْلِمِينَ وَعَامَّتِهِمْ."

Prophet Muhammad said, "The religion is *An Naseehah* (Sincerity)." We said, "To whom?" He said, "To Allah, His Book, His Messenger, and to the leaders of the Muslims and their common folk." [Sahih Muslim]

- What Prophet Muhammad meant here is that the essence of the religion lies in a sincere and truthful disposition.
- The hadith explains that this sincerity and goodwill are directed toward five key areas: Allah, His Words, the Messenger, the leaders, and the common people.

Surah Luqman: Verse 12-19

وَ لَقَدْ اٰتَيْنَا لُقْمٰنَ الْحِكْمَةَ اَنِ اشْكُرْ لِلّٰهِ ؕ وَ مَنْ يَّشْكُرْ فَاِنَّمَا يَشْكُرُ لِنَفْسِهٖ ۚ وَ مَنْ كَفَرَ فَاِنَّ اللّٰهَ غَنِيٌّ حَمِيْدٌ   وَ اِذْ قَالَ لُقْمٰنُ لِابْنِهٖ وَ هُوَ يَعِظُهٗ يٰبُنَيَّ لَا تُشْرِكْ بِاللّٰهِ ؕ اِنَّ الشِّرْكَ لَظُلْمٌ عَظِيْمٌ ....

يٰبُنَيَّ اِنَّهَا اِنْ تَكُ مِثْقَالَ حَبَّةٍ مِّنْ خَرْدَلٍ فَتَكُنْ فِيْ صَخْرَةٍ اَوْ فِي السَّمٰوٰتِ اَوْ فِي الْاَرْضِ يَاْتِ بِهَا اللّٰهُ ؕ اِنَّ اللّٰهَ لَطِيْفٌ خَبِيْرٌ

يٰبُنَيَّ اَقِمِ الصَّلٰوةَ وَ اْمُرْ بِالْمَعْرُوْفِ وَ انْهَ عَنِ الْمُنْكَرِ وَ اصْبِرْ عَلٰى مَا اَصَابَكَ ؕ اِنَّ ذٰلِكَ مِنْ عَزْمِ الْاُمُوْرِ   وَ لَا تُصَعِّرْ خَدَّكَ لِلنَّاسِ وَ لَا تَمْشِ فِي الْاَرْضِ مَرَحًا ؕ اِنَّ اللّٰهَ لَا يُحِبُّ كُلَّ مُخْتَالٍ فَخُوْرٍ

وَ اقْصِدْ فِيْ مَشْيِكَ وَ اغْضُضْ مِنْ صَوْتِكَ ؕ اِنَّ اَنْكَرَ الْاَصْوَاتِ لَصَوْتُ الْحَمِيْرِ

Recall when Luqman, while counseling his son, had said: "Son! Do not associate partners with God. In reality, polytheism is a great injustice." ..... "Son! If a deed is equal to even the grain of a mustard seed, whether it is hidden in a small mountain pass, in the heavens, or on the earth, God shall retrieve it. Indeed, God is discerning; He is aware of everything. Son! Be diligent in prayer, urge what is good, and forbid evil; whatever calamity strikes you, be steadfast. It is because these are the tasks that have been emphasized. And be not indifferent to people and not arrogant on the land because God does not like the arrogant and the conceited. Be moderate in your posture and keep your voice toned down. The donkey's braying is the most hideous of voices."

- The Surah begins by stating that these verses are revealed in a book full of wisdom. In that context, Allah told the disbelievers who were using all tactics to divert people from the Quran to pay attention to these verses.
- People in Arabia knew Luqman as a wise man in history and the leader of his nation. In these verses, Luqman is giving this advice to his son at the time of passing on leadership.
- The purpose of mentioning Luqman, the wise man, immediately after these verses is to show the disbelievers that what Prophet Muhammad is teaching is the same as what Luqman taught his son.
- In other words, if Luqman was wise with what he said, then what was the problem with Prophet Muhammad saying?

Key Pieces of Advice

Wisdom and Gratefulness

- Gratefulness to Allah is the first fruit of wisdom.
- This applies to other relationships.
- The recognition of others' rights must emerge from it.
- All Prophets who were kings and wise were grateful (Quran's theme).
- This attitude only benefits a believer.
- Allah does not need this and possesses whatever is in the heavens and earth.

Shirk is Injustice

- The gratefulness toward Allah requires that we dedicate it to Allah alone and not commit Shirk.
- When all blessings come from Him alone, then it makes no sense to treat anyone as His partner.
- Luqman called it a great injustice, which makes worshiping Allah alone a moral obligation.
- Luqman started his talk with Shirk, as this is the root of all evils.

You can't escape God

- This is the advice related to the Day of Judgment.
- Luqman told his son that they should live in this world with a sense of accountability.
- Allah is All-Capable and Powerful, and He will take into account every big or small deed.
- Even if your deed is hidden somewhere in the depths of a valley between mountains or somewhere up in the sky, Allah will bring it forth.
- This shows how careful we must be with our deeds.

Why is it wise for a person to be grateful all the time?

Key Pieces of Advice

Establish Salah

- Gratefulness must result in the form of performing Salah.
- Salah is the best way to thank our creator.
- Salah is more than the acts we do in Salah.
- In essence, we pray because we accept that Allah is our Lord.
- It is a symbol of humility before Him, a combination of His Greatness and our gratitude.
- Salah must be established in our lives.

Promote goodness

- If a person believes in Allah, then it is his/her duty to promote goodness and discourage evil.
- A believer cannot live his/her own life with no concern about others living around them.
- **Ma'aroof means:** what society, in general, considers good, like truthfulness, charity, and honesty.
- **Munkar means:** what society, in general, considers bad, like lying, cheating, dishonesty, etc.
- A society is as good as the people in that society.

Patience is key

- Promoting good and discouraging evil are not easy tasks.
- There will always be opposition to this in society.
- Luqman is advising his son to be patient and consistent when on this path.
- Patience is not a passive attribute.
- You continue to do what you consider is right without complaining all the time or losing hope.
- Allah loves patience.
- This determination and resolve only come from high-caliber people.

Key Pieces of Advise

Attitude toward people

- The next two attributes are the signs of a lack of gratefulness, which is the core message of Luqman.
- Dealing with people, especially those who are low in society, with a stern attitude.
- This stems from the arrogance in a person's heart.
- This is the complete opposite of humility, which results from gratefulness.
- Arrogance is the mother of all evils.

Don't be Arrogant

- One of the signs of arrogance is our style of walking and talking (which symbolizes the inner problem).
- Luqman is specifically talking about having an unjustified and magnified image of self – traits like vanity, pride, and show-off come from this.
- It is also called Satanic Attitude because it was first adopted by Satan, which cost him Allah's forgiveness and mercy.
- Arrogance can take many forms and sneak into our personalities without us even noticing.
- That's why Luqman talked about the symptoms of arrogance.
- Luqman told his son that Allah created humans as one of the best creations, but out of arrogance, we shout at other people, then we act like a donkey.

What are the different blessings of God that make a person arrogant?

What is Arrogance, and how can we avoid it?

Power	Knowledge	Lineage	Wealth	Beauty	Worship	Leadership

Abdullah ibn Masood reported that the Prophet said, "No one who has the tiniest amount of arrogance (size of a small seed) in his heart will enter Paradise." Someone asked, "But a man loves to have beautiful clothes and shoes." The Prophet said, "Verily, Allah is beautiful, and He loves beauty. That is not arrogance. Arrogance means rejecting the Truth and looking down on people.

Some practical tips:

1. Hide your good deeds as much as possible.
2. Look at the message, not the messenger.
3. Don't get angry when someone criticizes you.
4. Always ask for advice and feedback on anything you do.
5. Talk about things, characteristics, behavior, attributes, and issues, but not about specific people.
6. Always remember that whatever you have is a blessing from God, and He deserves all the praise and thanks for it.
7. If you are good at something, always be grateful to God.
8. Avoid argumentation even when you know you are right and the other person is wrong.
9. If you have bad feelings about someone, make dua for them and give them a gift.

Surah Baqarah: Verse 263-264

قَوْلٌ مَّعْرُوْفٌ وَّ مَغْفِرَةٌ خَيْرٌ مِّنْ صَدَقَةٍ يَّتْبَعُهَآ أَذًى ۗ وَ اللّٰهُ غَنِيٌّ حَلِيْمٌ

يٰٓأَيُّهَا الَّذِيْنَ اٰمَنُوْا لَا تُبْطِلُوْا صَدَقٰتِكُمْ بِالْمَنِّ وَ الْأَذٰى ۙ كَالَّذِيْ يُنْفِقُ مَالَهُ رِئَآءَ النَّاسِ

وَ لَا يُؤْمِنُ بِاللّٰهِ وَ الْيَوْمِ الْأٰخِرِ ۗ فَمَثَلُهُ كَمَثَلِ صَفْوَانٍ عَلَيْهِ تُرَابٌ فَأَصَابَهُ وَابِلٌ فَتَرَكَهُ

صَلْدًا ۗ لَا يَقْدِرُوْنَ عَلٰى شَيْءٍ مِّمَّا كَسَبُوْا ۗ وَ اللّٰهُ لَا يَهْدِى الْقَوْمَ الْكٰفِرِيْنَ

A kind word and, in unpleasant instances, a little forgiveness is better than charity, followed by inflicting hurt (reminding favors). And [you should know that] God is self-sufficient from such charity. [On such an attitude from you, He could have deprived you; however, such is He that] along with this, He is also very gracious. Believers! Do not waste your charity by reminders of generosity and by hurting [others] like those who spend their wealth to show off before others and believe neither in God nor the Last Day. So, the example of such people is like a large rock covered with soil: a heavy shower falls upon it, leaving it hard and bare. [On the Day of Judgement,] they will gain nothing from what they earned. And, in reality, God never guides such ungrateful people.

- The topic of spending in the path of Allah started from verse 254.
- Allah said in that verse that one should spend on others and on the path of Allah before a day comes when neither friendship nor favor will help.
- After that, Allah talked about His powers and His qualities, arguing that you are not giving this wealth to Allah – He owns everything and has the power to give life and death.
- In the same context, He reminded believers that the Day of Judgment is a reality, and the best way to save themselves on that day is to spend the wealth Allah has given them.
- The topic comes back to charity after these reminders – however, in these verses, the focus is on the etiquette of charity through an example.
- This is the best advice the Quran has given on charity: one would give away their money and time yet receive no reward if the etiquette of charity is not followed.

Etiquette of Charity

Kind Words
with forgiveness that promotes goodness
and provides emotional and moral support

is better
than

The Charity
that is followed by hurt and
reminding favors

- Charity is not restricted to wealth.
- Saying kind words, forgiving others, and spreading goodness are also acts of charity, especially in times of displeasure.
- However, when a person is charitable, they must be cautious not to hurt others' feelings, and reminders of favors must <u>not</u> be attached to it.
- Charity should be given with a feeling of responsibility that one has towards Allah's religion and others in society.
- It is better to give to charity in secrecy and with no intention to remind those you have helped of this favor – otherwise, it is better to say good words.

Don't waste your charity

- Allah warned believers not to waste their charity if they engaged in this behavior.
- This is not expected from a believer.
- This is the behavior of the disbelievers who spend to show off – they do not believe in Allah or the Hereafter.
- Their charity will not bear any fruit.
- An example of their charity is someone trying to grow a plant or tree on rocks because they found some soil on it.
- When heavy rain happens, nothing stays on those rocks, and the soil and the plants wash away.
- Smart people do not do that kind of planting.

Surah Ibrahim: Verse 22

وَ قَالَ الشَّيْطٰنُ لَمَّا قُضِيَ الْأَمْرُ إِنَّ اللهَ وَعَدَكُمْ وَعْدَ الْحَقِّ وَ وَعَدْتُّكُمْ فَأَخْلَفْتُكُمْ وَ مَا كَانَ لِيَ عَلَيْكُمْ مِّنْ سُلْطٰنٍ إِلَّا أَنْ دَعَوْتُكُمْ فَاسْتَجَبْتُمْ لِي ۖ فَلَا تَلُوْمُوْنِيْ وَ لُوْمُوْا أَنْفُسَكُمْ ۖ مَا أَنَا بِمُصْرِخِكُمْ وَ مَا أَنْتُمْ بِمُصْرِخِيَّ ۖ إِنِّيْ كَفَرْتُ بِمَا أَشْرَكْتُمُوْنِ مِنْ قَبْلُ ۗ إِنَّ الظّٰلِمِيْنَ لَهُمْ عَذَابٌ أَلِيْمٌ

And when the judgment shall be passed, Satan will say: "God, in reality, had made a true promise with you; [so, He fulfilled it] and I had also promised you, but I have gone back on my word. And I had no power over you; I only invited you, and you accepted. So, please do not blame me; blame yourselves. Now, neither can I respond to your pleading, nor can you respond to my pleading. I have already denied that you had made me a partner [of God]." In reality, it is such unjust people for whom there is painful torment.

- Before these verses, Allah talked about the judgment that was announced for the disbelievers on the Day of Judgment, and all of them saw the punishment coming.
- Satan was observing this, and he knew that once their judgment was announced, they would come toward him and start blaming him, as he is usually considered the leader of every evil deed.
- So, Allah recorded his statements in the Quran about what he would say to them and to everyone who followed him in this life.
- This is the best advice coming from Satan that we should all pay heed to.
- This verse describes his role and capabilities.
- It is out of the Mercy of Allah that He recorded these statements from Satan in the Quran.

There is a saying, "Tell me who your friends are, and I will tell you who you are." How true is this?

How does Satan trick us

He told them that Allah <u>warned</u> them about something, and I <u>promised</u> them something, but <u>only</u> Allah did what He said; I broke my promises.

- Satan has no control over us – he cannot FORCE us to do anything.
- All he does is invite people to evil and promises that following him will be in their favor.
- People respond to his invitation and commit evil.
- For evil deeds, he offers justifications so we don't feel bad about committing wrongs.
- So, he recused himself that day and gave us this advice: Do not pay heed to my invitation, do not listen to my justifications, and if you do, then blame yourselves, not me.
- He declared, "I cannot help you now, and you cannot help me."
- He turned away from those man-made gods that people were worshiping.

The fight with Satan

Cultivating an awareness of one's inner, harmful inclinations (enhanced by Satan) is vital for a Muslim's ultimate success in the Hereafter and their journey toward Allah. Through consistent acts of devotion—including prayer, remembrance, Quranic recitation, and contemplation—one can achieve greater mindfulness of God and self-awareness. Ibn al-Jawzi writes in his famous book *Talbis Iblis*:

Indeed, Iblis (Satan) only enters people by the measure he is able. His ability to do so is increased or decreased by the degree of their mindfulness, negligence, ignorance, and deeds. Know that the heart is like a fortress. Upon that fortress are walls, and the walls have gates, and in it are chambers in which the mind resides. The angels often visit that fortress. To its side are siege towers, in which are desires and devils frequently occupying them, with none to stop them. War is declared between the inhabitants of the fortress and the inhabitants of the siege towers. The devils continuously circle the fortress, seeking the guards' negligence and passage into some of its chambers. Thus, the guards should know all of the gates of the fortress, upon which its protection depends.

Hadith

Good and bad company

عن أبي مُوسَى عن النبي صلى الله عليه وسلم قال إنما مَثَلُ الجَلِيسِ الصَّالِحِ والجَلِيسِ السَّوْءِ كَحَامِلِ الْمِسْكِ وَنَافِخِ الْكِيرِ فَحَامِلُ الْمِسْكِ إِمَّا أَنْ يُحْذِيَكَ وَإِمَّا أَنْ تَبْتَاعَ منه وَإِمَّا أَنْ تَجِدَ منه رِيحًا طَيِّبَةً وَنَافِخُ الْكِيرِ إِمَّا أَنْ يُحْرِقَ ثِيَابَكَ وَإِمَّا أَنْ تَجِدَ رِيحًا خَبِيثَةً

Abu Musa reported that the Prophet said: "The example of the companionship of a good person and that of a bad one is that of the owner of the musk and of the one who ignites a furnace (for melting iron). As for the owner of the musk, he will either offer it to you free of charge, or you will buy it from him, or you will smell its sweet odor whenever he is nearby. The one who ignites a furnace [on the other hand] will either burn your clothes, or you shall have to smell its repulsive odor whenever he is nearby." (Sahih Muslim #2628)

Two Enviable People

عَبْدَ اللَّهِ بن مَسْعُودٍ يقول قال رسول اللَّهِ صلى الله عليه وسلم لَا حَسَدَ إلا في اثْنَتَيْنِ رَجُلٌ آتَاهُ الله مَالًا فَسَلَّطَهُ على هَلَكَتِهِ في الْحَقِّ وَرَجُلٌ آتَاهُ الله حِكْمَةً فَهُوَ يَقْضِي بها وَيُعَلِّمُهَا

Abdullah ibn Masud says that God's Messenger said: "Only two people are worthy of envy: a person whom God has given wealth, and he went about spending it for the cause of the truth, and a person whom God blessed with wisdom, and he decided [the affairs of people] through it and taught it [to them]." (Sahih Al Bukhari #816)

Leave what does not concern you

إِنَّ مِنْ حُسْنِ إِسْلَامِ الْمَرْءِ تَرْكَهُ مَا لَا يَعْنِيهِ

Ali ibn Husayn reported: The Messenger of Allah said, "Verily, among excellence in Islam is for a man/woman to leave what does not concern him/her." Sunan al-Tirmidhi #2318

BIBLE

True Friendship, Godly life

Perfume and incense bring joy to the heart, and the pleasantness of a friend springs from their heartfelt advice. (Proverbs, 27:9)

And one came to him and said, Master, what good thing do I have to do so that I may have eternal life? And he asked him, Why are you questioning me about what is good? One, there is who is good, but if you desire to go into life, keep the rules of the law. He says to him, Which? And Jesus said, Do not put anyone to death, Do not be untrue in married life, Do not take what is not yours, Do not give false witness, Give honor to your father and your mother: and, Have a love for your neighbor as for yourself. The young man says to him, All these things have I done: what more is there? Jesus told him If you desire to be complete, go, get money for your property, and give it to the poor, and you will have wealth in heaven, and come after me. But hearing these words, the young man went away sorrowing, for he had much property. (Matthew, 19:16-22)

Most people advise others to please the person who asked for the advice — why?

Chapter 13

Topic 8: The Day of Judgment in the Quran

This chapter introduces the concept of the Day of Judgment in the Quran and the details about it.

Why should there be a Day of Judgment?

- Believing in God without believing in the Day of Judgment is meaningless. This removes the need for accountability, and the entire concept of God is tied to the hope of receiving justice on the Day of Judgment.
- If you think about it, we need God for this reason alone.
- This need is reflected in many places.

Human Conscience

- By design, we are aware of good and evil.
- Our conscience chides us when we do wrong.
- We feel good when we do good.
- A small court is within us.
- If attention is not paid, evil lulls that voice.
- The same justice must also occur at a grand level.
- This is something common among humanity.

God's Attribute

- God is Merciful, but these attributes mean nothing without a concept of reward and punishment.
- Criminals kill millions of people with no accountability.
- A God must bring things to their conclusion.
- People who have suffered in this world must be compensated.

Concept of Justice

- We don't want anyone to commit injustice against us.
- We all love justice and hate injustice. For example, we do not go out into the market to be cheated. Then why should we cheat others?
- Injustice occurs when one is overwhelmed by desires and emotions.
- We all fight for justice.

Incomplete World

- A design with no purpose is meaningless.
- Humans don't even create a needle without a purpose.
- Everything is serving me; who should I serve?
- Things are in pairs; what is the pair of this life?
- Many desires remain unfulfilled.

Empirical Evidence

- Many Messengers before have demonstrated a DoJ on a smaller scale
- The true concept of reward and punishment was demonstrated
- God's power and scheme of things were made apparent
- The world has witnessed it many times
- Nations of Nuh, Aad, Thamud, and Pharaoh are all examples

Prophet Muhammad

- The last Messenger gave the news in the 7th century AD and recorded it in the Quran.
- Quraysh and neighboring nations saw their fate of rejecting Prophet Muhammad with their own eyes.
- He said at the very beginning that his companions would rule the earth, and it happened.

What arguments can be presented against a Day of Judgment?

Surah Zilzaal: Verse 1-8

اِذَا زُلْزِلَتِ الْاَرْضُ زِلْزَالَهَا ۙ وَ اَخْرَجَتِ الْاَرْضُ اَثْقَالَهَا ۙ وَ قَالَ الْاِنْسَانُ مَا لَهَا ۙ

يَوْمَئِذٍ تُحَدِّثُ اَخْبَارَهَا ۙ بِاَنَّ رَبَّكَ اَوْحٰى لَهَا ۙ يَوْمَئِذٍ يَّصْدُرُ النَّاسُ اَشْتَاتًا ۙ لِّيُرَوْا اَعْمَالَهُمْ ۙ

وَ مَنْ يَّعْمَلْ مِثْقَالَ ذَرَّةٍ شَرًّا يَّرَهٗ ۙ فَمَنْ يَّعْمَلْ مِثْقَالَ ذَرَّةٍ خَيْرًا يَّرَهٗ ۙ

When the Earth is shaken, the way it should be shaken, and the Earth will cast out all its burdens. And human beings will say: "What is the matter with this Earth?" On that day, the Earth will narrate all her story because your Lord would have asked it. On that day, people will emerge separately (individually) so that their deeds can be shown to them. Then, whoever has done the smallest bit of good shall see it, and whoever has done the smallest bit of evil shall also see it.

- Most of the Quran revealed in Makkah is about the Day of Judgment and the Hereafter.
- The Quraysh used to deny both.
- Surah Zilzaal and Aadiyaat form a pair and focus on the Day of Judgment.
- The Quran paints a dramatic picture of the Day of Judgment. The purpose is to convey the seriousness of the matter.
- Most people commit injustice and other evils because they either forget or don't believe in a Day when their actions and deeds will be exposed.
- The Quraysh of Makkah (and, in general, people) were doubtful about three things:
  - How could this universe be destroyed?
  - Who could record and cover every single deed of every human being?
  - Even if there is such a Day, our deities and elders will save us.
- Many of the verses that discuss the Day of Judgement fall into the category of *Mutashabihaat*. *Mutashabihaat* are those verses whose meaning is clear to us, but we don't know the reality behind them.

The Earth and other Planets will be destroyed

- NO ONE knows when the Day of Judgment will occur – not even Prophet Muhammad or Angel Jibrael.
- The Day of Judgment will be sudden - there will be no signs that the Earth is about to end physiologically.
- The Earth is the center of civilization and the human population, so the Day of Judgment will begin here.
- It will all start with an Angel blowing a horn.
- The Earth will rip apart, exposing all the 'secrets' inside it, including the dead.
- This is a symbolic statement that the Earth will expose all the secrets humans have been hiding, as if we hide things underground.
- Earth is the biggest witness to everything we do.
- It will be horrifying for humans to see that happening.
- The disbelievers at the time of Prophet Muhammad could not accept the fact that they would be resurrected to life. In other words, their main denial was about the Hereafter, which in essence negates the Day of Judgment.

اَئِذَا مِتْنَا وَ كُنَّا تُرَابًا وَّ عِظَامًا ءَاِنَّا لَمَبْعُوثُونَ

"When we are dead and have become dust and bones, shall we be raised again?" (Surah Waqiah:47)

We will see every deed in front of our eyes

- The resurrection will occur when the Angel blows a second horn.
- There is no concept of group accountability in Islam – Allah told us many places in the Quran that every human being would come alone because they would be so worried about their fate.
- Allah knows everything we have done, but His knowledge alone should never be the reason for our reward or punishment.
- In the court of justice, it's the witnesses who either get you punished or freed.
- On the Day of Judgment, our deeds, the Earth, and body parts will become witnesses for or against us.
- People will accept that they have committed wrongs and their punishment is justified.

وَ وُضِعَ الْكِتٰبُ فَتَرَى الْمُجْرِمِيْنَ مُشْفِقِيْنَ مِمَّا فِيْهِ وَ يَقُوْلُوْنَ يٰوَيْلَتَنَا مَالِ هٰذَا الْكِتٰبِ لَا يُغَادِرُ صَغِيْرَةً وَّ لَا كَبِيْرَةً اِلَّاۤ اَحْصٰىهَا ۚ وَ وَجَدُوْا مَا عَمِلُوْا حَاضِرًا ۗ وَ لَا يَظْلِمُ رَبُّكَ اَحَدًا

And the book of deeds will be presented. Then you will see the criminals fearing whatever is in it and will say: "Alas, our misfortune! What kind of a book is this that it has not omitted anything small or big from writing it down?" They found all they had done before them, and your Lord will not be unjust to anyone. (Surah Kahaf:49)

Small deeds

- Never underestimate any deed, no matter how small it is.
- Small things pile up into large things without us knowing.

عَنْ عَائِشَةَ، أَنَّ رَسُولَ اللَّهِ صلى الله عليه وسلم قَالَ " سَدِّدُوا وَقَارِبُوا، وَاعْلَمُوا أَنْ لَنْ يُدْخِلَ أَحَدَكُمْ عَمَلُهُ الْجَنَّةَ، وَأَنَّ أَحَبَّ الأَعْمَالِ أَدْوَمُهَا إِلَى اللَّهِ، وَإِنْ قَلَّ

Allah's Messenger said, "Do good deeds properly, sincerely, and moderately, and know that your deeds will not make you enter Paradise (it's the intention) and that the most beloved deed to Allah is the most regular and constant, even if it were little."

Surah Furqan: Verse 25-30

وَ يَوْمَ تَشَقَّقُ السَّمَآءُ بِالْغَمَامِ وَ نُزِّلَ الْمَلَٰٓئِكَةَ تَنْزِيْلًا

اَلْمُلْكُ يَوْمَئِذِ الْحَقُّ لِلرَّحْمٰنِ ۖ وَ كَانَ يَوْمًا عَلَى الْكٰفِرِيْنَ عَسِيْرًا

وَ يَوْمَ يَعَضُّ الظَّالِمُ عَلٰى يَدَيْهِ يَقُوْلُ يٰلَيْتَنِى اتَّخَذْتُ مَعَ الرَّسُوْلِ سَبِيْلًا

يٰوَيْلَتٰى لَيْتَنِىْ لَمْ اَتَّخِذْ فُلَانًا خَلِيْلًا

لَقَدْ اَضَلَّنِىْ عَنِ الذِّكْرِ بَعْدَ اِذْ جَآءَنِىْ ۖ وَ كَانَ الشَّيْطٰنُ لِلْاِنْسَانِ خَذُوْلًا

The Day when the sky shall split apart from above a cloud. [It will appear] and group after group of angels shall be sent [from within it.] True sovereignty shall only belong to the Most Merciful God on that Day. That Day shall be very harsh on the disbelievers. The Day when the oppressor (to his soul) shall longingly bite his hand and say: "Would that I had adopted the path [of truth] with the messenger. Alas! My misfortune! Would that I had not made so-and-so my friend! He had led me astray and diverted me from God's remembrance after it had come to me." It will be said: "Satan is very unfaithful (deceitful) to human beings!"

- Before these verses, the Quran stated some of the objections raised by the disbelievers:
  - Why did no angels descend on us instead of you being sent as a messenger?
  - Why can't we see God directly?
- The disbelievers sought an excuse to deny the Messenger and the Quran.
- Allah told them these questions were coming from an attitude of arrogance.
- The disbelievers will see both of them at a time when they will have no opportunity to mend their ways.
- Allah, keep all those things in Ghaib that go against the true spirit of the test and trial he has designed this life for. Allah, Himself, the angels, life after death, Allah's intervention in the daily affairs of this world, etc.

The Events on the Day of Judgment

- Like Earth (as explained in the previous verses), the sky (whatever is around us) will also experience destruction.
- Apparently, large white/grey clouds will appear as a result of that destruction.
- Angels will play a critical role on that day.
- People can see those angels busy preparing for the Day of Judgment, when everyone is dead and resurrected.
- That day will belong to Allah alone because He will be the sole authority on that day, and the authority given to humans will be taken away.
- All other kingdoms that humans are proud of will cease to exist.
- That day will be rough for the disbelievers as they will see whatever they have been denying

Wrongdoers will regret their attitude and company

- The Quran introduced a unique concept of injustice: committing injustice towards oneself.
- "Unjust" are those people who have committed wrong against themselves.
- People become unjust because they forget the Day of Judgment and accountability, or don't think it will happen.
- They will be biting their fingers with remorse and shame.
- The verses are specific to the people who rejected Prophet Muhammad, but they can be applied to anyone who faces a Truth (it becomes clear that it is the Truth) but ignores or rejects it due to temporary worldly benefits
- They will blame two people specifically:
  - Their companions, who helped them in doing evil and never reminded them about the consequences
  - Satan suggested excuses, but on the Day of Judgment, he betrayed and left the person alone

Remember that Satan never forces you to do wrong, but he creates excuses and justifications in your mind so you can agree to commit wrong. That is a very deceptive behavior.

Friend and companions

- We must surround ourselves with good companions, as they might decide our path in this life and the next.
- Find companions who share your life values.
- A good friend accepts your shortcomings but also guides you when they see you doing wrong. The Quran said in one place:

ٱلْأَخِلَّآءُ يَوْمَئِذٍ بَعْضُهُمْ لِبَعْضٍ عَدُوٌّ إِلَّا ٱلْمُتَّقِينَ

Except for those who fear God, all friends shall become enemies on that day. (Zukhruf:67)

- They should be your best advisors.
- Your companionship mostly influences you, so be careful and don't take it lightly when choosing one.
- Your friendship should strengthen your faith.
- We can be friends with anyone as long as they promote goodness and reject evil.
- Nothing stops us from befriending non-Muslims. Friendship with non-Muslims gives us an opportunity to share the message of Islam with them.

Surah Hajj: Verse 1-2

يَآ أَيُّهَا النَّاسُ اتَّقُوْا رَبَّكُمْ ۚ إِنَّ زَلْزَلَةَ السَّاعَةِ شَيْءٌ عَظِيْمٌ

يَوْمَ تَرَوْنَهَا تَذْهَلُ كُلُّ مُرْضِعَةٍ عَمَّا أَرْضَعَتْ وَ تَضَعُ كُلُّ ذَاتِ حَمْلٍ حَمْلَهَا وَ

تَرَى النَّاسَ سُكْرَى وَ مَا هُمْ بِسُكْرَى وَ لٰكِنَّ عَذَابَ اللهِ شَدِيْدٌ

People! Fear your Lord. In reality, the earthquake of the Day of Judgement is a very horrific thing. The day when you will see that every suckling mother will forget her suckled child and every pregnant one will shed her burden, you will see people drunk even though they will not be drunk. In fact, the torment of God shall be so severe (they would be so worried).

- Surah Hajj was one of the last Surahs of the Prophet's time in Makkah when he was about to migrate to Medinah.
- The main topic of the Surahs revealed in Makkah is the Day of Judgment and Accountability.
- As stated earlier, the disbelievers used to deny the Day of Judgment, which is why they adopted an arrogant attitude.
- The Quran constantly reminded them not to ignore this reality, and that day will be horrific for people who reject Allah and the Day of Judgment.
- These verses also bring the scene of the day before to their eyes.

The severity of the Day of Judgment

- These verses give us a good idea about the severity of the situation when the Day starts.
- The chaotic and terrifying imagery at the start of the Day of Judgment in the Quran, as in the first few verses of Surah Al-Hajj, serves several theological and psychological purposes. This vivid, dramatic portrayal is not meant to simply scare people, but to provide powerful lessons and warnings.
- As stated earlier, it would feel like a massive earthquake shaking the Earth violently.
- On one hand, this chaotic imagery illustrates that Allah's power is absolute and can dismantle creation with a single act, leaving no doubt about His ability to then resurrect all of humanity.
- On the other hand, it gives a clear message to human beings not to live a neglectful life. The event would be so horrific and terrifying that everyone would be concerned only with themselves.
- Today, when earthquakes happen, parents rush to save their children.
- However, on that Day, mothers would abandon their young nursing children.
- All pregnant women will suffer a miscarriage, and they would not want to carry their unborn children anymore.
- People would be worried about themselves and would only seek refuge.
- They would appear drunk because they would be running around directionless.
- This type of situation would be worse for people who have committed evil and injustice against other human beings.
- Some Ahadith describe righteous people feeling safe and secure on that Day as they await their accountability.

Seven types of people will get protection

"Seven people Allah will give them His Shade on the Day when there would be no shade but the Shade of His Throne (i.e., on the Day of Resurrection): And they are: a just ruler; a youth who grew up with the worship of Allah; a person whose heart is attached to the mosques, two men who love and meet each other and depart from each other for the sake of Allah; a man whom an extremely beautiful woman seduces (for illicit relation), but he (rejects this offer and) says: 'I fear Allah'; a man who gives in charity and conceals it (to such an extent) that the left hand does not know what the right has given; and a man who remembers Allah in solitude and his eyes become tearful".

Hadith

Who is poor?

عن أبي هُرَيْرَةَ أَنَّ رَسُولَ اللَّهِ صلى الله عليه وسلم قال أَتَدْرُونَ ما الْمُفْلِسُ قالوا الْمُفْلِسُ فِينَا من لَا دِرْهَمَ له ولا مَتَاعَ فقال إِنَّ الْمُفْلِسَ من أُمَّتِي يَأْتِي يوم الْقِيَامَةِ بِصَلَاةٍ وَصِيَامٍ وَزَكَاةٍ وَيَأْتِي قد شَتَمَ هذا وَقَذَفَ هذا وَأَكَلَ مَالَ هذا وَسَفَكَ دَمَ هذا وَضَرَبَ هذا فَيُعْطَى هذا من حَسَنَاتِهِ وَهَذَا من حَسَنَاتِهِ فَإِنْ فَنِيَتْ حَسَنَاتُهُ قبل أَنْ يُقْضَى ما عليه أُخِذَ من خَطَايَاهُمْ فَطُرِحَتْ عليه ثُمَّ طُرِحَ في النَّارِ

Abu Hurairah reported that God's Messenger said: "Do you know who is poor among us?" The companions replied: "A poor person is penniless and is without provisions. At this, the Prophet remarked: "The poor of my nation is one who would come on the Day of Judgement with prayers, fasts, and Zakah, but he would have abused some person and falsely accused another of immorality, devoured the wealth of a person and shed the blood of another, and beaten up another. Then one good deed after another will be given from his account and given [to the one he had oppressed]. If these good deeds fall short of paying back what he was liable for, the sins of those he had oppressed will be taken and credited into his account, and then he will be thrown into the Fire [of Hell]."
[Sahih Muslim #2581).

Sympathy

أَبَا قَتَادَةَ ... قال فَإِنِّي سمعت رَسُولَ اللَّهِ صلى الله عليه وسلم يقول من سَرَّهُ أَنْ يُنْجِيَهُ الله من كُرَبِ يَوْمِ الْقِيَامَةِ فَلْيُنَفِّسْ عن مُعْسِرٍ أو يَضَعْ عنه

Abu Qatadah reported: "... I heard God's Messenger as saying: "He who likes that God deliver a person from the suffering of the Day of Judgement should give respite to a poor borrower or reduce the burden of a loan from him." [Sahih Muslim #1563).

BIBLE

Words will count

You offspring of snakes, how are you, being evil, able to say good things? Because out of the heart's store come the words of the mouth. The good man, out of his excellent store, gives good things, and the evil man, out of his evil store, gives evil things. And I say to you that in that Day when they are judged, men will have to give an account of every foolish word they have said. For by your words will your righteousness be seen, and by your words, you will be judged.
(Matthew, 12:34-37)

How does the dramatic presentation of the Day of Judgment given by the Quran help deliver the message?

Read the Surah Qiyamah with translation and write a small summary of the Surah.

Chapter 14

Topic 9: Characteristics of a Believer

This chapter introduces the attributes a believer must possess, as outlined in the Quran.

Surah Muminoon: Verses 1-11

قَدْ اَفْلَحَ الْمُؤْمِنُوْنَ الَّذِيْنَ هُمْ فِيْ صَلَاتِهِمْ خٰشِعُوْنَ وَ الَّذِيْنَ هُمْ عَنِ اللَّغْوِ مُعْرِضُوْنَ

وَ الَّذِيْنَ هُمْ لِلزَّكٰوةِ فٰعِلُوْنَ وَ الَّذِيْنَ هُمْ لِفُرُوْجِهِمْ حٰفِظُوْنَ

اِلَّا عَلٰۤى اَزْوَاجِهِمْ اَوْ مَا مَلَكَتْ اَيْمَانُهُمْ فَاِنَّهُمْ غَيْرُ مَلُوْمِيْنَ

فَمَنِ ابْتَغٰى وَرَآءَ ذٰلِكَ فَاُولٰٓئِكَ هُمُ الْعٰدُوْنَ وَ الَّذِيْنَ هُمْ لِاَمٰنٰتِهِمْ وَ عَهْدِهِمْ رٰعُوْنَ

وَ الَّذِيْنَ هُمْ عَلٰى صَلَوٰتِهِمْ يُحَافِظُوْنَ اُولٰٓئِكَ هُمُ الْوٰرِثُوْنَ

الَّذِيْنَ يَرِثُوْنَ الْفِرْدَوْسَ ۗ هُمْ فِيْهَا خٰلِدُوْنَ

Those believers have succeeded who show humility in their prayer, who desist from nonsense talks/things and who pay Zakah, and who guard their private parts except for their wives and slave-maidens because, in their case, there is no blame on them; indeed, those who desire others besides them, it is they who exceed the limits and those who give due regard to their trusts and to their promises, and those who guard their prayers. It is these people who will be the owners. They will be the owners of the highest (Al-Firdaus). They shall abide in it forever.

- Surah Hajj and Muminoon pair on the topic of warnings and glad tidings.
- The warnings to the people of Makkah as the heir of Prophet Ibrahim / Ismail and as the custodian of the Kabaah are prominent in Surah Hajj.
- In Muminoon, the qualities and rewards of the believers are highlighted.
- Surah Hajj ends by stating that the Children of Ismail are now responsible for leading the nations of the earth and carrying the message of Islam to the world, as Prophet Muhammad did for them.
- Surah Muminoon begins with qualities that would enable them to discharge this grave responsibility.
- Without these qualities, they won't become a role model for this world.
- The Quran used the past tense to convey success, as if the believers had already succeeded. This is usually used in the Quran for assurance.

Why did Allah mention Salah at the beginning and the end of the list of attributes?

Qualities of a believer

- These verses explain the attributes of those believers who will be successful on the Day of Judgment.
- It is an excellent opportunity for us to see ourselves in the light of these attributes and determine how close we are to these attributes that Allah wants in a believer.
- Each attribute is explained in order.

 **Humility in Salah**

They express obedience, humility, and modesty in their prayers and pray with the presence of the mind. This is the true essence of the prayers.

 **Avoid Nonsense**

They completely avoid nonsense talk and actions that have no purpose. A believer does not live without objectives. Vain talks and acts only result in holding them responsible on the Day of Judgment.

 **Pay their Zakah (Charity)**

Along with Allah's rights, they also give human beings their right. Zakah is given to meet the needs of society in which there will always be people who are less fortunate than others

 **Guard their chastity**

They guard their chastity and only have relationships with their spouses, and what Islam allows them. This is necessary to build a pure society in which the family unit is healthy and prosperous.

Covenants and Trusts

They honor the covenants, promises, agreements, and any trust given to them in the best possible manner. A healthy society is formed when people trust one another.

Guard their prayers

They guard their prayers like a watchman. Their days revolve around prayer times. The Quran encompasses all the qualities in prayer because prayer is needed to maintain them.

- When it comes to fulfilling their promises and covenants, the Quran used the word "*Ra'un*" for those people.
- The Arabic word used, *ra'un*, is translated as "attentive" or "keeper" and is from the same root as the word for a shepherd (*Rai'i*)
- This linguistic and metaphorical connection, as explained by Islamic scholars, is meant to evoke the qualities of responsibility, diligence, and care associated with a shepherd.
- By using a term related to shepherding, the Quran links the simple act of fulfilling a promise to the deeper religious and moral duty of being a responsible steward over one's trusts.

The Reward

The ownership of the highest places in Paradise, called *Al Firdaus*, in which they will live forever.

Surah Al Maarij: Verses 19-35

إِنَّ الْإِنْسَانَ خُلِقَ هَلُوعًا ۞ إِذَا مَسَّهُ الشَّرُّ جَزُوعًا ۞ وَّ إِذَا مَسَّهُ الْخَيْرُ مَنُوعًا ۞ إِلَّا الْمُصَلِّيْنَ ۞

الَّذِيْنَ هُمْ عَلٰى صَلَاتِهِمْ دَآئِمُوْنَ ۞ وَ الَّذِيْنَ فِيْ اَمْوَالِهِمْ حَقٌّ مَّعْلُوْمٌ ۞ لِّلسَّآئِلِ وَ الْمَحْرُوْمِ ۞

وَ الَّذِيْنَ يُصَدِّقُوْنَ بِيَوْمِ الدِّيْنِ ۞ وَ الَّذِيْنَ هُمْ مِّنْ عَذَابِ رَبِّهِمْ مُّشْفِقُوْنَ ۞ اِنَّ عَذَابَ رَبِّهِمْ غَيْرُ مَأْمُوْنٍ ۞

وَ الَّذِيْنَ هُمْ لِفُرُوْجِهِمْ حٰفِظُوْنَ ۞ اِلَّا عَلٰى اَزْوَاجِهِمْ اَوْ مَا مَلَكَتْ اَيْمَانُهُمْ فَاِنَّهُمْ غَيْرُ مَلُوْمِيْنَ ۞

فَمَنِ ابْتَغٰى وَرَآءَ ذٰلِكَ فَأُولٰٓئِكَ هُمُ الْعٰدُوْنَ ۞ وَ الَّذِيْنَ هُمْ بِشَهٰدٰتِهِمْ قَآئِمُوْنَ ۞

وَ الَّذِيْنَ هُمْ لِاَمٰنٰتِهِمْ وَ عَهْدِهِمْ رٰعُوْنَ ۞ وَ الَّذِيْنَ هُمْ عَلٰى صَلَاتِهِمْ يُحَافِظُوْنَ ۞

اُولٰٓئِكَ فِيْ جَنّٰتٍ مُّكْرَمُوْنَ ۞

In reality, man has been created with a very impatient nature. Whenever some affliction befalls him, he complains, and when good fortune befalls him, he becomes very stingy. But not those who pray; who are always vigilant in the prayer; who have a fixed portion in their wealth for those who ask and for the deprived; who truly believe in the Day of Reckoning and keep dreading the punishment of their Lord because the punishment of their Lord is not something to be careless of; who preserve their chastity except with their wives and slave-girls, for in their matter they are not blameworthy, but those who seek to go beyond this, then it is they who are transgressors; who keep their trust and promises [both about God and about their fellow human beings] who stand firm in their testimonies and who guard their prayers. They will be in the gardens [of Paradise] with great honor.

- Surah Al-Maarij began with the disbelievers' demand for the punishment the Prophet had promised them if they continued to reject him.
- Allah told them that the punishment wouldn't be easy, and as soon as they saw it, they would start wailing about it.
- Instead of benefiting from the message, the messenger, and all the blessings given to them, they become arrogant and ask for punishment.
- The kind of affluent life that they have today won't be waiting for them in the Hereafter.
- All they would see is punishment and severe consequences for their actions.
- Then Allah explained the attitude of true believers who take heed from the warnings and act righteously.

Human beings are impatient

I want it
NOW!

- Impatience is one of the most dominant features in human beings.
- If one option is achievable today and another is a promise, we prefer the achievable one.
- It is not a bad feature; humans have achieved miracles because of it, but when it comes to ultimate success, it can be a disaster and become a big weakness.
- When some affliction befalls us, we start complaining and want the affliction to be removed immediately.
- However, when good things happen, we become arrogant and try to keep them to ourselves.
- An eye on the higher prize keeps a person patient and a righteous servant of Allah.
- It is interesting that Allah highlighted the inherent weaknesses of the human character before outlining the qualities of the believers who are an exception to this description.
- Sometimes, if we don't control this weakness, we tend to be restless and go into a state of distress and anxiety.
- On the other hand, when a person is blessed with good fortune, such as wealth or ease, their anxious nature manifests as stinginess, as they don't want to lose what they have.

Qualities of a believer

- After acknowledging human weakness, Allah outlines the qualities of the believers who are an exception to this kind of behavior, as they are God-conscious and control themselves through effort.

Vigilant in their Salah

Vigilant means consistent here. A small deed done regularly is more blessed than a big one done once. A steady light rain keeps the crops alive and yields a good crop.

Fixed portion for the needy

Along with Allah's rights, they also give human beings their right. Zakah (a fixed portion) is given to meet the needs of society, in which there will always be less fortunate people.

Beware of Accountability

They fear the Day of Judgment and the punishment in the Hereafter. Because of their strong belief in the Last Day, they judge their actions in the light of the guidance provided by their Lord.

Guard their chastity

They guard their chastity and only form relationships with their spouses, and what Islam allows them. This is necessary to build a pure society in which the unit of the family is healthy and prosperous

Allah SWT often uses the words "they guard their chastity." What steps can be taken to comply with this statement?

Covenants and Trusts

They honor the covenants, promises, agreements, and any trust given to them in the best possible manner. This is true with Allah and human beings. A healthy society is formed when people trust one another.

Guard their prayers

They guard their prayers like a watchman. Their days revolve around prayer times. The Quran encompasses all the qualities in prayer because prayer is needed to maintain them.

The Reward

They will be in the gardens of Paradise with great honor. It is specially prepared for them.

Surah Furqan: Verses 63-76

وَ عِبَادُ الرَّحْمٰنِ الَّذِيْنَ يَمْشُوْنَ عَلَى الْأَرْضِ هَوْنًا وَّ اِذَا خَاطَبَهُمُ الْجٰهِلُوْنَ قَالُوْا سَلٰمًا

وَ الَّذِيْنَ يَبِيْتُوْنَ لِرَبِّهِمْ سُجَّدًا وَّ قِيَامًا ۙ وَ الَّذِيْنَ يَقُوْلُوْنَ رَبَّنَا اصْرِفْ عَنَّا عَذَابَ جَهَنَّمَ ۖ

اِنَّ عَذَابَهَا كَانَ غَرَامًا ۖ اِنَّهَا سَآءَتْ مُسْتَقَرًّا وَّ مُقَامًا وَ الَّذِيْنَ اِذَآ اَنْفَقُوْا لَمْ يُسْرِفُوْا وَ لَمْ

يَقْتُرُوْا وَ كَانَ بَيْنَ ذٰلِكَ قَوَامًا وَ الَّذِيْنَ لَا يَدْعُوْنَ مَعَ اللّٰهِ اِلٰهًا اٰخَرَ وَ لَا يَقْتُلُوْنَ

النَّفْسَ الَّتِيْ حَرَّمَ اللّٰهُ اِلَّا بِالْحَقِّ وَ لَا يَزْنُوْنَ ۚ وَ مَنْ يَّفْعَلْ ذٰلِكَ يَلْقَ اَثَامًا ۙ

يُّضٰعَفْ لَهُ الْعَذَابُ يَوْمَ الْقِيٰمَةِ وَ يَخْلُدْ فِيْهِ مُهَانًا ۖ اِلَّا مَنْ تَابَ وَ اٰمَنَ وَ عَمِلَ عَمَلًا

صَالِحًا فَاُولٰٓئِكَ يُبَدِّلُ اللّٰهُ سَيِّاٰتِهِمْ حَسَنٰتٍ ؕ وَ كَانَ اللّٰهُ غَفُوْرًا رَّحِيْمًا

وَ مَنْ تَابَ وَ عَمِلَ صَالِحًا فَاِنَّهٗ يَتُوْبُ اِلَى اللّٰهِ مَتَابًا وَ الَّذِيْنَ لَا يَشْهَدُوْنَ الزُّوْرَ ۙ

وَ اِذَا مَرُّوْا بِاللَّغْوِ مَرُّوْا كِرَامًا وَ الَّذِيْنَ اِذَا ذُكِّرُوْا بِاٰيٰتِ رَبِّهِمْ لَمْ يَخِرُّوْا عَلَيْهَا صُمًّا

وَّ عُمْيَانًا وَ الَّذِيْنَ يَقُوْلُوْنَ رَبَّنَا هَبْ لَنَا مِنْ اَزْوَاجِنَا وَ ذُرِّيّٰتِنَا قُرَّةَ اَعْيُنٍ وَّ اجْعَلْنَا

لِلْمُتَّقِيْنَ اِمَامًا اُولٰٓئِكَ يُجْزَوْنَ الْغُرْفَةَ بِمَا صَبَرُوْا وَ يُلَقَّوْنَ فِيْهَا تَحِيَّةً وَّ سَلٰمًا ۙ

خٰلِدِيْنَ فِيْهَا ؕ حَسُنَتْ مُسْتَقَرًّا وَّ مُقَامًا

Surah Furqan: Verses 63-76

The servants of the Most Merciful are the ones who walk humbly on the earth, and when a person, overcome with emotions, tries to argue with them, they step aside by saying Salam to him. Those who spend their nights prostrating and standing before their Lord. Who prays: "Lord, ward off the torment of Hell from us. In reality, its torment holds fast. It is a very evil abode for staying and living." And [are those] who, when they spend, are neither extravagant nor stingy; their spending is in moderation. And [are those] who do not call any other deity besides God, do not kill any soul held sacred by God, and do not commit fornication–whosoever commits these sins shall bear their consequences. On the Day of Judgement, his torment shall continue to increase, and he shall forever abide in it disgraced. Except for those who repented, professed faith, and did good deeds, then it is such people whose bad deeds God shall transform into good ones. In reality, God is very Forgiving, Ever-Merciful. And he who repents and does good deeds should rest assured because he returns only to God with full success. And the servants of the Merciful are those who never participate in any evil, and when they have to pass by a frivolous thing, they pass with dignity. And are such that when they are reminded through their Lord's revelations, they do not fall blind and deaf. And who says: "Our Lord! Grant us the soothing of eyes from our wives and children, and [among these family members of ours] make us the leader of the pious." These people shall get lofty abodes in Paradise because of their perseverance and be welcomed there with salutations and greetings. They shall live in them forever. What a nice place to live and stay.

- Before these verses, Allah was talking about His attributes and why deities whom disbelievers worship other than Allah are not going to help them in any way.
- The verses emphasized one of Allah's most beloved attributes, Ar-Rahman (Most Gracious).
- Allah used this attribute in the Quran to draw attention to the one true God (whom people may call by different names).
- When the disbelievers were asked to prostrate to Ar-Rahman, they questioned," Who is Ar-Rahman"?
- In that context, Allah told them Ar-Rahman is your Lord who has created these Sun, Moon, and Stars, so you become grateful.
- Once you recognize Ar-Rahman, you behave as a servant of Ar-Rahman, and the qualities of those servants are described in these verses.

Who is Ar-Rahman?

- In the Quran, Allah used it as one of His names in place of Allah. This makes this name very special. It is usually translated as "the Most Merciful."
- This name carries three intrinsic aspects: Compassionate, Just, and Forgiving.
- His Mercy will not be void of justice and forgiveness, and only those who deserve His Mercy will get it.
- His Mercy is not like the mercy of a mother who is emotionally weak when it comes to delivering justice against her own children.

Qualities of the Servants of Ar-Rahman

 Humility in gait

Their gait does not reflect any sign of arrogance in their hearts. Many things can produce conceit in a person, as seen in how people walk. The believers walk with humility on earth.

 Disengage peacefully

Just as saying 'Salam' is to greet someone, it also helps us disengage from someone peacefully. Especially, when someone is debating and there are signs that he/she is not interested in knowing the Truth.

 Pray to ask for protection from Hellfire

They spend their days and nights prostrating and standing before their Lord. Asking Allah to ward off from them the torment of Hell, knowing that it is an evil abode for staying and living

 Balanced in spending

They are moderate in their spending, like many other things in life. They are neither extravagant nor stingy. Extravagant people do not find the opportunities to spend their wealth for the sake of Allah

No God except Allah

Monotheism is at the core of the beliefs of the believers. They do not call any other deities besides Allah, knowing that no one has power and only Allah can help them under any circumstances.

No Killing

Allah has made every human soul sacred, and the servants of Ar-Rahman know this fact very well. They do not allow their emotions to overtake them and kill someone without a justification (legal)

Guard their chastity

They guard their chastity and only form relationships with their wives, and what is allowed in Islam. This is necessary to build a pure society in which the unit of family is healthy and prosperous

The **BIG 3**

Shirk
Murder
Illicit relations

- Shirk, murder, and fornication are among the gravest sins in Islam, punishable both in the Hereafter and, for certain manifestations of the crime, in this life also. For example, for Shirk, people are punished when a Messenger is among them.
- Murder is a profound violation, not just against an individual but against the entire society, as it breaches God's law that protects all lives.
- Fornication (*zina*) is an explicit evil that undermines the institution of the family, which is fundamental to a healthy society.

Avoid Evil and Playful Things

They use their time and energy wisely with a sense of accountability. They are not engaged in evil & Laghw, which every upright person regards as one decent people should not engage in; cursing, immoral jokes, teasing, etc.

Pondering over Quran

They do not become blind or deaf to the verses of the Quran. When recited to them, they listen carefully and reflect to gain benefit. They take the verses of the Quran as reminders.

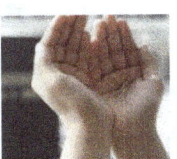

Making dua for the family

They are concerned about their family and constantly ask Allah to make them righteous. "Our Lord, make our wives and our children a source of coolness for our eyes and, on that Day, make them the leaders of the righteous.

The Rewards

If they repent,

- Have faith and decide to do good deeds, and then Allah will transform their evil deeds into good ones for reward.
- Allah will accept their return as the true return to Allah.

Due to patience,

- Lofty mansions in Paradise because they kept themselves low in this world by following the truth.
- They will be welcomed with beautiful greetings from angels
- They will live in those mansions forever.

Hadith

Qualities of a true believer

عن عبد اللّٰهِ بن عُمَرَ رضي الله عنهما قال أَخَذَ رسولُ اللّٰهِ صلى الله عليه وسلم بِمَنْكِبِي فقال كُنْ في الدُّنْيَا كَأَنَّكَ غَرِيبٌ أو عَابِرُ سَبِيلٍ

Abdullah ibn Umar said: "The Prophet held my shoulder and said: 'Live in this world as a stranger or as a traveler.'" (Sahih Muslim #6053)

عَنْ صُهَيْبٍ قَالَ قَالَ رَسُولُ اللّٰهِ صَلَّى اللّٰهُ عَلَيْهِ وَسَلَّمَ عَجَبًا لِأَمْرِ الْمُؤْمِنِ إِنَّ أَمْرَهُ كُلَّهُ خَيْرٌ وَلَيْسَ ذَاكَ لِأَحَدٍ إِلَّا لِلْمُؤْمِنِ إِنْ أَصَابَتْهُ سَرَّاءُ شَكَرَ فَكَانَ خَيْرًا لَهُ وَإِنْ أَصَابَتْهُ ضَرَّاءُ صَبَرَ فَكَانَ خَيْرًا لَهُ

Suhayb reported: The Messenger of Allah said, "Amazing are the affairs of a believer, as there is good for him in every matter; this is not the case for anyone but a **believer**. If he experiences good, he thanks Allah, and it is good for him. If he experiences bad, he shows patience, and it is good for him." (Sahih Muslim #2999)

وعن أبي الدرداء رضي الله عنه: أن النبي صلى الله عليه وسلم قال: ''ما من شيء أثقل في ميزان المؤمن يوم القيامة من حسن الخلق، وإن الله يبغض الفاحش البذي''

The Prophet said, "Nothing will be heavier on the Day of Resurrection in the Scale of the believer than good manners. Allah hates one who utters foul or coarse language." (Riyad as Saliheen #625)

BIBLE

Righteousness

For the Lord, your God is God of gods and Lord of lords, the great God, strong in power and greatly to be feared, who has no respect for any man's position and takes no rewards: Judging uprightly in the cause of the widow and of the child who has no father and giving food and clothing in his mercy to the man from a strange country. So be kind to the man from a strange country living among you, for you yourselves were living in a strange country in the land of Egypt. Let the fear of the Lord your God be before you, give him worship, and always be true to him, taking your oaths in his name.
(Deuteronomy, 10:17-20)

Collect three more verses about the qualities of a believer from the Quran besides what's already studied in this chapter.

Chapter 15

Topic 10: Features of a Muslim Society

This chapter introduces the attributes of a Muslim society as God describes in the Quran.

Surah Hujraat: Verse 6

يَٰٓأَيُّهَا ٱلَّذِينَ ءَامَنُوٓا إِن جَآءَكُمْ فَاسِقٌۢ بِنَبَإٍ فَتَبَيَّنُوٓا أَن تُصِيبُوا قَوْمًۢا بِجَهَٰلَةٍ فَتُصْبِحُوا عَلَىٰ مَا فَعَلْتُمْ نَٰدِمِينَ

Believers! If an evil-doer [unreliable sinning person] comes to you with important news (about something or someone), investigate it thoroughly so that you do not get overwhelmed by emotions and attack a nation; then, later, you feel ashamed of what you did.

- Surah Fath ends with a specific verse about the Prophet and his companions and how they treat each other.
- The same people who fight the disbelievers because of the firmness of their faith are compassionate and merciful toward one another.
- The Prophet's companions belonged to various tribes, and it was a miracle how they came together, putting aside their tribal differences.
- Surah Hujraat provides details of such a society and the main moral codes and behaviors upon which it must be built.
- This way, Surah Hujraat provides the recipe for a righteous Muslim society.
- According to some scholars, Allah revealed Surah Hujraat for the modern times that we live in.
- All the problems and ills we see in our societies today stem from our ignoring the message in Surah Hujraat.
- This background must be kept in mind when reading Surah Hujraat.

Why did Allah mention Salah at the beginning and the end of the list of attributes?

Verify everyone and everything you hear

Who is 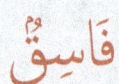 فَاسِقٌ	Anyone who is an evil-doer, not reliable, cannot be trusted, and is not considered upright in society

- Muslims in society must ask these three questions when they hear news that may have consequences when acted on.

Who?

- If the person is trustworthy, it is OK to investigate only the news and why they are telling you.
- If the person is known to be <u>not</u> upright and has no moral standing, then extra care should be taken in investigating the news and motives.
- If the person is unknown, they should be investigated first.

What?

- Everything that's been said must be verified.
- Especially the news that has major consequences, and the impact would be far-reaching if acted upon.
- It must be investigated through multiple independent means.
- The receiver must pay attention to the details and must not ignore anything.

Why?

- The motives for bringing the news are equally important and must not be ignored.
- Especially in tribal societies or in societies with factions, people used to spread rumors about specific people or tribes/factions to settle past scores.

Think before act

- We have heard about thinking before speaking, but what's more important is thinking before acting, because actions have far-reaching consequences.
- The Quran used the words "overwhelmed by emotions," meaning the nature of the news must not allow our emotions to take over our nerves or decision-making capabilities.
- The simple rule is that the more far-reaching the action's consequences, the more time is needed to think.
- Some actions' results cannot be undone, and the person or the group taking action will regret it forever.
- This advice is quite applicable to our current society, especially due to the prevalence of social media

A lion is crossing a bridge with a large, delicious piece of meat in its mouth. When he looks down, he sees his own reflection in the water. Mistaking the reflection for another lion with an even bigger piece of meat in its territory, he impulsively drops his own to attack the one in the water.

The small 'Forward' button

وَ لَا تَقۡفُ مَا لَیۡسَ لَکَ بِہٖ عِلۡمٌ ؕ اِنَّ السَّمۡعَ وَ الۡبَصَرَ وَ الۡفُؤَادَ کُلُّ اُولٰٓئِکَ کَانَ عَنۡہُ مَسۡئُوۡلًا

Do not go after what you know, not because eyes, ears, and hearts will all be questioned. (Surah Bani Israel #36)

كفى بالمرء كذبًا أن يحدث بكل ما سمع

Prophet Muhammad was reported to have said, "It is enough for a person to prove himself/herself a liar when he/she goes on narrating whatever he/she hears." (Sahih Muslim)

Surah Al Hujraat: Verses 9-10

وَ اِنْ طَآئِفَتٰنِ مِنَ الْمُؤْمِنِيْنَ اقْتَتَلُوْا فَاَصْلِحُوْا بَيْنَهُمَا ۚ فَاِنْۢ بَغَتْ اِحْدٰىهُمَا عَلَى الْاُخْرٰى فَقَاتِلُوا الَّتِيْ تَبْغِيْ حَتّٰى تَفِيْٓءَ اِلٰٓى اَمْرِ اللّٰهِ ۚ فَاِنْ فَآءَتْ فَاَصْلِحُوْا بَيْنَهُمَا بِالْعَدْلِ وَ اَقْسِطُوْا ۚ اِنَّ اللّٰهَ يُحِبُّ الْمُقْسِطِيْنَ ۚ اِنَّمَا الْمُؤْمِنُوْنَ اِخْوَةٌ فَاَصْلِحُوْا بَيْنَ اَخَوَيْكُمْ وَ اتَّقُوا اللّٰهَ لَعَلَّكُمْ تُرْحَمُوْنَ

[Your unity remains intact because of this; hence] if two groups of believers take up arms against one another, reconcile between them. Then, if one of the groups is unjust to the other, fight against the one who is unjust until it turns to God's verdict. Then, if it turns out, reconcile the two with justice and be very fair. Surely, God befriends the just. Believers are brothers to one another; thus, reconcile between two brothers and keep fearing God so that you are shown mercy.

Note: This conflict results from poor communication mentioned in verse 6.

Muslims are expected to play an active role in society, especially in those matters that affect society. They cannot just sit by and watch such conflicts grow, doing nothing about them. They must play a positive and constructive role in such matters.

- In a Muslim society, no circumstance should lead to an armed conflict between groups of believers.
- The verses explain the responsibility of society or the state as a whole in such a situation.
- Society, in general, cannot be indifferent to this situation because if it escalates into a war, its fire will engulf everyone around.
- The other Muslims should try to reconcile between the parties and avoid armed conflict at all costs.
- However, if they find that one party is committing injustice, is on the wrong side, and is not ready to make peace, the state should use force against that party until it comes to the table to talk or accepts what is right. This is not meant to punish them.
- But when they agree to talk and reconcile, no tribal or group inclination should stop the state from being just.

Muslims are brothers to each other

إِنَّمَا الْمُؤْمِنُونَ اِخْوَةٌ

- There is a common misunderstanding that Muslims are one nation – nowhere in the Quran has Allah said that.
- The Quran calls on Muslims to be brothers/sisters to one another.
- Muslims can maintain their nationality or identity on any other basis – nation, race, color, language, culture, etc.
- However, when it comes to religion, they become brothers and sisters of each other.

- The advice of Allah is not only applicable to nations but also to families and communities.
- First, brothers and sisters should not fight. But even if they had some conflict, it should not last long.
- In a Muslim society, people can't stay away from such conflicts that cause disharmony in a family or a community, just by saying that "this is not our concern".
- If the issue is within a family, some family members must serve as mediators; the same applies to a community or a neighborhood.
- In the end, as we are concerned about the well-being of our brothers and sisters, even if we fight with each other, we must be concerned about other Muslims regardless of the nation or race they belong to.

"The parable of the believers in their affection, mercy, and compassion for each other is that of a body. When any limb aches, the whole body reacts with sleeplessness and fever." (Sahih Bukhari #6011)

"None of you will believe until you love for your brother what you love for yourself." (Sahih Bukhari #13)

Surah Al Hujraat: Verses 11

يَـٰٓأَيُّهَا الَّذِينَ آمَنُوا لَا يَسْخَرْ قَوْمٌ مِّن قَوْمٍ عَسَىٰ أَن يَكُونُوا خَيْرًا مِّنْهُمْ وَ لَا نِسَآءٌ مِّن نِّسَآءٍ عَسَىٰ أَن يَكُنَّ خَيْرًا مِّنْهُنَّ ۖ وَ لَا تَلْمِزُوا أَنفُسَكُمْ وَ لَا تَنَابَزُوا بِالْأَلْقَابِ ۖ بِئْسَ الِاسْمُ الْفُسُوقُ بَعْدَ الْإِيمَانِ ۚ وَ مَن لَّمْ يَتُبْ فَأُولَـٰٓئِكَ هُمُ الظَّـٰلِمُونَ

Believers! [It is the requisite of this brotherhood that] neither [your] men make fun of other men; it may well be that they are better than them; nor should your women make fun of other women; it may well be that they are better than them. And neither defame your own people nor give bad names to one another. [All these are wrongdoings and] after faith, even the name of wrongdoing is evil. And those who do not repent [even after this warning], it is they who are unjust to their souls.

Why is there no brotherhood among Muslims?

- Right before this verse, Allah called Muslims brothers to each other (or sisters).
- In the next verse, 11, Allah told them the recipe for maintaining that bond—behavior and traits that Muslims must avoid to keep it healthy.
- Muslims allowed these vices to creep into their society and hence do not feel the bond of brotherhood and sisterhood.
- Unfortunately, all of these evils are associated with our tongues.
- The way Allah described them, these evils oppose our belief in Allah, and we must keep a check on them.
- Avoiding them is a sign of someone's belief.

Common issues in societies

Mockery

- This is one of the major causes of evil in society: when one group makes fun of another group and belittles them.
- This is especially true among people of one ethnicity, color, or language toward another.
- Our mockery is usually based on some worldly criteria – shortcomings, skin color, nature, status, nation, etc.
- Allah repeated the instructions for women to emphasize that this evil exists among men and women for various reasons.

Finger pointing

- At the same time, Allah said that a person or a group might be much closer to Allah in status while you are making fun of them.
- What matters in the sight of Allah is the status with Allah, regardless of the worldly status and situation.
- If we make fun of someone closer to Allah, the severity of consequences may become manifold.

Teasing and Taunting

- Teasing and taunting are usually done to other people to point out their faults or shortcomings.
- It could be that they have that fault or shortcoming, or we could assume they do — in either case, it's evil.
- This becomes especially despicable when done in front of others, as the intent is to ridicule or disgrace the person.

- This and similar evils are usually rooted in arrogance – the teaser thinks they are better than others.
- Making gestures without saying anything is the same.
- Islam teaches us the etiquette of letting others know their shortcomings – it must be done privately, with wisdom, for the betterment of the other person.
- Believers must pay attention to their faults and make efforts to fix them.

People who are targeted often have a more profound psychological impact as a result of receiving such behavior.

Calling names

- It is OK to have a nickname for other people if the nickname is good and respectable, and the other person prefers to be called by that name.
- However, calling names here means associating bad nicknames with others to hurt their feelings and disgrace them publicly.
- People often do that to demonize others whom they d not like for some reason.
- People involved in such evil are usually low and broug up in an unhealthy environment.
- Prophet Muhammad is reported to have said that it is the right of the believer to call his fellow believers by good names and titles that they like the best.

Hey this
Hey that ....

Lame
Dumbhead
Fat Hog
Brownie

Ali ibn Abi Talib said: The Messenger of Allah commanded Ibn Masood, so he climbed a tree to get something from the treetop for the Prophet. While climbing, his legs were exposed, and the Companions saw how thin they were, which made them laugh. The Messenger of Allah said, "What are you laughing at? At the legs of 'Abdullah? These legs will be heavier on the scale on the Day of Qiyamah than the weight of Mount Uhud."

بِئْسَ الِاسْمُ الْفُسُوقُ بَعْدَ الْاِيمَانِ

[All these are wrongdoings, and] after faith, even the name of wrongdoing (the slightest of it) is evil.

- Allah has exaggerated here by saying that after believing in Allah, how can you even consider doing it, let alone do it?
- This is similar to when we hate something; we say, "I don't want even to take its name."
- Allah is reminding us that after believing in Allah, we must hate these acts and should not even go close to this type of behavior

Surah Al Hujraat: Verses 12-13

يَا أَيُّهَا الَّذِينَ اٰمَنُوا اجْتَنِبُوا كَثِيرًا مِّنَ الظَّنِّ ۖ اِنَّ بَعْضَ الظَّنِّ اِثْمٌ وَّ لَا تَجَسَّسُوا وَ لَا يَغْتَبْ بَّعْضُكُمْ

بَعْضًا ۖ اَيُحِبُّ اَحَدُكُمْ اَنْ يَّاْكُلَ لَحْمَ اَخِيْهِ مَيْتًا فَكَرِهْتُمُوهُ ۖ وَ اتَّقُوا اللّٰهَ ۖ اِنَّ اللّٰهَ تَوَّابٌ رَّحِيْمٌ

يَا أَيُّهَا النَّاسُ اِنَّا خَلَقْنَاكُمْ مِّنْ ذَكَرٍ وَّ اُنْثٰى وَ جَعَلْنَاكُمْ شُعُوْبًا وَّ قَبَآئِلَ لِتَعَارَفُوْا ۖ اِنَّ اَكْرَمَكُمْ

عِنْدَ اللّٰهِ اَتْقَاكُمْ ۖ اِنَّ اللّٰهَ عَلِيْمٌ خَبِيْرٌ

Believers! Refrain from too much conjecture because some conjectures are pure sins. And do not spy [on others] and do not indulge in backbiting one another. Is there anyone among you who would like to eat the meat of his dead brother? So, if you do not tolerate this; [then why should backbiting be tolerated?] Fear God. God surely is quick in accepting repentance, Ever-Merciful. People! [If you do not regard one another as brothers, you will remain afflicted with these evils; so fully understand that] We have created you from a single man and a single woman and have divided you into families and tribes so that you recognize one another [distinctly]. In reality, the most honored among you in the sight of God is the one who is the most pious. [He will judge people on the Day of Judgement on this basis.] Surely, God is All-Knowing, All-Wise.

Suspicion

- In Islam, we are instructed to avoid unfounded suspicion or suspicion at all, unless we have strong evidence to do so.
- Today, we become suspicious of a person based on news or information that we have no way to prove.
- Islam asks us always to have positive thinking about people and give them the benefit of the doubt that we can.
- It becomes a sickness for some people, who suspect bad intentions in every other person's actions. It is more harmful to the person who is suspicious of everyone.
- Thinking positively about people keeps a person happy and free of sicknesses like jealousy and hatred.

مِنْ حُسْنِ إِسْلَامِ الْمَرْءِ تَرْكُهُ مَا لَا يَعْنِيهِ

"Part of the perfection of one's Islam is his leaving that which does not concern him." (Tirmidhi: 2318)

Backbiting and slander

- Regarding backbiting or slander, Allah used a very grave example, as if a person were eating the flesh of his brother.
- This is a disgusting act that no human being would like to do.
- The other person can't defend their position when someone is backbiting, which makes this act more severe.
- Backbiting, when it becomes an epidemic, destroys society.
- Gossiping usually leads to backbiting.
- Listening to the backbiting and not stopping it is the same as doing it.

A misunderstanding clarified

عَنْ أَبِي هُرَيْرَةَ أَنَّ رَسُولَ اللَّهِ صَلَّى اللَّهُ عَلَيْهِ وَسَلَّمَ قَالَ أَتَدْرُونَ مَا الْغِيبَةُ قَالُوا اللَّهُ وَرَسُولُهُ أَعْلَمُ قَالَ ذِكْرُكَ أَخَاكَ بِمَا يَكْرَهُ قِيلَ أَفَرَأَيْتَ إِنْ كَانَ فِي أَخِي مَا أَقُولُ قَالَ إِنْ كَانَ فِيهِ مَا تَقُولُ فَقَدِ اغْتَبْتَهُ وَإِنْ لَمْ يَكُنْ فِيهِ فَقَدْ بَهَتَّهُ

Abu Huraira reported: The Messenger of Allah said, "Do you know what backbiting is?" They said, "Allah and His Messenger know best." The Prophet said, "To mention your brother in a way he dislikes." It was said, "What if it is true about him?" The Prophet said, "If what you say about him is true, it is backbiting. If it is not true, it is slander." (Sahih Muslim 2589)

- The primary goal of these prohibitions is to preserve the integrity, harmony, and mutual respect of the community. By forbidding these actions, the Quran seeks to:
    - Cultivate a society built on trust, sincerity, and good faith.
    - Protect the honor and privacy of every individual.
    - Prevent discord and strife that arise from rumor-mongering, gossip, and suspicion.
- Spying on someone should not be confused with staying informed about people's situations when living in a community.
- Confusion can arise because both spying and informing a community about its needs involve gathering information, but the crucial difference lies in the intention, method, and impact of that gathering. The line is crossed from helpful awareness to forbidden spying (*tajassus*) when the motive becomes malicious, methods are secretive, and the impact is a violation of privacy and dignity.

Who is the best in the sight of Allah

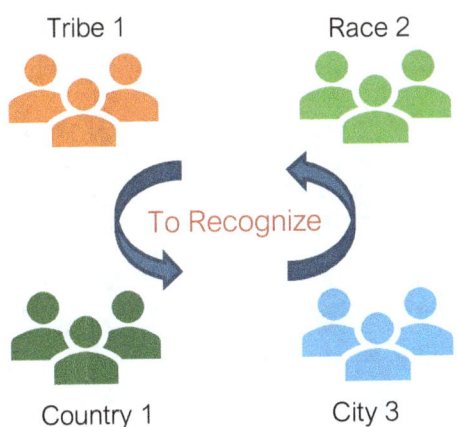

Tribe 1   Race 2

To Recognize

Country 1   City 3

"All humankind is from Adam and Hawa. An Arab has no superiority over a non-Arab, nor does a non-Arab have superiority over an Arab; also, a white has no superiority over a black, nor a black has any superiority over a white – except by piety and good action." (The Last Sermon of Prophet Muhammad)

- Allah destroyed the entire concept that people have about the superiority of their race or nation, which is at the root of many international issues.
- The groups, nations, and tribes exist, so they become unique and can easily recognize each other.
- Allah did not give anyone any superiority by default based on these factors.
- The best person in the sight of Allah is the one who is more God-conscious and does righteous deeds.
- All humans belong to one family because their parents are Adam and Eve.
- In the end, Allah also told us that no one knows who is more God-conscious, because this is an internal characteristic. So be careful when making fun of others, because you don't know their position with Allah.

The Last Sermon of Prophet Muhammad

- The final sermon of Prophet Muhammad, delivered in 632 CE, is regarded by many scholars as a charter of universal human rights that forms a core basis for justice and ethical conduct in Islam
- The principles articulated in this single speech addressed numerous pressing social and economic injustices, creating a framework for a more humane and equitable society.
- By prioritizing ethical duties over tribal loyalty, the sermon advanced the concept of universal human dignity long before similar ideas emerged in the Western world. Its principles are still referenced today in international human rights and social justice movements.

Hadith

An ideal Muslim Society

عن أبي مُوسَى قال قال رسول اللَّهِ صلى الله عليه وسلم الْمُؤْمِنُ لِلْمُؤْمِنِ كَالْبُنْيَانِ يَشُدُّ بَعْضُهُ بَعْضًا

Abu Musa stated that God's Messenger said: "A believer is like a building in which one brick supports the other." (Sahih Al-Muslim #2585)

عن النُّعْمَانِ بن بَشِيرٍ قال قال رسول اللَّهِ صلى الله عليه وسلم مَثَلُ الْمُؤْمِنِينَ في تَوَادِّهِمْ وَتَرَاحُمِهِمْ وَتَعَاطُفِهِمْ مَثَلُ الْجَسَدِ إذا اشْتَكَى منه عُضْوٌ تَدَاعَى له سَائِرُ الْجَسَدِ بِالسَّهَرِ وَالْحُمَّى

Numan ibn Bashir stated that God's Messenger said: "The example of believers about love, mercy, and affection between one another is that of one body; when any of its limbs aches, the whole body aches because of sleeplessness and fever." (Sahih Al-Muslim #2586)

عن أبي هُرَيْرَةَ أَنَّ رَسُولَ اللَّهِ صلى الله عليه وسلم قال حَقُّ الْمُسْلِمِ على الْمُسْلِمِ سِتٌّ قِيلَ ما هُنَّ يا رَسُولَ اللَّهِ قال إذا لَقِيتَهُ فَسَلِّمْ عليه وإذا دَعَاكَ فَأَجِبْهُ وإذا اسْتَنْصَحَكَ فَانْصَحْ له وإذا عَطَسَ فَحَمِدَ اللَّهَ فَشَمِّتْهُ وإذا مَرِضَ فَعُدْهُ وإذا مَاتَ فَاتَّبِعْهُ

Abu Hurairah reported that God's Messenger said: "A Muslim has six rights to a fellow Muslim." The companions asked: "What are they, O Messenger of God?" He replied: "When you meet him, say Salam to him; when he invites you, accept this invitation; when he asks for your advice, advise him sincerely; when he sneezes and thanks God [on this], you pray that God has mercy on him; when he falls sick, visit him; when he dies, follow his [funeral procession.]" (Sahih Al-Muslim #2162)

BIBLE

Acts of kindness

Do not seek to get even with one who has done you wrong, or harbor hard feelings toward the children of your people, but have a love for your neighbor as for yourself. (Leviticus: 19:18)

1. Discuss some practical tips on increasing the bond between you and a fellow Muslim brother or sister.
2. Read the complete Final Sermon of Prophet Muhammad and identify areas that help build a healthy and prosperous society.

Chapter 16

Topic 11: Satan (Shaytan)

This chapter introduces the concept of Satan and how God asked us to protect ourselves from his tricks.

Surah Aaraf: Verses 11-18

وَ لَقَدۡ خَلَقۡنٰكُمۡ ثُمَّ صَوَّرۡنٰكُمۡ ثُمَّ قُلۡنَا لِلۡمَلٰٓئِكَةِ اسۡجُدُوۡا لِاٰدَمَ فَسَجَدُوۡۤا اِلَّاۤ اِبۡلِيۡسَ ۖ لَمۡ يَكُنۡ مِّنَ السّٰجِدِيۡنَ

قَالَ مَا مَنَعَكَ اَلَّا تَسۡجُدَ اِذۡ اَمَرۡتُكَ ۖ قَالَ اَنَا خَيۡرٌ مِّنۡهُ ۚ خَلَقۡتَنِىۡ مِنۡ نَّارٍ وَّ خَلَقۡتَهٗ مِنۡ طِيۡنٍ

قَالَ اهۡبِطۡ مِنۡهَا ۚ قَالَ فَاَنۡظِرۡنِىۡۤ اِلٰى يَوۡمِ يُبۡعَثُوۡنَ

فَمَا يَكُوۡنُ لَكَ اَنۡ تَتَكَبَّرَ فِيۡهَا فَاخۡرُجۡ اِنَّكَ مِنَ الصّٰغِرِيۡنَ   قَالَ اِنَّكَ مِنَ الۡمُنۡظَرِيۡنَ   قَالَ فَبِمَاۤ اَغۡوَيۡتَنِىۡ لَاَقۡعُدَنَّ لَهُمۡ صِرَاطَكَ الۡمُسۡتَقِيۡمَ

ثُمَّ لَاٰتِيَنَّهُمۡ مِّنۡۢ بَيۡنِ اَيۡدِيۡهِمۡ وَ مِنۡ خَلۡفِهِمۡ وَ عَنۡ اَيۡمَانِهِمۡ وَ عَنۡ شَمَآئِلِهِمۡ ۖ وَ لَا تَجِدُ اَكۡثَرَهُمۡ شٰكِرِيۡنَ

قَالَ اخۡرُجۡ مِنۡهَا مَذۡءُوۡمًا مَّدۡحُوۡرًا ۚ لَمَنۡ تَبِعَكَ مِنۡهُمۡ لَاَمۡلَـَٔنَّ جَهَنَّمَ مِنۡكُمۡ اَجۡمَعِيۡنَ

We created you and then gave you a special form. Then We had said to the angels: "Prostrate before Adam." So, except Satan, all prostrated. He was not among those who prostrated. God said: "What stopped you from prostrating when I had ordered you?" He replied: "I am better than him. You have created me from fire and created him from clay." He said: "Get you down from here because you do not have the right to show arrogance here. So, away with you! Surely, you are disgraceful." He replied: "Give me respite until the Day people are raised up." God said: "You have this respite." He replied: "Then because you have led me astray, I too shall surely lie in ambush at Your straight path for the progeny of Adam. Then I shall certainly pounce upon them from their front and behind, from their right and left – from all sides. And You will find most of them to be ungrateful to You." God said: "Go away from here, disgraced and accursed. [Remember that] those of them who follow you, I also shall definitely fill Hell with you all."

- Allah had given power and resources to many nations before, but most of them were ungrateful and caused corruption on the land.
- The primary reason behind that attitude was following the path of Satan.
- Through this story, the Quran wanted to remind the addressees of the Quran that if their attitude towards Allah's blessings, especially the biggest blessing of all, the Messengers, is one of rejection and denial, then they need to check if they are following the path of Satan.
- It is an excellent reminder for all of us to stop complaining and be grateful for Allah's blessings.

Satan's Revenge

Why did Allah instruct angels and jinns to prostrate?

- There is a misconception that Allah instructed angels and jinns to prostrate to Adam because Adam is the most superior creation of Allah. This is not true.
- Allah said in Surah Bani Israel, verse 70, that Allah has made Adam superior to many creations but not all creations.
- Allah instructed both angels and jinns to prostrate to Adam as a trial and to give Adam and his wife a lifelong lesson. With Allah, the matter was not about who was superior to whom.
- Satan only used his superior creation as an excuse to satisfy his pride.
- What's more important for the creation of Allah is to obey the Creator once a command is fully understood.
- The creation may not understand the wisdom behind it, but it can make an effort to do that.

Why did Satan ask for the time?

- Arrogance leads to all kinds of vices, and jealousy is at the top of the list.
- Surprisingly, he blamed Allah for misguidance.
- Satan could not tolerate that Allah punished him because of Adam.
- His jealousy inspired him to take revenge.
- He took it as a challenge that he would lead human beings to destruction and make them end up in Hellfire, his final abode.

What are his plans for human beings?

- He would lie in ambush on the straight path that Allah has set for the progeny of Adam.
- That means he would spend all his time and energy on people who want to remain on the straight path.
- He will pounce upon them from their front and behind, from their right and left – from all sides.
- Without forcing anyone, he will entice them into sins from all sides by manufacturing justification.
- The goal is to make them ungrateful by disobeying Allah.

> The moral of this story is that arrogance is the main hurdle in accepting the truth, even when it is coming from Allah

Surah Bani Israel: Verses 71-75

وَ اِذْ قُلْنَا لِلْمَلٰٓئِكَةِ اسْجُدُوْا لِاٰدَمَ فَسَجَدُوْٓا اِلَّآ اِبْلِيْسَ ۔ قَالَ ءَاَسْجُدُ لِمَنْ خَلَقْتَ طِيْنًا

قَالَ اَرَءَيْتَكَ هٰذَا الَّذِيْ كَرَّمْتَ عَلَيَّ ۚ لَئِنْ اَخَّرْتَنِ اِلٰى يَوْمِ الْقِيٰمَةِ لَاَحْتَنِكَنَّ ذُرِّيَّتَهٗٓ اِلَّا قَلِيْلًا

قَالَ اذْهَبْ فَمَنْ تَبِعَكَ مِنْهُمْ فَاِنَّ جَهَنَّمَ جَزَآؤُكُمْ جَزَآءً مَّوْفُوْرًا

وَ اسْتَفْزِزْ مَنِ اسْتَطَعْتَ مِنْهُمْ بِصَوْتِكَ وَ اَجْلِبْ عَلَيْهِمْ بِخَيْلِكَ وَ رَجِلِكَ

وَ شَارِكْهُمْ فِى الْاَمْوَالِ وَ الْاَوْلَادِ وَ عِدْهُمْ ۚ وَ مَا يَعِدُهُمُ الشَّيْطٰنُ اِلَّا غُرُوْرًا

اِنَّ عِبَادِيْ لَيْسَ لَكَ عَلَيْهِمْ سُلْطٰنٌ ۚ وَ كَفٰى بِرَبِّكَ وَكِيْلًا

[There is no reason for this except that they have adopted the way of Satan.] Remind them when We had said to the angels: "Prostrate before Adam." Thus, all of them prostrated except Iblis. He said, "Should I prostrate to him whom you have created from clay?" He further said: "Look! Is this the one whom you honored above me? If you give me respite until the Day of Judgement, I shall consume all his progeny except a few." God said: "Very well! Go; then all those among them who follow you are the fuel of Hell because it is Hell which is the full recompense for you all. Whoever among them you can overpower, make them anxious with your commotion; bring upon them your riders and pedestrians; become partners in their wealth and children, and make promises with them. In reality, the promises Satan makes with them are nothing but deception. You will not have any power whatsoever over My servants, and as a guardian, sufficient is your Lord alone [O Prophet!]"

- It is very similar to the previous passage of the Quran, where Allah reminds the people who are adamant about their behavior of rejection that it is because of arrogance, which makes people blind to the truth.
- The context of these verses also speaks to the addressees of the Quran, asking them to accept the messenger as a sign. Allah told them that many nations before them had been given clear signs, yet they still rejected the message.
- Their main problem is arrogance, not lack of signs.
- Arrogance is one of the signs of Satanic behavior.
- That's why Allah repeats the story of Satan over and over to remind his addressees and us that it was Satan who made excuses to reject the truth, even when he was directly conversing with Allah.
- Arrogance makes a person bold (in a negative way), and he/she does not fear the consequences because they become blind.

Arrogance is the root of all evil

Satan's Arrogant Behavior

- Satan made fun of Adam because Adam was created from clay, whereas he was created from a superior form of energy: smokeless fire.
- One of the major signs of arrogance is looking down on people for one reason or another.
- He said, "Look! Is this the one whom you honored above me?" … it was a statement of scorn and tease.

His Threat to Human Beings

- He said he would use every means to "consume" most human beings, except for a few.
- "Consume" means he will create so many attractions for them that they will forget about Allah.
- It also refers to the fact that they will be meeting the same fate as Satan due to listening to him.

Tools used by Satan and His Agents

- Satan and his agents, among Jinns and humans, use many tools to keep people from the straight path:
    - Polytheistic myths and superstitions
    - False hopes with saints and their shrines
    - Propaganda and emotional appeals towards polytheistic beliefs and practices.
    - All types of amusement and entertainment that completely consume people.
    - Keep them dissatisfied with what Allah has given them and become envious of others for what they have. This is a form of disbelief.

Satan has no power over human beings

- The Quran's statement that Satan has no power over human beings means that Satan cannot force anyone to commit evil. His influence is limited to whispering suggestions, tempting individuals, and making wrongful actions seem appealing. Ultimately, humans have free will and are responsible for choosing whether to follow Satan's temptations or to obey God.

Surah An Nahl: Verse 63

تَاللَّهِ لَقَدْ أَرْسَلْنَآ إِلَى أُمَمٍ مِّن قَبْلِكَ فَزَيَّنَ لَهُمُ الشَّيْطَنُ أَعْمَالَهُمْ فَهُوَ وَلِيُّهُمُ الْيَوْمَ وَ لَهُمْ عَذَابٌ اَلِيّمٌ

By God! [O Prophet!] We had sent messengers to many nations before you also; so, Satan made their deeds seem fair to them [in a similar way]. So, now he is their companion, which is a painful torment for them.

- This particular theme has appeared in the Quran on multiple occasions.
- In this particular context, Allah talked about the deviated concept of the Pagans about Allah.
- They were worshipping idols to get closer to Allah, but at the same time, they used to call angels daughters of Allah.
- Allah rejected the idea by saying that it is Satan who is making things fair and pleasing to them.
- In that context, Allah told the Prophet that their behavior was not strange because many nations before them had similar problems, and Satan was making their deeds pleasing and fair to them; hence, Allah sent messengers to correct their beliefs.
- Through this, Allah pointed out an important fact and how Satan works for humans to pay attention to.

Self-Serving Justification

- From the Quran, we learn that Satan has no control over us. In Surah Ibrahim, Verse 22, he was quoted as saying:

وَ مَا كَانَ لِيَ عَلَيْكُمْ مِّنْ سُلْطَانٍ اِلَّاۤ اَنْ دَعَوْتُكُمْ فَاسْتَجَبْتُمْ لِيۡ

And I had no power over you; I only invited you, and you accepted.

What is Self-Serving Justification

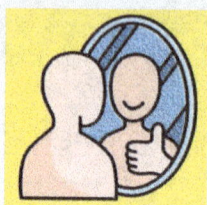

Self-serving justification refers to the cognitive process where a person rationalizes his/her actions or beliefs to serve their interests or preserve their self-image. It involves interpreting events or behaviors in a manner that portrays oneself in a positive light, even if it means ignoring contradictory evidence or downplaying one's faults.

https://www.psychologytoday.com/us/blog/in-love-and-war/202008/six-common-ways-people-justify-unethical-behavior

- As part of his invitation, he suggests excuses and justifications for an evil deed.
- Those who continue to pay attention to his suggestions start to see a 'goodness' in what they do, and it seems fair to them.
- This is the stage when it's hard to fix a problem because people do not see any problem with their actions.

Other Satan Tactics

1. He wants us to worship and depend on others besides Allah.
2. He encourages people to corrupt religion by introducing innovations.
3. He entices people to commit major sins because he knows that Allah may forgive minor sins if a person stays away from major ones.
4. He encourages people to indulge in minor sins by giving the excuse that they are minor and OK to commit.
5. He keeps people engaged in things that are neither halal nor haram but useless. People waste hours on them.
6. He keeps you satisfied with lesser things, even though you intended to do better.
7. He puts negative thoughts in our minds about other people to create discord.

Hadith

Avoiding suspicion & idle thoughts

عن أَنَسٍ أَنَّ النبي صلى الله عليه وسلم ان مع إِحْدَى نِسَائِهِ فَمَرَّ بِهِ رَجُلٌ
فَدَعَاهُ فَجَاءَ فقال يا فُلَانُ هذه زَوْجَتِي فُلَانَةُ فقال يا رَسُولَ اللَّهِ من كنت أَظُنُّ
بِهِ فلم أَكُنْ أَظُنُّ بِكَ فقال رسول اللَّهِ صلى الله عليه وسلم إِنَّ الشَّيْطَانَ يَجْرِي
من الْإِنْسَانِ مَجْرَى الدَّمِ

Anas ibn Malik reported that [once] the Prophet was with one of his wives when a person passed by him. So, the Prophet called him over. The person came to him. At this, the Prophet said: "O you! This is my such and such wife." The person then replied: "O Messenger of God! Who am I to think in this way? I would never think about you (suspiciously) in such a manner?" At this, God's Messenger replied: "Indeed, Satan is found in a person like the blood that circulates [in his body]."(Sahih Muslim #2174).

Note: He meant that a malicious thought could come to your mind, so I clarified it.

" يَأْتِي الشَّيْطَانُ أَحَدَكُمْ فَيَقُولُ مَنْ خَلَقَ كَذَا وَكَذَا حَتَّى يَقُولَ لَهُ مَنْ خَلَقَ
رَبَّكَ فَإِذَا بَلَغَ ذَلِكَ فَلْيَسْتَعِذْ بِاللَّهِ وَلْيَنْتَهِ

Satan comes to every one of you and says: Who created this? Who created that? Till he questions: Then who created your Lord? When he comes to that, one should seek refuge in Allah and keep away (from such idle thoughts). (Sahih Al-Muslim Book 1 Hadith 252)

BIBLE

Spend even if you have little

And he [Jesus] took a seat by where the money was kept and saw how the people put money into the boxes: a person with wealth put in a lot. And a poor widow put in two little bits of money (equal to a quarter of a penny today). And he made his disciples come to him, and said to them, Truly I say to you, This poor widow has put in more than all those who are putting money into the box: Because they all put in something out of what they did not need for; but she out of her need put in all she had, even all her living. (Mark, 12:41-44).

Showing off Generosity

Take care not to do your good works before men, to be seen by them, or you will have no reward from your Father in heaven. When you give money to the poor, do not make a noise about it, as false-hearted men do in the Synagogues and the streets, so that they may have glory from men. Truly, I say to you, they already have their reward (but from men). (Matthew, 6:1-2).

Note: "Father" is used metaphorically for God on such occasions.

Discuss some practical tips to fight the tricks of Shaytan

Chapter 17

Topic 12: Quran's guidance on morals and morality

This chapter introduces a selection of verses from the Quran that address God's moral guidance.

The Knowledge of Good and Evil is innate

> وَ نَفْسٍ وَّ مَا سَوّٰىهَا ۙ فَاَلْهَمَهَا فُجُوْرَهَا وَ تَقْوٰىهَا ۙ
>
> قَدْ اَفْلَحَ مَنْ زَكّٰىهَا ۙ وَ قَدْ خَابَ مَنْ دَسّٰىهَا ۙ
>
> And (witness is) the soul and the way it is perfected (over time), then <u>inspired it with its evil, and it's good </u>(that the Day of Judgement is certain to come); [hence,] he succeeded who purified his soul, and he failed who corrupted it. (Surah Ash-Shams: 6-10)

- In this Surah, until verse 5, the various oaths depict the testimony of the majesty and exaltedness, gradual progression and elaborate arrangement, power and wisdom that we observe in the rising and setting of the sun and the moon, in the alternation of day and night, and in the way the heavens and the earth have been created.

- After this, the testimony of the soul is presented, emphasizing the importance of self-reflection and the power of one's conscience.

- Our self or soul is a creation full of amazing abilities and intelligence.

- This soul also has a conscience that distinguishes between right and wrong.

- This conscience acts like an unbiased judge inside our mind, telling us when we've done something wrong.

- This internal judgment is constant, unless we become so corrupted by wrongdoing that we can no longer hear that inner voice of truth.

- After directing attention to all these manifestations of soul and matter, the Quran has argued that this world is not an accidental creation or a place of amusement.

- No one will go scot-free without being held accountable for their deeds. He shall definitely be held answerable. God has appointed the Day of Judgement to fulfil this purpose. Hence, the Day of Judgement is bound to come.

Cherish the inner guidance

- The picture below summarizes what we are born with, and the results and consequences of our behavior and attitude towards what we are given. The guidance from external sources will only help if we first cherish the God-given conscience.

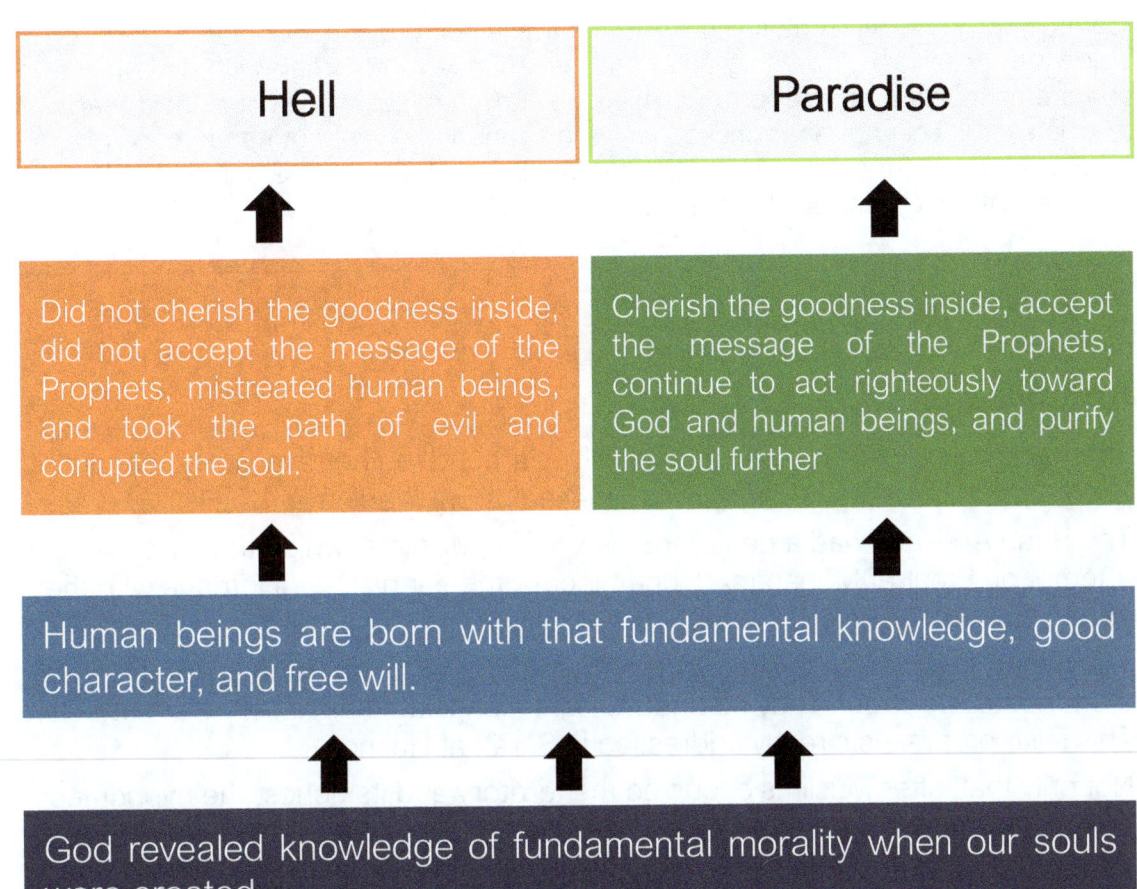

Hell | **Paradise**

Did not cherish the goodness inside, did not accept the message of the Prophets, mistreated human beings, and took the path of evil and corrupted the soul.

Cherish the goodness inside, accept the message of the Prophets, continue to act righteously toward God and human beings, and purify the soul further

Human beings are born with that fundamental knowledge, good character, and free will.

God revealed knowledge of fundamental morality when our souls were created.

No source other than the divine can give us the information that we are born with knowledge of fundamental morality and that we fully understand the concepts of good and evil. Our experience only verifies that knowledge comes from the divine. Without believing in the divine, humans struggle to find its true source.

Selflessness

وَ الَّذِيْنَ تَبَوَّؤُ الدَّارَ وَ الْاِيْمَانَ مِنْ قَبْلِهِمْ يُحِبُّوْنَ مَنْ هَاجَرَ اِلَيْهِمْ وَ لَا يَجِدُوْنَ فِيْ صُدُوْرِهِمْ حَاجَةً مِّمَّآ اُوْتُوْا وَ يُؤْثِرُوْنَ عَلٰٓى اَنْفُسِهِمْ وَ لَوْ كَانَ بِهِمْ خَصَاصَةٌ ۚ وَ مَنْ يُّوْقَ شُحَّ نَفْسِهٖ فَاُولٰٓئِكَ هُمُ الْمُفْلِحُوْنَ

[Contrary to these hypocrites,] those who have already made this land a place of residence (Ansar and initial migrants) and have firmly rooted their faith, love those who are migrating to them [now after them] and do not feel any ill-will in their hearts on whatever is being given to these immigrants, and they give them preference over themselves even if they are in need. In reality, those who have been protected from selfishness it is they who shall succeed. (Surah Hashr: 9)

Background

- The background of Surah al-Hashr revolves around the betrayal and subsequent expulsion of the Jewish tribe of Banu an-Nadir from Medina in 4 A.H.

- The Banu An-Nadir had a peace treaty with the Muslims, which the assassination attempt on Prophet Muhammad, combined with their history of intrigue with the pagan Quraysh, violated.

- The hypocrites in Medina secretly promised support to the Banu an-Nadir, urging them not to surrender. They pledged to fight alongside them if they were attacked. This false promise is directly addressed in Surah al-Hashr.

- Not only that, after Muslims occupied the territory and its riches, the hypocrites complained about the war booty that the Muslim army got hold of after defeating the Jewish tribes.

- They wanted a share of it, and Allah told them that neither Muslims nor hypocrites made any efforts for this war. This dominance is given solely by Allah to the Prophet and his companions.

- Whatever was distributed after a portion was kept under the protection of the state for unprivileged people in society, the true believers showed no inclination or greed towards it, but rather were happy that much was distributed to new Muslims to win their hearts to Islam.

- These verses contrast the selflessness of the true believers with the hypocrisy of the hypocrites.

Selflessness

- This was a great example of selflessness in the verses.
- The true believers focus on the Hereafter and take only an appropriate share of the blessings of this world, as needed.
- They enjoy the blessings of this world, but are not greedy for them.
- They are selfless, always look after the people around them, and play an important role in society.
- In times of difficulty, they prefer others over themselves, even when they are in need.
- The character they have built as a believer helps them take the lead and become selfless in such situations.
- True believers bargain the temporary blessings of this world for the permanent blessings of the next.
- It builds the bond that every family and community needs.

Every creation of God is
Selfless

Be like them!

Golde Rule
None of you is a believer until he loves for his brother that which he loves for himself." (Hadith –Bukhari & Muslim)

Be with Truthful People

يَا أَيُّهَا الَّذِينَ آمَنُوا اتَّقُوا اللهَ وَ كُونُوا مَعَ الصَّادِقِينَ

Believers! fear God and be in the company of the truthful. (Surah Taubah: 119)

- The actual word is *Sadiqeen,* which is the opposite of hypocrites, and it is combined with God consciousness (*Taqwa*).
- It refers to people whose words and deeds are in complete harmony. This verse urges people to fear God and to remain in the company of the truthful to secure themselves from the wrongs mentioned earlier in the Surah.
- *Taqwa* protects a person from within, and the truthfulness helps him against Satan from without.
- Truthfulness is one of the manifestations of *Taqwa*.
- If a person spends a good part of his time with liars, the corrupt, and the ignorant, even a strong-willed person can be influenced by them, let alone the weak.
- In a similar way, the company and affection of those who are men of truthfulness instill the strength and will in the weak to overcome their shortcomings, and they gradually are transformed into one of them.

Truthfulness is larger than the action of the tongue
- The outside should be what's inside
- Actions based on what you believe
- Practice before preaching

وَمَن يُطِعِ اللَّهَ وَالرَّسُولَ فَأُولَٰئِكَ مَعَ الَّذِينَ أَنْعَمَ اللَّهُ عَلَيْهِم مِّنَ النَّبِيِّينَ وَالصِّدِّيقِينَ وَالشُّهَدَاءِ وَالصَّالِحِينَ ۚ وَحَسُنَ أُولَٰئِكَ رَفِيقًا

And whosoever obeys God and His messenger, such will be in the company of those whom God has blessed: the Prophets, **the truthful ones**, the martyrs, and the righteous. And how excellent a company of such people is (Quran 4:69)

Justice, Justice …. Justice

يَٰٓأَيُّهَا ٱلَّذِينَ ءَامَنُوا۟ كُونُوا۟ قَوَّٰمِينَ لِلّٰهِ شُهَدَآءَ بِٱلْقِسْطِ ۖ وَ لَا يَجْرِمَنَّكُمْ شَنَـَٔانُ قَوْمٍ عَلَىٰٓ أَلَّا

تَعْدِلُوا۟ ۚ ٱعْدِلُوا۟ هُوَ أَقْرَبُ لِلتَّقْوَىٰ ۖ وَ ٱتَّقُوا۟ ٱللّٰهَ ۚ إِنَّ ٱللّٰهَ خَبِيرٌۢ بِمَا تَعْمَلُونَ

Believers! Stand up for God bearing witness to justice. Even your animosity toward a people should not induce you to turn away from justice. Be just; this is nearer to piety. And keep fearing God because God is well aware of all your deeds. (Surah Al Maidah Verse 8)

يَٰٓأَيُّهَا ٱلَّذِينَ ءَامَنُوا۟ كُونُوا۟ قَوَّٰمِينَ بِٱلْقِسْطِ شُهَدَآءَ لِلّٰهِ وَ لَوْ عَلَىٰٓ أَنفُسِكُمْ أَوِ ٱلْوَٰلِدَيْنِ وَ ٱلْأَقْرَبِينَ ۚ

إِن يَكُنْ غَنِيًّا أَوْ فَقِيرًا فَٱللّٰهُ أَوْلَىٰ بِهِمَا ۖ فَلَا تَتَّبِعُوا۟ ٱلْهَوَىٰٓ أَن تَعْدِلُوا۟ ۚ وَ إِن تَلْوُۥٓا۟ أَوْ تُعْرِضُوا۟

فَإِنَّ ٱللّٰهَ كَانَ بِمَا تَعْمَلُونَ خَبِيرًا

Believers! Adhere to justice, bearing witness to it for God, even if this evidence is against yourselves, your parents, and your kinsfolk. If someone is rich or poor, God is more worthy that His law be followed. So, do not be led by desires [by leaving His guidance], lest, as a result, you deviate from the truth. And [remember that] if you try to distort [what is true and just] or evade [it], you shall definitely be punished for it because God is well aware of what you do. (Surah An-Nisaa Verse 135)

Background

- Taken together, the two verses above establish a comprehensive Islamic concept of justice that God desires.
- Justice must <u>not</u> be compromised by any relationship, whether with family, friends, or enemies, at the national level.
- The motivation for justice is not worldly gain but sincere devotion to God.
- The practice of justice is not merely a legal or social obligation but an essential component of one's religious character and God-consciousness. God is just, and He wants us to uphold justice at any cost.

Justice in Islam

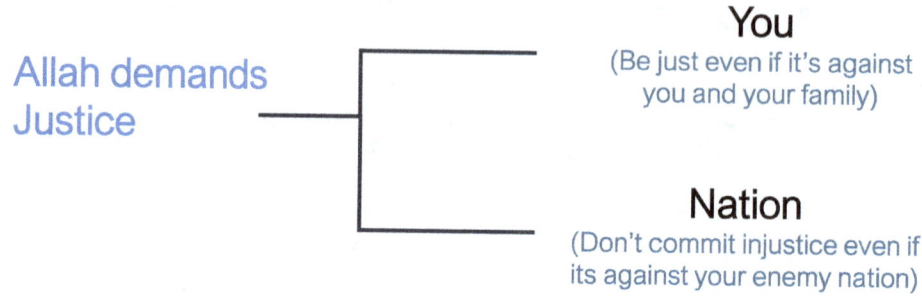

Justice means *placing things in their __rightful__ place*

Allah demands Justice

You
(Be just even if it's against you and your family)

Nation
(Don't commit injustice even if its against your enemy nation)

- The word justice is usually construed as something done in the courtroom or at the king or ruler level, and never related to a common man and his/her daily life.
- In Islam, justice starts with you and me before it applies to the court or ruler.
- We praise justice because justice is an attribute of Allah, and for this reason, its likeness has been ordained in our nature – this is a universal concept within humanity.
- The Quran made justice the necessary outcome and mandatory requirement of faith in the heart – a seed properly sown and taken care of will always bear fruit.
- The Quran talks about justice in two aspects:
    - Justice in personal matters, regarding one's own family or relatives.
    - Justice in collective matters, regarding our nation and tribe
- In personal matters, a person must testify honestly, even if it harms their own kin, because their testimony is for God, not for family.
- The second one is a tougher command, requiring justice toward those one dislikes or who have shown hostility at the national level. It establishes a high moral standard that prevents personal enmity from corrupting a person's or nation's judgment.

Prophet Muhammad is reported to have said: "People, beware of injustice, for injustice will be darkness on the Day of Judgment." (Musnad Ahmed)

Sincerity with God

وَ يُطْعِمُونَ الطَّعَامَ عَلَى حُبِّهٖ مِسْكِينًا وَّ يَتِيْمًا وَّ اَسِيْرًا ۝ اِنَّمَا نُطْعِمُكُمْ لِوَجْهِ اللّٰهِ لَا نُرِيْدُ مِنْكُمْ جَزَآءً

وَّ لَا شُكُوْرًا ۝ اِنَّا نَخَافُ مِنْ رَّبِّنَا يَوْمًا عَبُوْسًا قَمْطَرِيْرًا

They feed the poor, the orphan, and the captive, even though they themselves are in need of it. They provided them with the intention, saying: "We are feeding you for the sake of God only. We do not desire any reward from you nor expect gratitude. We dread that day from our Lord, which will be extremely grim and distressful." (Surah Insaan Verses 8-10)

Background

- Surah Insaan starts with a question about the existence of human beings in the first place.
- This question is meant to make a person reflect on why they have been so fortunate in life, a blessing.
- Why do they have such great capabilities? Is their only purpose to eat, drink, and die? Don't they have a duty to use their blessings responsibly? Don't they have an obligation to their Creator? Everyone who thinks about their life should consider these questions."
- Then it talks about the free will God has given human beings, so they can be grateful or ungrateful to God.
- When talking about grateful people, God highlighted a few of their attributes, including their sincerity in their actions towards God.

Sincerity with God

- The first condition for all religious acts in Islam is sincerity.
- Sincerity is a core value in Islam that permeates all aspects of a believer's life, ensuring that their actions align with their faith and are done solely for the pleasure of Allah.
- The sincerity of one's actions will be a crucial factor on the Day of Judgment.

"Verily, reward of the deeds are only by intentions." (Hadith)

- In Islam, individuals will be judged not only by their deeds but also by the sincerity of their intentions.
- Acts of worship and charity lacking sincerity may not be accepted.
- A community built on sincere individuals is more likely to be harmonious and cooperative because they have no expectations from others. How good would society be if everybody gave without expecting anything in return?
- God said in the Quran:

لَنْ يَّنَالَ اللهَ لُحُومُهَا وَ لَا دِمَاؤُهَا وَ لٰكِنْ يَّنَالُهُ التَّقْوَى مِنْكُمْ

Neither does their (sacrificial animal) flesh reach God nor their blood; in fact, only your piety reaches Him. (Surah Hajj: 37)

The first of the people against whom judgment will be pronounced on the Day of Resurrection will be a man who died a martyr. He will be brought, and Allah will make known to him His favors, and he will recognize them. [The Almighty] will say: And what did you do about them? He will say: I fought for you until I died a martyr. God will say: You have lied – you fought so that it might be said about you: He is courageous. And so it was said. Then he will be ordered to be dragged along on his face until he is cast into Hellfire. (Part of Sahih Muslim #4688).

Repel evil with good

وَ مَنْ أَحْسَنُ قَوْلًا مِّمَّنْ دَعَآ إِلَى اللهِ وَ عَمِلَ صَالِحًا وَّ قَالَ إِنَّنِى مِنَ الْمُسْلِمِيْنَ

وَ لَا تَسْتَوِى الْحَسَنَةُ وَ لَا السَّيِّئَةُ اِدْفَعْ بِالَّتِى هِىَ اَحْسَنُ فَاِذَا الَّذِىْ بَيْنَكَ وَ

بَيْنَهُ عَدَاوَةٌ كَاَنَّهُ وَلِىٌّ حَمِيْمٌ وَ مَا يُلَقَّهَآ اِلَّا الَّذِيْنَ صَبَرُوْا وَ مَا يُلَقَّهَآ اِلَّا ذُوْحَظٍّ عَظِيْمٍ

وَ اِمَّا يَنْزَغَنَّكَ مِنَ الشَّيْطٰنِ نَزْغٌ فَاسْتَعِذْ بِاللهِ اِنَّهُ هُوَ السَّمِيْعُ الْعَلِيْمُ

Whose call can be better than the person who calls people to God, does righteous deeds, and says, "I am among the obedient." In reality, good and evil are not equal. **You do that which is good in response to evil**. Then you will see that the very person with whom you had an enmity has become a close friend. And [remember that] this wisdom is acquired only by steadfast people and is given to only those very fortunate. And [if at some instance] you feel temptation in your heart from Satan, seek God's refuge. Indeed, it is He Who hears and knows. (Surah Fussilat Verses 33-36)

Background

- These verses compare the attitude of Prophet Muhammad and his companions with the attitude of the disbelievers about the Quran and God's message.
- They used to incite people to make noises or talk about other petty things when the Prophet would recite the Quran to invite people to Islam.
- The objective was that their conversation remain dominant, and that whatever Prophet Muhammad is reciting be lost in the noise and commotion.
- God warned those people that at this moment, they do not realize the intensity of their crime by trying to stop people from the call of the Quran. When the severe punishment of God comes before them, only then will they realize the terrible nature of their actions.
- In comparison, God talks about the attitude of Prophet Muhammad and his companions, who are calling people to Islam and taking a forgiving attitude towards their enemies.

Repel evil with good

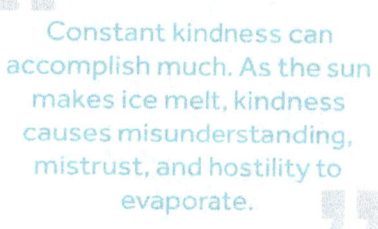

> Constant kindness can accomplish much. As the sun makes ice melt, kindness causes misunderstanding, mistrust, and hostility to evaporate.

- Albert Schweitzer

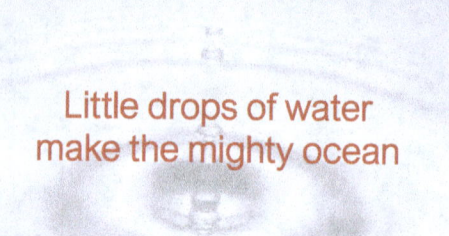

Little drops of water make the mighty ocean

- People who call others toward Allah face many challenges in this task.
- It is quite expected that they will be treated in an evil manner, and that behavior becomes a test of their patience in this cause.
- Allah asked them to repel the evil with continued goodness.
- People who have done that have seen tremendous results of such behavior.
- The enemies turn into best and admiring friends after seeing this positive behavior from the believers.
- However, this is not an easy task, and only the fortunate will gain this wisdom.
- Through this wisdom, they avoid the traps of Satan, who wanted discord among people.

How kindness gives you the upper hand

- You may be concerned that responding to evil with kindness will make you appear weak. However, kindness doesn't mean backing down or letting yourself be walked over.
- When the other person is aggressive, it's a natural survival response to react with anger — it's counterintuitive to choose a different reaction. Deciding to respond with kindness requires both restraint and emotional intelligence.
- Reacting to charged situations with kindness is a vulnerable act and takes courage. Kindness is so powerful because its roots lie in connecting to one's humanity and empathizing with the other person.
- When you don't fuel the fire with anger, it's likely to surprise the other person and make them step back to reflect on their actions and behaviors.
- Your unconventional response of kindness will remind them that they also have the agency to decide how they want to react to such situations.

Trust in God

> اَلَّذِيْنَ قَالَ لَهُمُ النَّاسُ اِنَّ النَّاسَ قَدْ جَمَعُوْا لَكُمْ فَاخْشَوْهُمْ فَزَادَهُمْ اِيْمَانًا * وَّ قَالُوْا
>
> حَسْبُنَا اللّٰهُ وَ نِعْمَ الْوَكِيْلُ
>
> They (believers entrapped in Medinah) are those who, on being told by people: "The enemy has mustered a great force against you: so, fear it," grew more in their faith [on hearing this] and replied: "God is all-sufficient for us, and He is the best protector." (Aal-e-Imran:173)

- After several defeats, all the enemies of Islam joined hands and agreed to crush the Muslims and their progress by attacking Medinah at once in the Battle of Ahzab.
- Later in this battle, the situation became extremely challenging for the Muslims due to the harsh weather conditions, shortage of food, and the psychological pressure of the siege.
- Despite these difficulties, the Muslims under the leadership of Prophet Muhammad demonstrated unwavering faith and commitment to their cause, which is unheard of.
- Even when they were told that enemies were gathering outside Medinah to crush them, it increased their faith in God, and they declared that God is sufficient for them against anyone in the world.
- True believers always trust in God and rely on Him for guidance and protection when they are certain that they are on the right path.
- This trust must be evident in their actions and prayers during such difficult times.

The Concept of Trust in God

- Sometimes Muslims misunderstand the concept of Trust in God, which should be clarified.
- Often, verses related to the Prophet Muhammad and his companions that speak of trusting in God are not directly applicable to our situations because a Messenger was among them, and God promised victory to the Muslims if they show firm belief and trust in God.
- For the matters that are more general in nature today, we are asked to do our best first before putting our trust in God. So, we can't slack in our efforts before putting our trust in God.
- When you put your trust in God, it is not necessary that the result will be as per your wishes or desires. It will be as it fits in the overall scheme of God.

Contentment

وَ لَا تَتَمَنَّوْا مَا فَضَّلَ اللهُ بِهِ بَعْضَكُمْ عَلَى بَعْضٍ ۚ لِلرِّجَالِ نَصِيبٌ مِّمَّا اكْتَسَبُوْا ۚ وَ لِلنِّسَآءِ

نَصِيبٌ مِّمَّا اكْتَسَبْنَ ۚ وَ سْئَلُوا اللهَ مِنْ فَضْلِهِ ۚ إِنَّ اللهَ كَانَ بِكُلِّ شَىْءٍ عَلِيْمًا

And do not desire things in which God has given preference to some of you over others, because whatever men have earned, they shall get their share, and whatever women have earned, they shall also necessarily get their share and ask God of His bounty. Surely, God has full knowledge of all things. (Surah Nisa:32)

- The sphere of inborn abilities and characteristics is not the right one to compete in, because people have different strengths.
- God has created some people superior to others as regards their mental, physical, economic, and social status – the same is true in the case of a man and a woman.
- They have been created as counterparts, with one serving as the active member and the other as the passive one. While the former trait needs domination, vigor, and force, the latter needs gentleness, subtlety, and acquiescence.
- Each possesses relative superiority to the other. These are inborn characteristics, and any effort to surpass one another in this area would be tantamount to waging war against nature.
- God has directed attention to another sphere in which people should strive to outdo one another. This is the sphere of earning reward for oneself through good deeds, high character, worship, diligence, and virtue.
- The Quran, at various places, refers to this sphere using terms such as "faith" and "righteous deeds." This is the sphere in which people should try to outdo one another. There is no restriction on anyone in striving to outdo others in this sphere; in fact, trying to surpass others in this sphere is as desirable as it is condemnable in the sphere of innate abilities.

The role of husband and wife

In the sight of Allah

For roles and responsibilities

MEN = WOMEN   HUSBAND ≠ WIFE

- The natural abilities of men and women are very different, and hence, their roles in a family and in a society.
- Even within men or women, some people are created superior to others in talent, mental and physical abilities, and economic and social status
- That is also true between husband and wife, given this relationship. Husbands are made responsible for the house because they are given the responsibility to earn a living for the family.
- Despite being in charge, Muslim husbands are told to run the affairs of the house with mutual consultation. That is best for any family that wants to live with love and harmony.
- However, both men and women should be content with whatever duties and roles they have been given, and they can change them, if required, with mutual consultation.
- The sphere where husband and wife should strive to outdo each other is the sphere of earning rewards from Allah through the best of morals and good deeds. This field of competition is open to everyone, including husbands and wives.

Arrogance

إِنَّ الَّذِينَ كَذَّبُوا بِآيَاتِنَا وَ اسْتَكْبَرُوا عَنْهَا لَا تُفَتَّحُ لَهُمْ أَبْوَابُ السَّمَاءِ وَ لَا يَدْخُلُونَ الْجَنَّةَ حَتَّى يَلِجَ الْجَمَلُ فِي سَمِّ الْخِيَاطِ ۚ وَ كَذَلِكَ نَجْزِي الْمُجْرِمِينَ

This is certain that those who have denied Our revelations (or signs) and have arrogantly turned away from them, for them the doors of the heavens <u>shall not be opened,</u> and they shall never enter Paradise unless a camel passes through the eye of a needle. [Listen!] This is how we punish criminals. (Surah Aaraf:40)

- When it comes to rejecting Prophet Muhammad and the Quran, God declared very clearly in the Quran on multiple occasions that the only reason these disbelievers can't accept this truth is because of their arrogant behavior.
- God pointed out that this is the same attitude the People of the Book have toward accepting the truth. They created divisions among themselves after receiving clear signs, due to rivalry and arrogance.
- God dislikes arrogance so much so that He declared that there is **no** chance for an arrogant person to come near paradise.

What is arrogance?

- Arrogance is the epitome of all these negative traits: pride, vanity, and show-off. It is the root of all evils, and an attitude of superiority and self-importance showed through an overbearing pride. It is usually within people's hearts and is displayed in various forms.
- Arrogance keeps one away from any good a person can do
- Sometimes it is difficult for us to figure out what arrogance is and how it differs from other human traits that appear to be arrogance. This is explained in one of the Ahadith by Prophet Muhammad:

Abdullah ibn Masood reported that the Prophet said, "No one who has the tiniest amount of arrogance (size of a small seed) in his heart will enter Paradise." Someone asked, "But a man loves to have beautiful clothes and shoes." The Prophet said, "Verily, Allah is beautiful, and he loves beauty. That is not arrogance. **Arrogance** means:

1. <u>Rejecting the truth (which you know is the truth)</u>
2. <u>Look down on people (I am greater than everyone)</u>

Patience

وَ اسْتَعِينُوا بِالصَّبْرِ وَ الصَّلوةِ

Seek help with patience and prayers. (Surah Al-Baqarah:45)

قُلْ يٰعِبَادِ الَّذِينَ ءَامَنُوا اتَّقُوا رَبَّكُمْ لِلَّذِينَ أَحْسَنُوا فِى هٰذِهِ الدُّنْيَا حَسَنَةٌ وَأَرْضُ اللَّهِ وَاسِعَةٌ
إِنَّمَا يُوَفَّى الصّٰبِرُونَ أَجْرَهُمْ بِغَيْرِ حِسَابٍ

Say "O My servants who believe! Be mindful of your Lord. Those who do good in this world will have a good reward. And Allah's earth is spacious. Only those who endure patiently will be given their reward without limit."
(Surah Zumur: 10)

- In the Quran, patience means 'to remain steadfast on a principle or course of action for a stand that one considers is right while seeking help from God.'
- The Quran gave us the recipe for being steadfast in such situations: seek help through prayer and with patience/perseverance.
- There is no single moral quality appreciated and promised paradise in the Quran more than PATIENCE.

Patience is developed over time

Patience or *Sabr* is not a passive waiting

- Any reader of the Quran cannot fail to notice that patience is the key to paradise.
- In Islam, patience is required even when someone is given the blessing to undergo the test of gratitude – it requires patience not to become arrogant.
- The believers who were patient are glorified in the Quran, so much so that when they enter into paradise, they will be told that they are there because of their faith and the patience they displayed.
- Patience is a very vast concept, and it is required in almost every aspect of our lives. It DOES NOT mean sitting and passively waiting for something.
- Patience means making your best effort to do what you believe is right, and then facing the challenges and opposition that come your way without complaining.

The foundation of morality and moral behavior

إِنَّ اللهَ يَأْمُرُ بِالْعَدْلِ وَ الْإِحْسَانِ وَ اِيتَآئِ ذِى الْقُرْبٰى وَ يَنْهٰى عَنِ الْفَحْشَآءِ وَ الْمُنْكَرِ وَ الْبَغْيِ ۚ يَعِظُكُمْ لَعَلَّكُمْ تَذَكَّرُوْنَ

Indeed, God directs you to <u>justice</u> and <u>excellence</u> and <u>to give to the kin</u>, stopping you from <u>lewdness</u>, <u>evil</u>, and <u>rebellion</u>. He counsels you so that you receive a reminder. (Surah Nahl:90)

- This verse is a miracle in itself, as it is very comprehensive.
- The foundation of all good morals one wants to acquire and the evil traits one wants to avoid are described in this verse of the Quran.
- If someone wants to know if something is morally right or wrong, then that something must be seen in the light of this verse to get the answer.
- All moral instructions are rooted in three positives and three negatives:

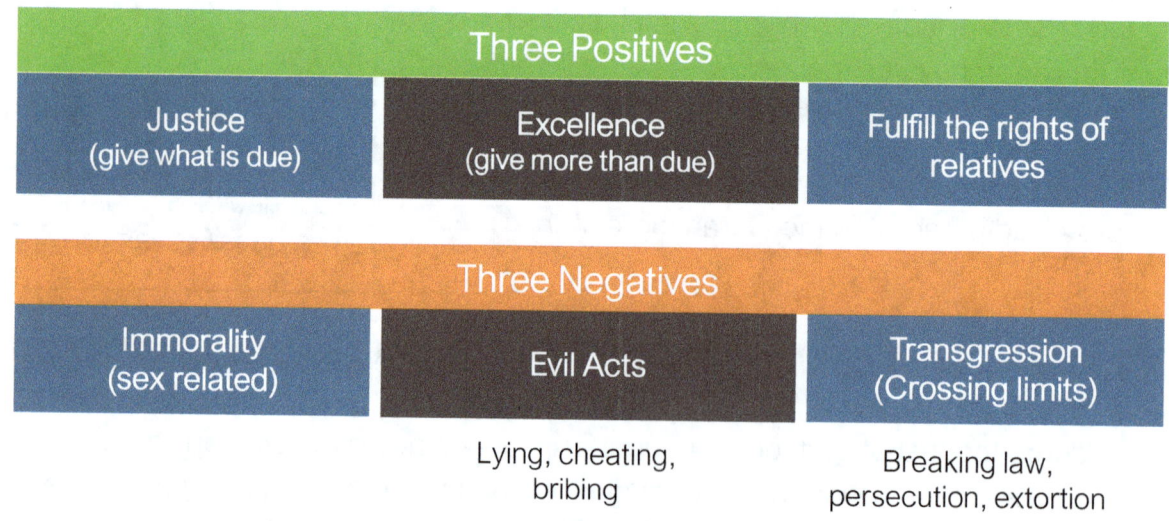

Three Positives		
Justice (give what is due)	Excellence (give more than due)	Fulfill the rights of relatives

Three Negatives		
Immorality (sex related)	Evil Acts	Transgression (Crossing limits)
	Lying, cheating, bribing	Breaking law, persecution, extortion

What is the difference between justice and excellence? Give some examples.

www.ingramcontent.com/pod-product-compliance
Lightning Source LLC
Chambersburg PA
CBHW081325120626
46546CB00011B/3222